Lost Paradise

A harree ta fow,
A toro ta farraro,
A now ta tararta.

The palm tree grows,
The coral spreads,
But man shall vanish.

POLYNESIAN
SAYING

Lost Paradise

The Exploration of the Pacific

By Ian Cameron

Salem House Publishers
Topsfield, Massachusetts

First Published in the United States
By Salem House Publishers, 1987
462 Boston Street, Topsfield, MA 01983

Originally Published in Great Britain By Century Hutchinson Ltd
Brookmount House, 62-65 Chandos Place, Covent Garden,
London Wc2N 4nw
Library of Congress Cataloguing In Publication Data
Cameron, IAN, 1924 –
Lost Paradise.
Bibliography: p.
Includes index.
1. Oceania – Discovery and Exploration.
I. Title.
DU19.C35 1987 919′.04 87-4280
ISBN 0-88162-275-3

Manufactured in Great Britain
10 9 8 7 6 5 4 3 2 1
First American Edition

CONTENTS

Frontispiece of Dumont D'Urville's atlas
Voyage to the South Pole, volume 1.

INTRODUCTION

The truest picture of an Arcadia.

It was dawn off the island of Tahiti, and mist was coiling up in little spirals out of a quiet sea. As the mist rose, it thinned out in the warmth of the sun, and feature by feature Tahiti was unveiled: first the cone of an extinct volcano, then a jumble of forest-covered hills 'uneven as crumpled paper', then an arc of beaches fringed with palms, and finally the encircling waters of a lagoon. Never had the crew of the ship which was running under shortened sail about a mile offshore seen so beautiful an island.

By 6 am the mist had cleared sufficiently for Lieutenant James Cook to stand in towards the land. There was little wind, but the swell was heavy and the reef a hazard not to be taken lightly. Cook lowered his pinnace, and with the leadsman taking soundings every few cables, the *Endeavour* edged into Matavai Bay.

Matavai is beautiful by any standards. To a ship's company who had been cooped-up for eight months in the cramped and squalid confines of an eighteenth-century ship,

A beach scene in Samoa, taken by an amateur photographer in the late nineteenth century.

it must have seemed beautiful beyond dreams. We can imagine the seamen's delight as they stared at the sandy beaches and steep-sided hills: hills which were here and there silvered with waterfalls and everywhere bejewelled with flowers – red hibiscus, yellow jasmine and the ubiquitous *tiare Tahiti*. Wherever the ground was level, the crew could make out little palm-thatched homesteads, scattered among fruit trees and fields. It was, to say the least, a wonderfully attractive haven in which to drop anchor.

And the people who came out in their canoes to welcome the *Endeavour* were every bit as attractive as the land they lived in. The men were tall, well-proportioned and agile, their skins the pale honey colour of a south European's. The women were graceful and lissom, with long dark hair and bodies they were clearly not ashamed of – for, we are told, 'they endeavoured to engage the attention of [the] sailors by exposing their

The *Astrolabe* at anchor off Mangaréva (Isles Gambier) from a painting by D'Urville's artist Le Breton.

beauties to their view.' To say the crew of the *Endeavour* responded with enthusiasm would be an understatement. In the words of that doyen of Pacific studies, Dr Beaglehole, they thought themselves 'imparadised'.

Imparadised is not a word often used nowadays, but it describes very precisely how almost all the early explorers felt and wrote about the islands of the Pacific. They regarded them as that earthly paradise which seamen from time immemorial have dreamed of: a port-of-call where the sun is ever shining, food and water are ever abundant, and the women are beautiful and ever eager to make love. Never before or since have explorers waxed so enthusiastic over the lands they have discovered.

It is not so easy to be sure about the other side of the coin – to know how the islanders felt about the Europeans who descended on them as unexpectedly as aliens from outer space. For the Pacific islanders had no written language; there are therefore no contemporary records to tell us what their feelings were, and we have always to judge their reaction at second hand, through the eyes of those who discovered them. Probably Alan Moorehead has summed up as well as anyone how they must have felt. He writes: 'They might have been compared to village children at the arrival of a travelling circus; they came forward to the encounter with a sort of timid, wondering excitement, eager to see the show, ready to be amazed, but a little fearful of approaching too close until they were sure that all was well.'

So we have some idea of how both Europeans and Tahitians felt that morning as Cook led his landing party across the sands of Matavai Bay. It was an historic moment, the first meaningful confrontation between two totally different peoples with totally different ways of life. Earlier explorers had of course made contact previously with the people of other Polynesian islands. Such contacts, however, had been fleeting. This was the first occasion on which an explorer was landing with the intention of spending not a few hours or a few days ashore, but several months. This therefore was the moment of truth.

The Europeans advanced over the fine black sand with confidence. The Tahitians, in contrast, were apprehensive. They had already, a couple of years earlier, been peppered with grapeshot by Wallis and bayoneted to death by Bougainville. They *wanted* to be friends with the strangers, but found it difficult to understand their *taboos*, their filthiness and the terrible rages they flew into for no apparent reason. So they now came forward, virtually on hands and knees, offering a cornucopia of coconuts and green branches – their symbol of peace. 'No[t] one of the Natives,' wrote Cook, 'made the least opposition at our landing, but came to us with all imaginable marks of friendship and submission.'

So far so good; the auguries for friendship could hardly have been more favourable, and it wasn't long before the Tahitians were inviting the Europeans into their homes. 'We proceeded for four or five miles,' wrote Cook's naturalist Joseph Banks, 'under groves of coconut and breadfruit trees. Beneath these were the habitations of the people, most of them without walls; the scene was the truest picture of an Arcadia . . .' If Banks had ended his description here, there might have been some hope for the people of the Pacific. However, that night aboard the *Endeavour* he added another eight words to the entry in his diary, words which transformed his eulogy into a valediction. 'The scene was the truest picture of an Arcadia,' he wrote, 'of which we were going to be kings.'

This sting in the tail epitomizes not only Banks's personal arrogance (which was considerable!), but the arrogance with which the people of Europe in general had, for the previous two centuries, been leaving their heartland to dominate the world.

There are two schools of thought about the pre-European people of the Pacific islands. Were they Noble Savages, living lives of happy innocence, as in the top picture; or were they simply savages, addicted to murder and cannibalism, as in the bottom?

In 1513, when Balboa became the first European to set eyes on the Pacific, he waded into the ocean and 'took possession of these seas and lands and islands and all thereunto annexed until the final day of judgement.' The fact that the seas and lands and islands might belong to somebody else seems not to have occurred to him; he claimed them as by divine right. A couple of centuries later when Banks and his companions landed in Tahiti, they took it for granted that they were going to be 'kings' of the demi-paradise into which they had stumbled. The fact that Tahiti already had kings of its own seems to have carried no weight with them; they never doubted that their presumed superiority entitled them to rule.

Before we condemn Balboa and Banks for a pride which on the face of it seems as consuming as Lucifer's, it is worth reminding ourselves that we are all children of our times; and the fact is that for over 400 years (from roughly 1500 to well past 1900) Europeans thought of themselves as an élite who were doing the rest of the world a favour by imposing on it *their* standards, *their* values and *their* beliefs. This they had the military muscle to do. It is also worth remembering that Balboa was perhaps the most honest and humane of the conquistadors, and that Banks was a dedicated scientist and a man of great intelligence and high ideals. This serves to underline the fact that the Europeans who so tragically destroyed the Polynesians and their culture were often neither bad nor cruel men; they were simply men of their times. It is easy for us to condemn them; but when one looks closely at the sort of people the islanders were and the sort of people the sixteenth- to eighteenth-century seamen were, then the opening up of the Pacific can be seen to have the inevitability of a Greek tragedy – a tale whose end is writ plain in its beginning.

For the Polynesians and the Europeans worshipped gods who were not only different but incompatible. The former were content to be happy, the latter were ever-striving to progress. It would seem from all the accounts that have come down to us that

Double canoes *(vaa-taie)* of Tahati,
painted by Sydney Parkinson, 1769.

the pre-European Polynesians were a gentle and happy people; however, because of the lack of written records we are in possession of few hard facts about them. Carbon dating of bones and artefacts may tell us when they first settled on their islands. Computer analysis of currents and winds may tell us the most likely routes by which they arrived. Sophisticated techniques of historical research may tell us what they ate, what they wore, what tools they used. But we have no certain way of assessing the quality of their lives. This is a matter of conjecture and there are two opposing schools of thought on the subject.

The romantically-minded believe that the islands really *were* a latter-day paradise, and the islanders a sweet-tempered and happy people who led lives of primordial innocence like Adam and Eve before the Fall. In support of this view they quote the early explorers. Cook wrote:

The soil is rich, fertile and well-water'd. Benevolent nature has not only supply'd them with necessarys but with an abundance of superfluities. Their behaviour to strangers and to each other is affable and courteous.

Forster wrote:

Food and drink, the two great wants of the human species are easily supplied, and the character of the people is amiable; their friendly behaviour to us would have done honour to the most civilized nation, and all their actions bespoke of a noble mind and a charming simplicity of manners.

Bougainville wrote:

I felt as though I had been transported to the Garden of Eden. Everywhere we found hospitality, peace, innocent joy and every appearance of happiness. What a country! What a people!

Captain Wallis's first meeting with the people of Tahiti, June 1767, from John Hawkesworth's *Voyages*.

It is worth repeating that never before or since have explorers gone into such rhapsodies over the land and the people they discovered. It would therefore seem, at least on the face of it, that life in the pre-European Pacific islands had much to commend it.

However, those with a less romantic and more realistic approach to history feel that the explorers make everything sound too good to be true. Isn't it possible, the realists argue, that the early seamen were so delighted to exchange the squalor and abstinence of their ships for the beauty and promiscuity of the islands, that they saw everything through rose-coloured spectacles? And isn't it possible that when they returned to Europe the accounts they brought back of their adventures were used by intellectuals to promote the myth of 'the Noble Savage' – the idea, very popular in eighteenth-century drawing rooms, that man in his natural state was free from sin, and that sin was a product of the greed and sophistry of civilization? The realists also point out that not all the islands were as overflowing with milk and honey as Tahiti – many were little more than outcrops of coral devoid of life – and that the islanders, far from living in a state of blissful innocence, had frequent wars, and were not averse to infanticide and human sacrifice. They even, on occasions, ate one another. All of which obviously adds up to something less than paradise.

We may never be able to prove which school of thought is nearer to the truth. What *is* beyond dispute is that over a period of some 2,000 years the Polynesians discovered and settled on virtually every island in the mid-Pacific, until by AD 1500 they had become by far the most widely-spread people on Earth; and that on these remote islands, cut off from the rest of the world, they established civilizations which were lacking in material artefacts, but where the way of life would seem from all accounts to have been idyllically happy. This was a great achievement.

We know far more about the European explorers who followed them.

First on the scene were the Spaniards. *Their* voyages were inspired by motives both sacred and profane. On one hand, an obsession with proselytizing, and on the other a lust for spices and gold – a combination which may strike us today as distasteful, but one which was not only widely accepted but widely applauded in the sixteenth century. For some 100 years the Pacific was to all intents and purposes a Spanish lake. Towards the end of the sixteenth century, however, its waters came under increasing threat from the Dutch and the British. The Dutch were less interested in exploration than the Spaniards, and had little zeal for proselytizing. Their forte was trade; they had the unenviable reputation of 'always offering too little and asking too much' – and getting away with it. Those lands they discovered and considered unsuitable for trade, like Australia, they abandoned. They did, however, establish a number of long-lived and highly profitable emporia in Indonesia, and played a major role in exploring and making known to the rest of the world the southernmost reaches of the Pacific. British interest in the ocean tended to be spasmodic and ambivalent in motive. Drake's crossing, for example, was inspired by both the wish to explore *and* the wish to plunder. Cook's three great voyages – which transformed the map of the Pacific from a maze of medieval misconception to an outline that was recognizably modern – were inspired by both the wish to acquire scientific knowledge *and* the wish to acquire strategic bases. The nineteenth century, however, saw two great British voyages which were purely scientific; Darwin's voyage in the *Beagle,* which inspired the modern theory of evolution, and Nares's voyage in the *Challenger,* which led to the birth of oceanography as a practical science. The most enlightened explorers of the Pacific were probably the French. It is true that they never really understood the Polynesians, and often praised them for the wrong reasons. Yet they, more than any other nation, seemed to appreciate that the islanders had something of value to offer the rest of the world. If the Napoleonic Wars had been won by the forces of the French revolutionary left and not by the forces of the British reactionary right, then the myth of the Noble Savage *might* have metamorphosed into a sort of reality.

But history is full of ifs. . . By the time the Americans and the Russians arrived on the scene, the central reaches of the Pacific had been explored. Both nations were therefore obliged to concentrate their voyaging around the ocean's near-polar extremities. The Russians Bering, Chirikov, Kotzebue and Lutke mapped the approaches to the Bering Strait. The American Wilkes, in one of the most hazardous and physically demanding voyages of all time, mapped a large part of the coast of Antarctica, and with the discovery of this last continent the delineation of the Pacific was complete. It had taken the European explorers more than 300 years simply to define the limits of this greatest of oceans.

Most of these European explorers who came to the Pacific had one thing in common. They were filled with an almost daemonic energy – Magellan risking (and finding) death in a frenzy of religious fervour, Cook striving, in his own words, always 'to go farther than man had ever gone before', Wilkes driving his near-foundering ship and mutinous crew to the very limit of human endurance. They were all men of action, ever striving to learn about and, as they saw it, to improve the world. It is one of the tragedies of history that many of them mistook knowledge for wisdom, and that the changes they brought about were not always for the better.

And if this is true of the explorers, it is even more true of those who followed them: the exploiters.

The Pacific islands had little, except copra, that was instantly exploitable – none of the gold of the Incas or the grazing land of the American Indians. The Polynesians therefore suffered comparatively little in the way of cruel or deliberate exploitation. But the privateers who used their harbours as bases were predatory, the whalers who decimated their herds of sperm and right whales were brutal, the missionaries who forbade them to sing, dance or play music were bigoted, and today's tourists tend to destroy the very things that they came in search of. Many of these exploiters were filled with almost as great an energy as the explorers who preceded them – witness the tourist who today rushes around Papeete taking photographs, then boasts that he or she has 'done' Tahiti! What chance of survival did the easy-going Polynesians have in the face of such a whirlwind of Westernization?

A few of the islanders did of course survive; although there was a time about 100 years ago, when it seemed that the whole race might, as the Polynesians themselves put it, drift apathetically into the night to be absorbed by the multitude of their ancestors, dying of accidie simply because all the things that they valued and loved had been taken from them, and they had no wish to go on living. That crisis passed, and the Polynesians today are increasing in number. But their traditional way of life has gone for ever, gone almost as completely as though it had never been, and the world is the poorer for its going.

Some people say the idea that the islanders once lived lives of innocence and happiness is a myth. But this does not seem to have been the case. The concept of the Noble Savage was myth. The happiness of the Polynesians' traditional way of life – for all its flaws, idiosyncracies and intellectual naievety – was real. To understand just *how* real we need to go back to the very beginning of things, to the forming of the Pacific. For the way the Pacific was formed determined the layout of its islands; and in turn the layout of its islands determined how, when and by what sort of people they came to be populated.

The Forming Of The Pacific

Kio was the original god. It was he who created the universe by means of his divine powers.
Kio slept in the darkness, and darkness covered the universe. Then Kio spoke saying, 'Who will cause the night to be infused with the soft light of dawn and the glow of twilight?' . . . And it was done. . .
And when there was light, Kio commanded the Sand to lie with the Water, saying 'Be fertile.' And they heard him, and made children.

Traditional Polynesian chant describing the creation, sung by the people of the Tuamotus many centuries before Christians came to the Pacific.

The forming of the Pacific has been going on for something like 4,000 million years. In the beginning, according to Genesis and the geologists – and according too to Polynesian legend – there was no sea, only the molten orb of the Earth, endlessly spinning, imperceptibly cooling. As the Earth cooled, so its heavier rocks like nickel and iron coalesced around the centre, while its lighter rocks like the silicon-compounds formed a crust round the surface. The lightweight rocks of the surface contained moisture, and it is with this moisture that the story of the Pacific begins.

As our planet cooled, its surface rocks contracted and the moisture was squeezed out of them; this moisture was then evaporated by the heat of the Earth and metamorphosed to atmosphere. Because Earth was large enough to have sufficient gravity to retain this atmosphere, it didn't drift away into space (which is what happens to the atmosphere of smaller celestial bodies like the moon) but developed into a protective mantle of cloud: cloud which eventually became so impregnated with water-vapour that it voided rain. The rain didn't settle to start with, for the rocks of Earth were still hotter than the boiling point of water, and the raindrops as they hit the surface were simply converted to steam and sucked back into the atmosphere. There came a time, however, when the rocks became so cool that the rain as it hit them no longer boiled away. It settled. It collected in little pools. Ever seeking the lowest levels, it began to form into seas.

We don't know for how long these first primordial rains poured down from the clouds, maybe a million years, maybe 100 million. Nor do we know if the rain fell gently or in sudden tempests which scoured away the very surface of the Earth. All we know is that it rained and rained and rained, until our planet became – as it remains to this day – a world of water.

All this took place about 4,000 million years ago. Our oceans, in other words, are so old as to be almost ageless, an agelessness summed up by that fine writer of the sea, Joseph Conrad: 'No man can in truth declare that he ever saw the sea look young, as the Earth looks young in spring.' Another characteristic of the oceans is their apparent unchangeability. In the last 1,000 million years the land-masses have changed out of all recognition, while the oceans appear to have changed hardly at all. There would be little difference between being caught in a storm at sea in the Palaeozoic era and being caught in a storm at sea today, and many of the 60,000,000,000,000,000,000,000,000,000,000,000,000,000,000,000-odd molecules of water which go to make up the world's oceans have been continuously circulating, unaltered in structure, since the time of the first rains. No wonder priests and poets extol 'the eternal deep' and 'the everlasting sea'. But although the oceans' appearance and water-content have changed little, their structure – the position, size and shape of them – has changed a great deal. To understand how the primordial sheets of water developed into the oceans as we know them today, we need to know something of the elemental forces which have been constantly restructuring the layout of land and sea.

It is best not to be too dogmatic about the early history of our planet. Until comparatively recently it was thought that the oceans were the result of cataclysmic disasters: that the Atlantic resulted from the sinking of the lost continent of Atlantis after an earthquake and the Pacific was a crater left behind when matter whirled off the Earth to form the moon. These ideas have few supporters today, and most scientists now agree that our oceans' present structure can be attributed to continental drift, and that continental drift can in turn be attributed to plate tectonics.

The theory of continental drift is delightfully simple. It was as long ago as 1858 that Antoine Snider pointed out that the continents are rather like the pieces of a jig-saw puzzle; if you compress them they fit very neatly one into the other – the bulge of Africa, for example, fits almost exactly into the bight of the Caribbean. Snider was trying to prove the limited point that the coal seams of Europe run along the same parallels of latitude as the coal seams of North America. He drew maps to demonstrate this, and

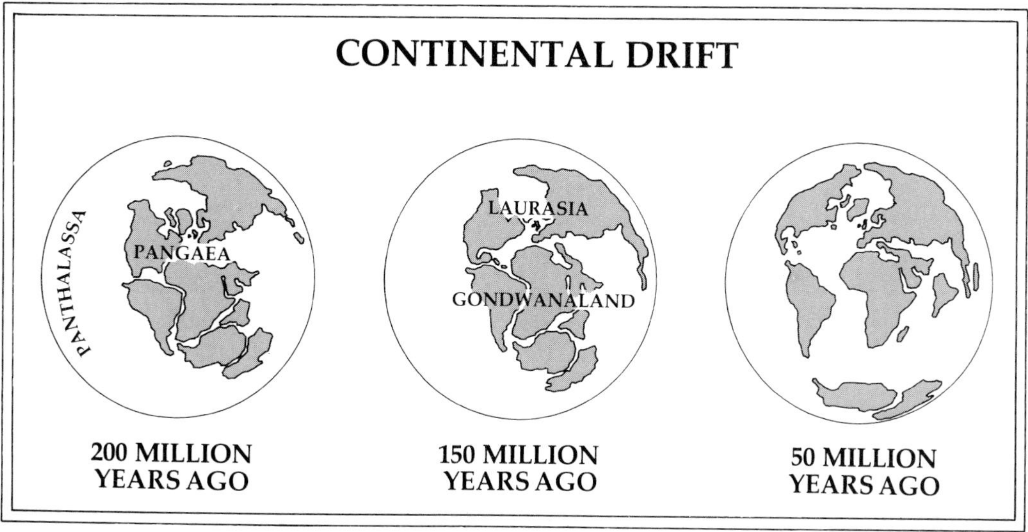

these seem to have been the first ever published to show the continents in juxtaposition. He made no attempt to explain how the various pieces of his jig-saw might have drifted apart. This was left to Alfred Wegener, who read his famous paper to the Geological Society of Frankfurt in 1912. Wegener envisaged a supercontinent (Pangaea) which began to break up about 250 million years ago, with its fragments drifting slowly into their present positions under the influence of thermal convection from the interior of the Earth. He was too far ahead of his times. His father-in-law warned him, 'to work at subjects outside the traditionally defined bounds of science exposes one to being regarded with mistrust and being considered an outsider', and this warning was prophetic. For 50 years geologists were reluctant to believe that Wegener, a mere meteorologist, could have come up with so simple and so revolutionary a theory, and be right. As recently as 1964 the *Time-Life Nature Library* wrote, with something approaching contempt, 'Unfortunately for Wegener's daring hypothesis there are no known forces strong enough to move the continents around the earth, let along split them into fragments. . . For these reasons the theory of continental drift has been abandoned by nearly all geologists'.

Then came a discovery which gave Wegener's ideas a new lease of life, the discovery of plate tectonics. Our understanding of plate tectonics has grown steadily over the last couple of decades as a result of research by scientists all over the world. It has

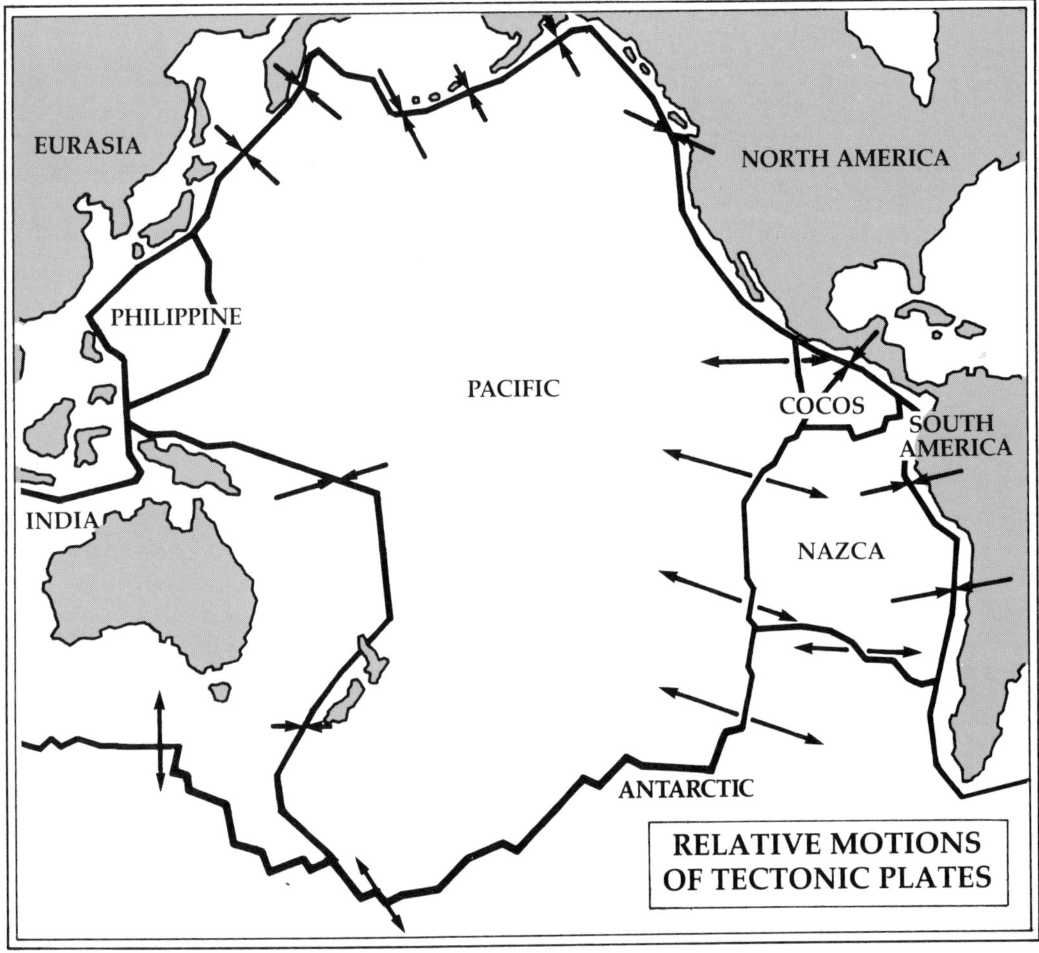

RELATIVE MOTIONS OF TECTONIC PLATES

been established that the crust of the Earth consists of five or six major plates and roughly the same number of minor ones. Some plates are continental and the crust of these is relatively thick, some are oceanic and the crust of these is relatively thin. All of them rest on the ostenosphere, which is a layer of semi-molten matter sandwiched between the Earth's cold and solid outer crust and its hot and liquid inner core. The ostenosphere forms a viscous surface across which the plates are being fractionally but continuously moved by convection-currents welling up from the molten innards of the Earth.

This concept of plate tectonics has added enormously to our understanding of the world. Now that we realize the continents are forever on the move we can understand how regions which were near-polar 100-million years ago are near-tropical today. We can also appreciate how, as plates have collided, great mountain ranges such as the Himalayas and the Andes have been prised up from the bed of the sea. Our knowledge of the oceans has been similarly increased, and we can see that far from being static sheets of water which have lain inert from time immemorial, they are 'restless and dynamic seas . . . which are being continuously created and at the same time continuously destroyed'.

A typical Pacific atoll: Wilson Island in the Great Barrier Reef.

The Pacific has attained its present position, shape and size as a result of this process of creation and destruction. It consists of four light oceanic plates – the huge plate of the Pacific itself, and the small plates of Nazca, Cocos and Philippines – surrounded by five heavy continental plates – Eurasia, North America, South America, Antarctica and India (for geological purposes India includes the extension of Australasia). Where these plates meet, great fracture-lines split open the crust of the Earth. The fracture-lines are areas of instability and hence of volcanic activity. In places where the plates are drifting apart, there is little friction, and here volcanic activity tends to be continuous but peaceful. In places where the plates are boring into or sliding past one another, the story is very different. Here there is friction. And here, as the oceanic plates crumble and disintegrate under the impact of their heavier neighbours, volcanic activity is often catastrophically violent.

To reduce a complex subject to the simplest possible terms, the Pacific Ocean consists of two totally different areas. In the south, the east and the centre is a stable area of quietly forming ridges and deep-sea basins which is being created as the oceanic plates drift apart. In the north, the west and the periphery is a highly unstable area of deep-sea trenches and island-arcs which is being destroyed as the oceanic and continental plates grind together.

The south, east and centre of the Pacific are dominated by the great fracture-line which marks the boundary between the Pacific plate on one side, and the plates of the Cocos, Nazca and Antarctica on the other side. This fracture-line runs diagonally across the ocean from the Ross Sea to the Gulf of California, and the Pacific plate is ever edging away from it to the north-west, while the other plates are ever edging away from it to the south-east. As the plates move apart, so magma from the core of the Earth comes welling up between them in an almost continuous flow. This therefore is an area of much movement and much heat; but because the plates are moving apart there is no friction; and because there is no friction there is no violent seismic activity – no earth tremors, no volcanic eruptions, simply a controlled and continuous outpouring of magma from the bed of the sea. As this magma has continued over millions of years to ooze out from the sea-bed, it has formed an ever-expanding ridge (the Pacific-Antarctic and the East Pacific Rises) immediately above the fracture-line. Eventually this ridge became so heavy that the sea bed subsided beneath its weight, and this led to the formation, along either flank of the ridge, of deep-sea basins. Because this process, which is known as sea-floor spreading, has been slow, continuous and gentle, there are, in this part of the Pacific, no volcanoes, and because there are no volcanoes there are none of those progeny of volcanoes, islands.

Here therefore is an area where the ocean-floor consists of a quietly spreading ridge and stable basins, while the ocean-surface consists of a vast expanse of water uncluttered by island, atoll or reef. In this part of the Pacific, as Magellan and many subsequent voyagers found to their cost, it is possible to sail for two months and 3,000 miles without ever sighting land. No other ocean contains so vast an expanse of featureless sea.

It is partly because this area of the Pacific *is* so featureless that its winds and currents – unchecked and undiverted by land – have a basic simplicity. At the approaches to the South Pole, winds and currents blow and flow non-stop and strongly from west to east; at the approaches to the equator they blow and flow non-stop, though not so strongly, from east to west. These basic characteristics have prevailed in this part of the Pacific if not from the dawn of time at least from the dawn of recorded history.

A paucity of islands, strong and continuous one-way winds and currents, vast distances . . . it would be hard to imagine greater disincentives to voyaging. No wonder therefore that these lonely reaches of the south, east and central Pacific were the last habitable parts of Earth to witness the coming of man. No wonder they were explored and populated only recently and only with the greatest difficulty.

It has been a different story elsewhere in the Pacific. Moving to the ocean's north, west and periphery is like moving to another world; one dominated by a fracture-line that is not crust-creating, but crust-consuming – the Andesite Line.

The Andesite Line is the longest and most active fracture-line on Earth. It all but encircles the Pacific and throughout the whole of its length it is either compressional or transform. In other words, the plates which adjoin it are either meeting head-on, or are sliding past one another. Compressional or transform, the result is the same. Friction. Friction which leads to violent seismic activity, as the crust of the lightweight oceanic

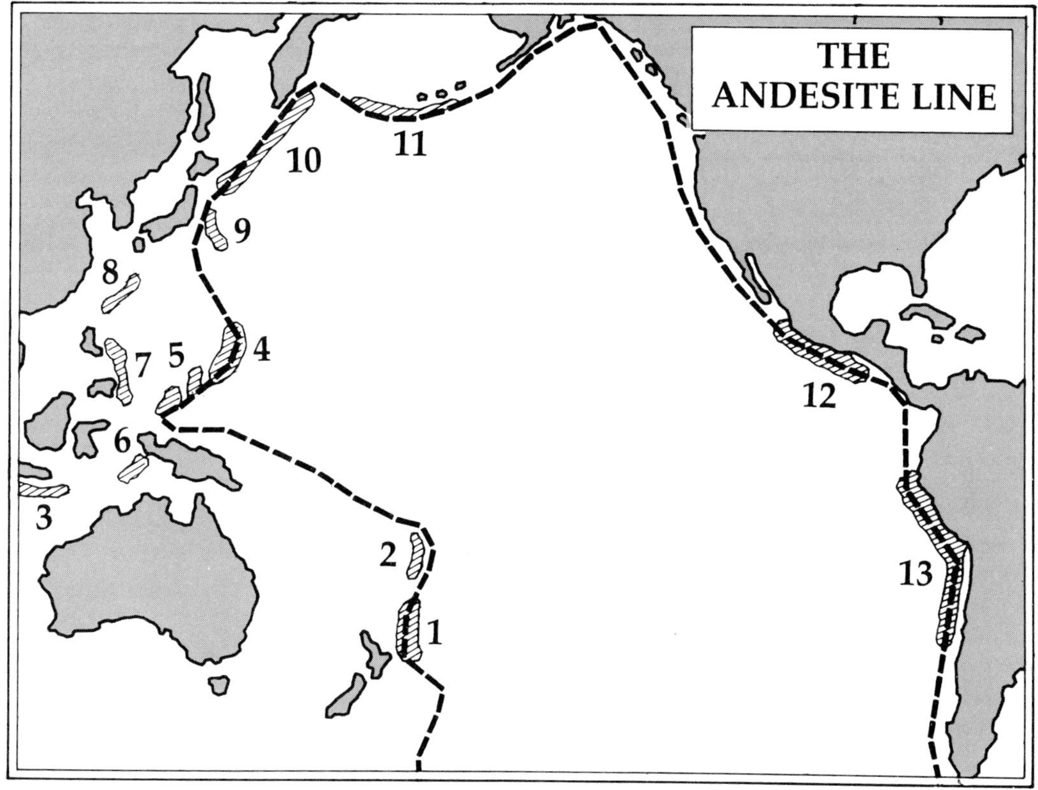

The dotted Andesite Line and the girdle of deep sea trenches round the Pacific: 1 Puerto Rico 2 Aleutian 3 Kuril 4 Japanese 5 Rin Kin 6 Nero 7 Yap 8 Pelen 9 Philippine 10 Sunda 11 Tonga 12 Kermadec 13 Peru and Chile 14 Middle American.

plates are being forever pulverized, fragmented and forced either down to form deep-sea trenches, or up to form ranges of volcanic mountains.

Along most of the length of the Andesite Line we have a situation where a continental plate is grinding into an oceanic plate, and the result is that girdle of trenches and volcanoes which encircles the Pacific, from Japan to Tierra del Fuego, with the deepest trenches often lying within the shadow of the highest mountains. (The Japanese and Kuril Trenches, 34,472ft (10,542m), for example, lie alongside the great volcanic peaks of Japan and Kamchatka; the Mid-American Trench, 21,784ft (6,662m), lies alongside the volcanoes of Mexico, while the Peru-Chile Trench, 26,375ft (8,066m), lies alongside the volcanoes of the Andes.)

However, in the south-west section of the Andesite Line, there is collision between two oceanic plates and the result here has been a skein of deep-sea trenches and a plethora of islands – more islands than in all the rest of the world put together.

About 80 per cent of all the islands in the world lie within a triangle whose apexes are Tokyo, Jakarta and Pitcairn. These islands have been spawned by violent seismic activity in an area where the plates of Eurasia, the Philippines, India and the Pacific have for millions of years been boring into or grinding past one another. This part of the world has witnessed the most catastrophic natural disasters ever recorded. The eruption of Krakatoa hurled rocks 34 miles into the air, dust fell for eleven days, and the

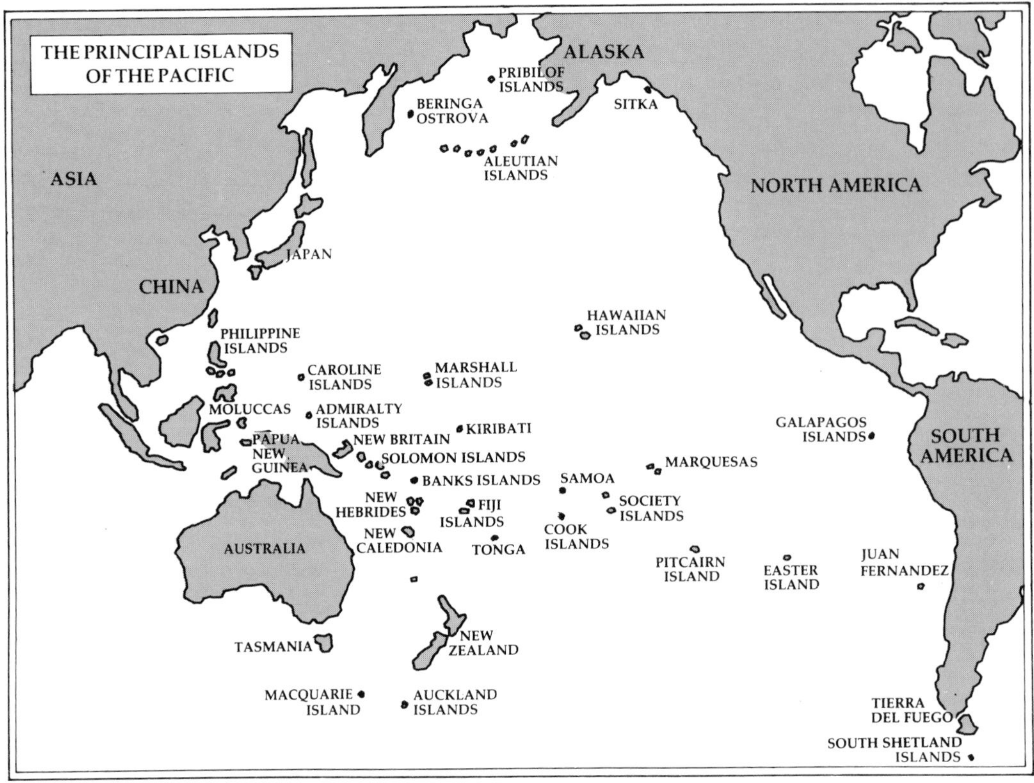

explosion, like the roar of heavy guns, was heard 3,000 miles away. The earthquake of Kwanto killed some 150,000 people and the sea-bed subsided a thousand feet. In the wake of such activity literally thousands of volcanic cones have erupted from the bed of the sea with the vigour of Jason's legendary corn. And the volcanic cones of yesterday are the islands of today.

These islands – some major land masses in their own right, some part of huge archipelagos and some isolated specks in an infinity of sea – have been a key factor in how, when and by whom the Pacific was first explored and occupied.

In the west, off the coast of Asia, the islands, large and close knit, are clustered together in two great archipelagos, Indonesia and the Philippines. Geologically they consist of mixed rocks, faulted and folded; their flora and fauna are essentially Asiatic, so too are their people. A little farther to the east lie the islands of Melanesia – the Solomons, New Guinea, New Hebrides, New Caledonia and Fiji. They too are fairly large, but are more widely scattered than their westerly neighbours. Although they too are basically continental, their flora, fauna and people tend to be more idiosyncratic. Farther still to the north and to the east lie the islands of Micronesia and Polynesia – the Marianas, the Marshalls, Samoa, Tonga, the Society Islands and the Tuamotu Archipelago. These islands are altogether different. All of them are fashioned out of the one type of basaltic rock which has been extruded from the sea-bed of the plate of the Pacific; most (but not all) of them are small, infertile and able to support only the most basic types of flora and fauna. They are widely scattered, and the farther east one sails into the Pacific the more remote and isolated the islands become.

Around these islands, 'like confetti scattered across the surface of a vast blue lake', are to be found another phenomenon of the Pacific, its atolls. As volcanoes spawn

The volcanoes of the Andesite Line encircle much of the Pacific. *Top* Mount Fiji-San, Japan; *below* Mount Egmont, New Zealand.

islands, so islands spawn atolls – low flat strips of coral strung out like the beads of a necklace around a central lagoon. They are reefs of living creatures which have survived the subsidence of the volcano to which they were originally attached, and have established a precarious but viable existence of their own. In appearance many of them are beautiful, but since they lack soil and surface water and are prone to devastation by hurricanes, they are not the easiest environment for human settlement. Frequently they degenerate to wave-swept reefs, which are a hazard to navigation.

These western and peripheral reaches of the Pacific are completely different from the eastern and central reaches, the one being stable, simple and devoid of islands, the other unstable, complex and boasting the greatest concentration of islands in the world. It is partly because the west Pacific *is* so complex that its winds and currents are complex too.

Here the prevailing winds are the South-east and the North-east Trades, which blow steadily for most of the year. However, during the summer there is a reversal, and for several months the prevailing wind is from west to east. The major oceanic current, the South Equatorial, also flows steadily from east to west; but here too there is a complication; between roughly 0° and 5° North the Equatorial Counter Current flows strongly in the opposite direction.

A multitude of islands, winds and currents which blow and flow at different times of the year in different directions. . . It would be hard to imagine conditions that could be more favourable for deep-sea voyaging. No wonder therefore that these south-western reaches of the Pacific were the first part of the ocean to witness the coming of man. Certainly people were living here at least a couple of millennia before the birth of Christ.

So far we have stressed the differences between the various parts of the Pacific. However, one feature is common to all parts. Everything is constructed, everything happens, on a vast scale. The Pacific is an ocean of superlatives. Here is the deepest trench in the world – the Marianas, 35,806ft (10,950m), and the highest base-to-summit mountain – Mount Kea in Hawaii, 33,476ft (10,177m). Here are the most violent storms and the most breathless calms, the most active volcanoes and the most stable and featureless deep-sea basins. And everywhere the distances are enormous. The Pacific covers a greater area than all the land in the world put together; it is 9,500 miles from the Bering Strait in the north to the Ross Sea in the south, and 12,500 miles from Panama in the east to the Malay Peninsula in the west – that is almost exactly halfway round the world. Imagine yourself setting sail from Easter Island. You could sail south for 3,250 miles without sighting land, north for 3,000 miles without sighting land, and east for 1,750 miles without sighting land. Your nearest land to the west would be the miniscule speck of Ducie Island 750 miles away, and even with modern navigational aids you would have to be a first-class seaman to make a landfall. Many other Pacific islands are almost equally remote – Clipperton, Lisienski, Campbell, Sala y Gomez; it is doubtful if one person in a million has heard of them, let alone could place them on the map. Nowhere else on Earth are the distances so vast, the sense of loneliness and isolation so aching.

How, one wonders, did early man manage to penetrate into even the most far-flung reaches of this huge ocean, and not only survive but establish in this alien environment happy and successful civilizations?

CHAPTER TWO

THE PEOPLE OF THE PACIFIC

They are without vice (COOK)... *They know no other god than love* (COMMERSON)... *Both their bodies and souls are moulded to perfection* (BANKS)... *Their stature is small, their eyes too prominent. In my opinion their Characters have been as much depreciated as their beauties have been Magnefyed.* (WALES)

The people of the Pacific have always been an enigma to the rest of the world. Where did they come from? What sort of people were they? How did they manage to discover and settle on even the remotest of the Pacific atolls. Only the first of these questions is easy to answer.

The people of the Pacific came from the west, from Indonesia and the Philippines.

About 20,000 years ago Indonesia and the Philippines were occupied by an Australoid people – small, dark-skinned hunter-gatherers, who had established themselves over most of south-east Asia. Today all that is left of these once ubiquitous people are a few isolated remnants in the forests of Malaya, the Philippines and the Andaman Islands; for something like 10,000 years ago they were overrun by a more technically advanced and warlike race, the Mongoloids. The Mongoloids, who originated in present-day China, were taller, paler-skinned and more heavily-built than the Australoids. They were cultivators – mainly of the yam and the taro – and husbanders – mainly of poultry and pigs; they were also fishermen, and this implies that they had some expertise in boat building and some knowledge of the sea. The two races intermingled and intermarried, and their descendants fanned out across the Pacific in search of new fishing grounds and new lands. In his *Geography of the Pacific* Kenneth Emory makes this point very clearly. 'From ancient times the great islands close to south-east Asia have drawn forth their people and converted them into searfarers. As these people developed skill and daring they struck out eastward across the seas, eventually reaching even the most remote islands in the Pacific.' Emory may have written this thirty years ago, but recent research has strengthened rather than weakened his fundamental premise, that the Pacific islands were populated by the purposeful migration of people sailing east from Asia.

This, it should be said, is not the only interpretation of how the Pacific came to be populated. Thor Heyerdahl and, to a lesser degree, Andrew Sharp have put forward very different theories.

In 1947 Thor Heyerdahl and five Scandinavian companions built a balsa-wood raft, the *Kon-Tiki*, and set out from Peru to try to prove that South American Indians could have drifted west across the Pacific and so reached the islands of Polynesia. They succeeded. After a voyage of 100 days and 4,000 miles, they beached their raft on an atoll in the Tuamotus. Thor Heyerdahl not only wrote a best-seller about this voyage – *The Kon-Tiki Expedition* – he also wrote a number of scholarly works – *American Indians in*

The people of the Pacific include many different ethnic types: *inset* a man of Oonalashka (Aleutian Islands), from a drawing by John Webber; *lower* a man, woman and child, natives of Tierra del Fuego (Straits of Magellan), from a drawing by Sydney Parkinson; *above left* a Maori chief, the face 'curiously tataow'd' (New Zealand), from a drawing by Sydney Parkinson; *above right* a young woman of the Sandwich Islands (Hawaii), from a drawing by John Webber.

the Pacific, *Sea Routes to Polynesia* and *The Art of Easter Island*. In these he very persuasively advanced the theory that the Pacific islands were settled not by Asians sailing east, but by American Indians drifting west. This caused a considerable ripple in the academic pond, for Heyerdahl was both a practical seaman who had proved his point and a forceful scholar who had a point to prove.

South American Indians undoubtedly *did* reach some islands in the central Pacific. There is no other explanation for the fact that the Polynesians cultivated the sweet potato (*Ipomoea batatas*) which was unknown in Asia and had its origins, both linguistically and botanically, in the Andes. There is also the evidence of the *ahus*, or statue-platforms, of Easter Island, several of which contain masonry so exactly similar to Inca masonry that it can only by explained by direct contact. There is, however, a world of difference between saying that *some* islands in Polynesia were visited by *some* people from South America, and saying that *all* the islands of the Pacific were populated by people of South American origin. Common sense makes the latter view untenable. For the layout of the Pacific archipelagos is such that the voyager from the west is offered a succession of island stepping-stones into the unknown, whereas the voyager from the east is faced immediately by a vast expanse of featureless, islandless sea. Also the currents are more favourable for voyaging from the west – *Kon-Tiki* had to be towed out to sea for more than 70 miles before her drift could begin. Most people today feel that Thor Heyerdahl had a good hand to play but overplayed it, a view endorsed by a senior lecturer in prehistory at the Australian National University, Peter Bellwood, who writes: 'Modern opinion on the Polynesians is that they derive from somewhere in eastern Indonesia or the Philippines, and that they migrated through Melanesia into Polynesia between 2000 and 1000 BC. This view is soundly supported by archaeology and linguistics.'

It is easier to say where the people of the Pacific came from than to say what sort of people they are, or rather were, before they suffered the trauma of Europeanization.

Not all Pacific islanders belong to the same ethnic group; there are obvious and very basic differences between the inhabitants of New Zealand, Papua New Guinea and the Aleutian Islands. However, within the huge and ill-defined triangle of Polynesia, an area roughly the size of the USSR, there is a close ethnic homogeneity between the people of *all* the islands, even those as far apart as New Zealand, Easter Island and Hawaii. The people within this enormous triangle are one race. This was noticed as long ago as 1774 by Cook, who wrote, 'Is it not remarkable that the same Nation should have spread themselves over all the isles in this vast Ocean?'

Even more remarkable is the fact that Cook's one 'Nation' managed, in a far from easy environment, to establish civilizations which may have been flawed and idiosyncratic, but which were undeniably successful.

Students of archaeology and linguistics are all agreed that the Polynesians first arrived in the more westerly of their islands – Tonga and Samoa – about 1200 BC and that they had settled into the whole of their island-kingdom, except New Zealand, by about AD 500. In other words, when an eighteenth-century European explorer stepped on to a Pacific island he was often making contact with a people and a civilization more ancient than his own. It is of course true that Polynesian civilization was nothing like as technically advanced as its European counterpart, and this was especially the case with regard to material artefacts and weapons. It was, however, a civilization which had enabled its people to lead contented lives for thousands of years, and it hadn't collapsed under either internal or external pressures. Any civilization which meets these criteria must be considered a success.

'The manner in which the New Zealand Warriors defy their Enemies', from a drawing by Sydney Parkinson, 1769 and *left* 'A man of the Sandwich Islands, dancing,' from a drawing by John Webber, 1799.

It is not so easy to say *why* the early Polynesians were a success. The difficulty here is that we can only see them through other people's eyes and other people's prejudices, the romanticism of Banks and Commerson, the spiritual arrogance of the missionaries, or the sexual preoccupation of the seamen, traders and whalers. To get a true picture of the early Polynesians we need to ignore these prejudices and concentrate on facts. What did they eat? What sort of homes did they live in? What laws were they governed by? What gods did they worship? What was the structure of their society? What pastimes did they indulge in? From these bare bones should emerge a portrait based not on myth but on reality.

The pre-European Polynesians ate little meat and less grain. Their diet was sea food, tubers and fruit. The first people to arrive in the islands relied almost wholly on seafood – 'fish, turtles, crabs, sea-birds and porpoises', the archaeologists tell us. Tropical lagoons and their encircling reefs are generally regarded as an excellent habitat for molluscs, crustaceans and fish; but although fish may have been many in variety, they were usually few in number – nowhere in the central Pacific is there anything like the enormous shoals of salmon and anchovy which are found off the coasts of Alaska and Chile. Also less than one type of reef-fish in ten is edible. The harvest of the sea was not won easily.

Since seafishing was so much a part of their lives, it is not surprising that the Polynesians became expert builders of canoes and makers of fishing gear. Their basic canoes were dugouts with a balancing outrigger; fast, manoeuvrable and seaworthy craft which could be either paddled or sailed, and easily beached. Their fishing tackle was technically sophisticated and often aesthetically beautiful, with different types of hook, line and sinker for different types of fish, usually made out of bone, pearl-shell or obsidian. In time the Polynesians became the most versatile and proficient fishermen on Earth. They could not, however, have survived if they had depended entirely on the sea for sustenance, and horticulture first supplemented seafishing, then gradually superseded it as the Polynesians' main occupation.

The smaller islands of Polynesia contain virtually no indigenous edible plants or land animals. It is true that some of the larger islands contain both, but only in small number. Nowhere, except in New Zealand, did the land provide sufficient food to sustain human life. So when Cook wrote that 'benevolent nature has not only supply'd them with necessarys, but with an abundance of superfluities', he had – for once – got it wrong. Virtually all the food-producing trees and plants which flourished in the pre-European Pacific islands – the coconut palm, the taro, the sweet potato, the yam, breadfruit, banana, pandanus, gourd, chestnut and arrowroot – were brought there by the early settlers. It was not 'benevolent nature' which provided the Polynesians with their wealth of tubers and fruit, but industrious man.

The most important of the Polynesians' trees was the coconut palm, which had a wide range of uses; its trunk provided (poor quality) wood for building, its leaves were used for roofing and mats, its fibre was used for cordage, its roots provided the ingredients for medicines and dyes, while its fruit provided not only food and drink but a number of valuable by-products such as copra and soap. The coconut palm is tolerant of saline conditions, and will flourish on even the most infertile and wave-swept atoll. Their staple crop was the taro, a tuberous and nutritious aroid – both roots and leaves can be eaten – which is easy to grow so long as it has moisture and warmth. The taro was cultivated in carefully irrigated fields, or in pits dug out to below the level of the water-table. Propagation was by cuttings, as with vines. Over the years the Polynesians perfected a system of shifting horticulture which may have *looked* simple, but was in fact a sophisticated form of crop rotation. A plot would be cleared, planted for two or three consecutive years with mixed or rotated crops, then allowed to lie fallow for something like twelve years, thus allowing the soil to regenerate. Fields were screened with plantations of breadfruit and pandanus and made attractive with borders of flowering shrubs. It would therefore be true to say that the beauty of the Polynesian countryside bears little more relation to Nature than the beauty of the English countryside. The pre-European islanders may indeed have lived in a Garden of Eden, but the garden was planted and tended by man.

There is no word in the Polynesian language for village or town, for the pre-European islanders had neither. They lived in small, single-storey, single-room homesteads which were scattered at random throughout the whole of their tribal territory. These homesteads were made of wood and thatched with palm; some were open-sided, but most had walls of loosely-woven wickerwork. Such buildings may have been simple, but they were well suited to their environment, being cool, dry, airy and able to withstand the hurricanes which swept many of the islands. They were usually surrounded by small, fenced-in gardens, and joined one to another by paths. Most homes were handed down from father to son, although on a few islands inheritance was from mother to son. Occasionally houses were clustered together around some chiefly residence or particularly favoured site, but by and large homesteads were spread evenly throughout all land which was suitable for cultivation, with families and their dependants tending to congregate together to form little loosely-connected sub-communities within the main tribe.

Polynesian laws were simple. Since the islanders didn't write, there was no formal legal code; in its place was a strong traditional knowledge of what was right and what was wrong. What was wrong was *taboo* – one of the few Polynesian words to have become part of the English language – and everything that wasn't *taboo* was acceptable. People knew by their upbringing what things were *taboo*; anything contrary to their religion was *taboo*, so was anything contrary to established custom, so was anything unkind. Those who broke *taboo* were publicly rebuked by the tribal elders, and, what

Polynesian homesteads: *top* the house of a Maori chief, Bay of Islands, New Zealand and *above* other local houses, both from Dumont D'Urville's atlas. *Right* A ghost house, used for storing ancestral relics, Matema, Solomon Islands, photographed by John Watt Beattie in 1906.

was more to the point, the whole family was made to share the miscreant's humiliation and disgrace. Physical punishments were often hinted at but seldom carried out, since every family, zealous of its good name, felt obliged to see that whatever crime had been committed was not repeated. This system has been described, with some justification, as 'inflexible and open to abuse'. However, one might reasonably argue that it was more civilized than stoning adulterers to death, cutting off thieves' hands or transporting prostitutes to the other side of the world.

The writer who lays down the law about Polynesian religion is asking for trouble, for we know tantalizingly little about this aspect of the islanders' lives. All Polynesians, however, appear to have held certain fundamental beliefs. They all believed in one god, or perhaps godhead would be a more accurate term; one supreme 'Creator of Life', who could not be personified but was usually referred to as Te Atua. Subordinate to Te Atua were a number of lesser gods and folk heroes – rather like those of Greek and Roman mythology – who were associated with particular activities. There was Tangaroa, the god of the sea, Tu, the god of war, Rongo, the god of horticulture, and Tane, the god of procreation. Still farther down the scale were a number of what might be termed local or specialized gods, like Pele, the volcano goddess of Hawaii. Finally there were the not so important spirits, the spirits of well-loved ancestors who were revered, and the spirits of evil-doers who were feared.

None of these gods or spirits was particularly demanding. They were remembered and propitiated at the occasional ceremony; several crafts such as tattooing and canoe-building involved religious rituals. On some islands, notably the Societies, temples were built in the gods' honour, and they were offered the occasional sacrifice, sometimes human. All this demanded few acolytes.

However, in the sixteenth century a privileged priesthood known as the Arioi seems to have emerged in and around the Society Islands. As well as outraging Western observers by killing their children at birth, the Arioi have been accused of 'a degree of rapacity, cruelty and promiscuity unparalleled in Polynesia'. Although there is never smoke without fire, in my opinion outsiders should be wary of passing judgement on other people's religious practices. The Ariois' infanticide, for example, was probably due in part to their efforts to prevent a population explosion which they knew the economy of the islands could not support. It is also worth bearing in mind that almost all we know about the Arioi stems from the writings of the early missionaries, who were hardly likely to look with favour on a rival priestly élite.

Polynesian religion had many imperfections, both in theory and practice. However, it never sparked off the sort of religious wars which bedevilled Europe, nor did it ever demand anything remotely like the mass sacrifices which cast so dark a shadow over the lives of the Aztecs. By and large it kept most of the people happy most of the time; and it is, I think, significant that the pre-European islanders were firm believers in heaven, but had no concept of hell. Hell was something they learned about from the West.

The structure of Polynesian society was often misunderstood by the early explorers. It may at first sight have appeared to be democratic – this is certainly the way romantics like Banks and Bougainville *wanted* to see it. However, first impressions can be misleading; and in spite of the panegyrics of those who believed in the myth of the Noble Savage, the pre-European Polynesians' lives were controlled by a system which was tribal and feudal, and had more in common with medieval England than with the Arcadia of Greek legend. Each tribe had its own territory; this was usually a single atoll, or, in the larger islands, a clearly-defined segment of land with a large, fertile coastal area, and a smaller, infertile inland area tapering off into the central hills. A tribe was ruled by its hereditary god-descended royal family and its powerful heriditary aristocracy. Outside of this élite a person's status depended largely on his or her birth, although status could to a certain degree be improved by personal skill and ambition. The different classes were stratified fairly rigidly, and were kept apart by marriage-barriers, *taboos*, and a wide variety of deterrents which in some tribes included the death penalty. As well as being ruled by their overall chief, the ancient Polynesians also came under the aegis of the head of their family. Different families had – within the overall laws laid down by their chief – slightly different codes of ethics and slightly different sets of *taboos* which makes it dangerous to generalize about details. Such a system was, again, open to abuse, and to Western eyes patently unjust. However, it suited the Polynesians tolerably well. This was partly because their chiefs were usually more interested in the trappings of their power than in using it for self-aggrandizement, and partly because the heads of their families were in most cases genuinely paternal.

The Polynesians' pastimes have been nicely summed up in a single sentence by Alan Moorehead. 'They lived from day to day in an endlessly repeated cycle, controlled only by their hunger and their desires, ashamed of nothing, eating, sleeping, dancing, fishing, bathing, cooking, talking and making love, always together and always in the open air.' From this it can be seen that their interests were active rather than contemplative. They were a people who set unusual store by the physical things of life. They admired strength, grace, agility, beauty and sexual skill. They were proud of their bodies and took great care of them, washing themselves at least twice and sometimes three times a day; indeed washing seems to have become something of a fetish, and there are reports of old people dying as they staggered down to the rivers determined not to miss the obligatory bathe. Their clothes were hygienic, and were kept scrupulously clean. They suffered from few illnesses, apart from a skin disease which was probably a form of benign sun-cancer. 'They know no sickness,' wrote one of the early missionaries, 'apart from that gradual decline which brings old age and death.' They invented games, such as surf-riding and wrestling, which were tests of physical courage and co-ordination. And of all the games they indulged in the one they practised most and enjoyed best was sex.

What a lot of nonsense has been written about the sex life of the Polynesians:

> *They know no other god than love,* Commerson would have us believe. *Every day is consecrated to him, the whole island is his temple, the women are his idols and the men his worshippers. And what women! They rival the Georgians in beauty and the muses in grace. Here modesty and prudery are unknown. The act of procreation is an act of religion, its preludes are encouraged by the songs of the assembled people, and its climax greeted by universal applause.*

All this, however, is very wide of the mark. The Polynesians didn't make such a song and dance about sex – they simply regarded it as one of the natural pleasures of life – and it had nothing whatsoever to do with their religion. It was the sex-starved Europeans who turned a commonplace happening into a romantic legend, and it is none too easy now to separate legend from fact.

The fact, however, seems to be that nobody in pre-European Polynesia ever thought of sex as sinful, much less as a matter for secrecy, salacity or self-restraint. When Polynesians felt the desire for sex they had intercourse, in much the same way that they ate when hungry, or drank when thirsty. This seemed perfectly natural to them, and it never occurred to them that other people wouldn't consider it natural too. So, as David Howarth points out in his book *Tahiti*, from an early age Polynesian children were taught the pleasures of sex by their elders, and as teenagers they were encouraged to put into practice what they had learned. Any chance encounter between a boy and a girl or between groups of boys and groups of girls was likely to lead to sex; and sexual skill was as much admired and as openly acclaimed as skill at wrestling or canoeing. The more lovers young people had, the better their parents were pleased; and if a girl became pregnant this was a cause for rejoicing, since it proved she was fertile. For some ten or twelve years this cheerful promiscuity continued. Then when a boy or a girl married, it ended. Or, to be precise, promiscuity in general was superseded by promiscuity within the family.

When a Polynesian married, he or she married the whole family, that is to say marriage was monogamous, but it was neither exclusive not possessive. It was considered perfectly proper for a husband or a wife to have sexual relations with their partner's relatives, also with their *taio* or special friend. Women who, when they married already had children, brought them into the new family where the children were readily accepted and accorded full status. Only two things were *taboo*, marriage across the class barrier, and incest. This system may appear curious to Western eyes, but it worked. Divorce in pre-European Polynesia was easy and involved no great social stigma, yet it seems hardly ever to have happened. Statistics are hard to come by, but recent research indicates that before the European invasion, less than one Polynesian marriage in 100 ended in divorce. When one compares this to the one marriage in four which now breaks up in the Western world, there is little doubt which system an impartial observer would consider the better.

It is easy to see how these facts were misinterpreted by the early seamen and writers, and were gradually metamorphosed into a legend which bore little resemblance to truth.

The seamen got things wrong from the start. When the first European explorers arrived in the Pacific they were clearly hungry, so the islanders offered them food, and offered it freely, expecting nothing in return. When the Europeans – as a sort of barter – gave them cloth and nails they were delighted. As well as being in need of food the Europeans appeared also to be in need of sex, so this too the islanders offered them freely, as an act of hospitality, again expecting nothing in return. When the Europeans – again as a sort of barter – offered them cloth and nails they naturally didn't refuse them. However, the island girls were not stupid. Once they had been given cloth and nails they began to expect them and to ask for them, and thus their happy gift (at least in the eyes of the seamen) became a sort of prostitution. Some seamen, it is true, were perspicacious enough to realize that few of their sexual partners were married women, and fewer still women from the Polynesian aristocracy. Most men, however, took what pleasures they were offered without a great deal of thought, assuming that the Polynesians all believed in free love and lived in a state of perpetual and uninhibited orgy. They were wrong. In the same way that those who have plenty of food don't need to overeat, so those who have plenty of sex don't need to indulge in orgies. The orgies were in the minds of the Europeans.

These misconceptions of the seamen were, in the eighteenth century, seized on and magnified by contemporary writers, many of whom were eager to give credence to a myth which became very popular towards the middle of the century: the myth of the Noble Savage.

The idea of the Noble Savage is old as time, as old, if you like, as the idea of the Garden of Eden. For millennia philosophers have been intrigued by the concept that primitive man, before he became shackled by the material trivia of civilization, was intrinsically without sin. In the middle of the eighteenth century this concept was distilled and popularized by Rousseau:

> *Man in his natural state was born essentially good and free of all prejudices; he followed the impulses of an instinct which remained sure because it had not yet degenerated into reason. . . Men were meant to remain in this simple state, which was the true youth of the world, and all subsequent steps towards the aggrandizement of the individual have in fact been retrogressive steps, leading towards the decline of the species.*

This was heady stuff. And mid-eighteenth-century Europe, effervescing with the ideas which were soon to spark off the French Revolution, was in a mood to listen.

This idea of the Noble Savage seemed transformed from intellectual theory to material fact by the discovery of the Pacific islands, and Tahiti in particular. For here was what appeared to be an earthly paradise where the people were indeed as Rousseau argued they ought to be, physically beautiful, peaceful, compassionate and above all happy; a race caught and preserved in a state of primordial innocence. With the publication of popular versions of Bougainville's and Cook's *Journals*, and with the arrival in Paris and London of two Noble Savages in the flesh, the islands of the Pacific became the most fashionable and controversial talking point in the coffee-houses and salons of Europe. 'Now,' to quote Dr Beaglehole, 'rose up within Natural History something incomparably exciting, Man in the state of nature; the Noble Savage entered the study and the drawing room of Europe in naked majesty to shake the preconceptions of morals and of politics.'

It was unfortunate, but perhaps inevitable, that most of the coffee-house conversation and most of the intellectual theorizing about the Noble Savages of the Pacific was based on misconceptions:

> Boswell: *I do not think the people of Otaheite can be reckoned savages.*
>
> Johnson: *Don't cant in defence of savages.*
>
> Boswell: *I am assured that they have the bread tree, the fruit of which serves them for bread, and that they laughed very heartily when they were informed of the tedious process necessary with us to have bread.*
>
> Johnson: *Why, Sir, all ignorant savages will laugh when they are told of the advantages of civilized life. When you tell men who live without houses how we pile brick upon brick and rafter upon rafter, they would laugh heartily at our folly in building; but it does not follow that men are better without houses. No, Sir, (holding up a slice of a good loaf) this is better than the bread tree.*

Boswell was typical of the naive romantics who were ever anxious (often for the wrong reasons) to put the Pacific islanders on a pedestal. Johnson was typical of the down-to-earth sceptics who were ever anxious (again often for the wrong reasons) to cut them down to size. Both, in the conversation quoted, got just about everything wrong. The people of Tahiti were far too courteous and far too sensible to laugh at something they didn't understand; this they *never* did. As for Johnson, his comparison was valueless, for he had never set eyes on, let alone tasted, a breadfruit in his life.

The intellectuals were often equally ill-informed. Rousseau's friend Denis Diderot wrote a widely read *Supplement* to Bougainville's voyage in which he extolled the islanders' natural innocence and railed against those who threatened to disturb their idyllic life. Why, Diderot argued, *shouldn't* love govern all? Was it not natural sometimes for brother to desire sister, or father daughter; for were we not all incestuous descendants of Adam and Eve? This was about as wide of the mark as it was possible to get. Incest, throughout Polynesia, was *taboo*.

Top A group of Inuit of Alaska, photographed in 1914 when they visited the camp of the Stefanson expedition near Point Barron. *Above* Aborigines of Tasmania, from the original painting by R. Dowling presented by the artist to the town hall, Launceston.

The propagation of such misconceptions led to a great deal of muddled thinking about the Pacific islanders. Fact and legend became inextricably intertwined and have remained intertwined to this day, so that even now the old fallacies cloud our judgement, making it difficult for us to say with certainty how close the pre-European islanders really were to paradise. This has to be a matter of personal opinion. Mine – for what it is worth – is that they were closer to paradise than it is comfortable for us to admit.

In his book *Tahiti*, David Howarth manages very well to separate fact from legend, and his portrait of the islanders is perceptive and full of sound common sense. He writes:

> *The Polynesian islands had a combination of qualities that was unique. They had been left entirely alone since mankind first came to live in them, and they had all the needs of human life and comfort. So their people had an opportunity nobody else had ever had. Unthreatened and untaught, they created a society and a religion on the basis that there was plenty of everything for everyone, and nobody had to be either poor or rich. They were content with what they had, and never yearned for more. They made sure that everyone had what he (or she) needed by a custom of mutual giving. It was not trade, because they had no money; nor was it barter. A Tahitian would give anything to anyone who needed it, and expected nothing in exchange except the knowledge that if ever he was in need himself somebody would do the same for him. As a matter of course they gave food to anyone who was hungry, and with equal innocence they gave the pleasure of sex to anyone who was hungry for that. . . Nobody thought of himself as the permanent owner of anything. They had never heard of private property: so they were never tempted into the sins of envy, selfishness or avarice. Nor were they cruel or unkind, either by nature or example. Therefore the religion they created did not have to assume that mankind was sinful, as European religions did; they conceived a heaven but no hell. . . They found it easy to satisfy their gods' demands. Reverence was no trouble nor was kindness towards each other, because this was the general habit. Some Tahitians must have had better brains than others, but nobody's intellect had to be stretched above the norm because there was (little) call for innovation or inventiveness. On the contrary, everyone's experience of life was the same and everyone could understand his environment and his place in it. . . So the uneventful days passed by in endless summer and prolific natural beauty. As a deeply religious people they must have felt that their gods had been good to them in the shade of the fruit trees, the curve of the palms, the unsullied sand of the beaches, and always, glimpsed between the boles of the trees, the placid blue lagoon and the flashing breakers on the reef beyond. Everyone who met them said they were happy.*

If this wasn't paradise, it was surely as close to it as man has ever been. Yet within a century of Cook's landing in Matavai Bay the Pacific islanders' traditional way of life had been destroyed beyond hope of resurrection. They had been deprived of their gods, their culture and their happiness, and left (to quote a contemporary writer) 'with nothing to look forward to but "going into the night" to join the spirits of their ancestors'. Those who have nothing to live for, die. Within three generations the population of Tahiti plummeted from over 140,000 to under 5,000.

The exploration of the Pacific is not only a story of epic voyages; it is a story too of the spoliation of a demi-paradise. Some people may feel that spoliation is too strong a word, that what happened to the Polynesians was either inevitable, or of little consequence since their culture was largely myth and barely worth the saving. The first argument has a grain – but no more than a grain – of truth in it. The nineteenth century was not a good time for a people as innocent as the Polynesians. This was the period in world history when something like a million whales and seals were butchered annually in the Southern Ocean, and American Indians and Australian Aborigines were hunted with dogs and poisoned like vermin with arsenic.

It was unfortunate for the gentle people of the Pacific that they suffered Europeanization at a time when the Europeans were at their most complacent, expansionist and material-minded. In the eighteenth century a fair number of Westerners had questioned the ethics of disturbing the Noble Savages; in the nineteenth century most people were less interested in ethics than in bêche-de-mer, sperm oil, copra and strategic bases. Yet man can see and rectify his errors, and there were those living in the Pacific in the nineteenth century who gave warning of the tragedy that was taking place – artists like Gauguin and writers like Melville. The fact that their warnings went unheeded was tragic, but the tragedy itself was not inevitable.

The argument that Polynesian culture was largely myth and not worth saving

Watching the preparations for a feast on Raiatea, in the Society Islands.

is simply not true. A great many things about the Pacific islanders and their culture was myth – the doctrine of the Noble Savage for example – but the quality of their lives was praised too often by too many people to be anything other than fact. The pre-European Polynesians were kind and they were happy, and the world is a poorer place for their passing.

It is poorer because in the same way that 'no man is an island (but) a peece of the Continent', so no race is an isolated limb but part of the human body as a whole; and as 'any man's death diminishes me', so the death of any people diminishes mankind. And mankind was particularly diminished by the disappearance of the Pacific islanders because they had a unique contribution to make to the well-being of our species.

No people in history have ever enjoyed such physical happiness. Mentally, the Polynesians were not remarkable. It has been said with some truth that because they were so alike in character and intelligence, their life-style must have been dull. They bred no geniuses. They wrote no epics, composed or painted no masterpieces (although their carving and sculpture was remarkably fine). They never even attempted the sort of technological advances which many people today equate with civilization; not in a thousand years would they have split the atom, designed a computer or landed on the moon. It would therefore probably be true to say that mentally they represented no more than a backwater in man's evolution, a gentle meander far removed from the vital mainstream of progress.

Physically, they were on a different and altogether higher plane. Their environment helped. They lived in a perpetual sun-drenched summer which was seldom too hot and never too cold, with a sea-breeze ever rustling the palms. Their rainfall was adequate, their diet was well-balanced, and the sea was on their doorstep – the lagoons to swim in, the breakers to surf in, the beaches to play on. They had enough work to preclude the decadence of idleness, but not enough to exhaust them. No wonder they developed into a strong, agile, healthy and beautiful people who excelled at all things physical.

It might be argued that in our essentially cerebral civilization there is little room for such physical and primitive skills as the Polynesians delighted in. Yet can we in honesty look back on the pre-European islanders and not be haunted by the vision of Adam and Eve walking hand-in-hand along the unsullied beaches, naked and unashamed, as they were in the days of their innocence?.

CHAPTER THREE

'VIKINGS OF THE SUNRISE'

THE VOYAGES OF THE POLYNESIANS

He wanka ururu kapua
(A canoe in which to dare the clouds of heaven)

Few mysteries are as beguiling as the presence of the Polynesian in his islands. How did he get there? There are two theories: one that he arrived by drift and by chance; the other that he arrived as a result of planned and purposeful migration.

The layman might well feel the truth lies somewhere in between; that some islands were settled by chance, some by deliberate voyaging, and some by a combination of both. However, the champions of each theory have dug their toes in, and a somewhat acrimonious dispute has transformed the usually placid waters of Pacific scholarship into a maelstrom. These are seas into which the outsider ventures at peril. The question, however, is too important to be begged, and the differences appear at first sight too fundamental to be reconciled. So how *did* the Polynesians spread throughout the Pacific?

In the old days people pictured the Polynesians as 'intrepid voyagers, ever pushing boldly into the unknown', and it was generally assumed that their migrations were intentional. This uncritical and romantic view was challenged in the 1950s by Andrew Sharp. Sharp was a gifted and meticulous New Zealand scholar who had no time for flights of fancy. History to him consisted of facts which could be proved. He was sceptical about the extent of ancient voyaging in general – 'the tales of Viking visits to America (he wrote) are broken reeds' – and he was sceptical about the extent of Polynesian voyaging in particular. For as he rightly pointed out, the islanders had no compasses and no sextants; they were unable to determine longitude, and unable to measure the displacement caused by winds and currents. In bad weather they quickly became disorientated and lost. Sharp was therefore convinced that they would have lacked the ability to reach distant islands by design, and that if they happened to reach them by chance they would have lacked the ability to find their way home again. Most Pacific islands, he contended, could only have been settled as a result of one-way voyages, many of which would have been accidental-or-drift-voyages. The idea of deliberate migration was anathema to him. 'The notion,' he wrote, 'that fleets of brown-skinned colonists pushed into and through these islands impelled by a mysterious (migratory) urge, is purely mythical, is belied by the evidence, and flies in the face of the well-known facts of the evolution of human cultures everywhere.'

Sharp's theory of population by drift voyaging was better received by academics than Heyerdahl's theory of population from the Americas had been. While Heyerdahl had appeared as the eloquent champion of a lost cause, Sharp appeared as the novel interpreter of facts which were already proven. Also his thesis was meticulously

An engraving of a canoe of the Sandwich Islands (Hawaii), from a drawing by John Webber, the artist on Cook's third voyage.

researched and supported by a wealth of statistics, and so provided a much needed corrective to the spate of vague and ill-informed romanticizing about the Polynesians which was in vogue immediately after World War II.

Partly perhaps because of the war, and partly because of man's growing concern with ethnology, the early 1950s saw a revival of interest in the Polynesians and their legends. It was all to the good that these legends were collected and recorded before they disappeared into limbo. Unfortunately, however, legend, myth and apocryphal story were often dressed up and presented, without justification, as historical fact. A legend would be unearthed describing 'petals of white flowers scattered all over the sea', and this would be taken to mean that Polynesian canoes had penetrated deep into the Antarctic and been brought up short by pack-ice. Another legend was found describing the edge of the world as 'a great wall of rock rising sheer from the sea'. This was taken to mean that Polynesian canoes had traversed the Pacific and been brought up short by the Andes. Such flights of fancy wilted under the astringent blast of Sharp's scepticism and statistics.

So was he right? *Were* the Polynesians overrated as voyagers?

To decide this question we need to look at what might be called the component parts of their voyaging: their ships, their crews, their provisions, their ability at navigation, and the motives which might have triggered off their journeys. If any of these are found wanting, Sharp's theory will be strengthened.

All Polynesian vessels were known to the early explorers as canoes – the word (which comes from the Carib *canaoa*) was introduced to Europe by Columbus, and for the next 300 years was used indiscriminately to describe any native vessel from a flimsy birch bark to a 100-foot carvel-built sailing ship. The Polynesians had many types of ocean-going craft, some of which bore little resemblance to the image conjured up by the word canoe. The main categories were the *vaa*, a small paddling outrigger about 15 feet long used for fishing inside or close to the reef; the *vaa-taie*, a 25-35-foot outrigger with a single sail used primarily for deep-sea fishing or short-distance voyages between the islands, and the *pahi*, twin-hulled, twin-masted ocean-going vessels, the smallest of which were about 60 feet in length and the largest about 100.

Pahi were described by the early explorers as 'unwieldy (and) too clumsy for fishing'. This was right. However, for deep-sea voyaging *pahi* had a lot to commend them. They could be paddled or sailed – an adaptability they shared with those other great sea-going vessels, the Phoenician traders and the Viking longships. They were fast – Cook reckoned they could outsail the *Endeavour*, and 'might with ease make 40 leagues a day'; this would give them a fair-wind sailing speed of about 7 knots. They were good at tacking; indeed some *pahi* (those of the Gilbert Islands for example) could be sailed from either bow or stern. They were stronger than they looked. Their construction may have appeared 'rickety and ramshackle'; they may have leaked like the proverbial sieve, and to European eyes it may have seemed obvious that 'canoes held together with bits of vegetable fibre must be less seaworthy than craft fastened with bolts and nails'. Appearances, however, can be deceptive, and it was in fact partly *because* of their loose-knit construction and their yielding lashings that the *pahis* were so seaworthy. They were flexible, they bent to the sea as a reed to the wind, they soaked up punishment under which a more rigidly-built vessel would have disintegrated; in time of storm or in heavy seas they had a unique propensity for staying afloat.

Pahis were good load-carriers, with their twin-hulls providing stability and buoyancy, and their deckhouses providing shelter and storage space. Ton for ton they almost certainly carried more men and more provisions than a contemporary European ship.

By the time Western explorers arrived in the Pacific not many *pahis* were being built; for by this time all the islands had been discovered, and the incentive for long-distance voyaging had waned. A few of the great oceangoing vessels, however, were still in existence, and one of these was measured and sketched by John Webber, Cook's artist aboard the *Resolution*. From this and similar drawings it would appear that the larger *pahis* would almost certainly have possessed both the seagoing ability and the carrying capacity to make long-distance voyages, although the fact that by the eighteenth century such voyages were rare indicates they were hazardous.

It is an old axiom that a ship is only as good as its ship's company; so how competent a deep-water crew would the early Polynesians have been? No one doubts their ability at working close inshore; their skill in negotiating the reefs around their lagoons, their skill in fishing, and in making short journeys from island to island. What *is* in doubt is their ability in deep water. Some writers would have us believe they possessed 'a mystical almost spiritual affinity with the ocean . . . a *rapport* with blue water'. Those who believe this are seeing the prehistory of the Pacific through rose-tinted spectacles; for all available evidence points to the fact that the Polynesians regarded deep-sea voyaging in much the same way that mountain-dwellers regard high peaks – as hazards best avoided.

The idea of a spiritual affinity between the Polynesians and the Pacific may be myth, but there can be no denying the fact that the islanders had a unique knowledge of the sea; for they alone of all the people on Earth lived in a world which was sea-orientated rather than land-orientated. Other races living in river deltas or desolate coastlines may have depended for their livelihood on the sea, but the land was always the hub of their lives. It was a different story for those who lived in mid-Pacific; the hub of *their* lives was the sea – there are 500 parts of ocean in Polynesia to every single part of land. No wonder therefore the islanders developed special seafaring skills, just as bush-

Top A double canoe in its construction shed – almost the size of a small aircraft hangar – on one of the Vava's Islands (Tonga).
Above Five men in a canoe on River Aramia, Papua New Guinea, photographed by Frank Hurley, 1922.

men developed special skills in their desert or hunter-gatherers in their rain forest.

These skills were neither mystic nor magic; they were strictly practical, and they would have been invaluable on long-distance voyages. Take their knowledge of birds. . . For thousands of years Polynesians fishing in deep water beyond their lagoons would have watched and learned from the ever-wheeling kaleidoscope of sea birds. They would have seen the terns flying purposefully from one shoal of tuna to another, and the pelagic petrels passing high overhead on their annual migrations, and these they would have ignored. But they would have seen too, just before sunset, the frigate-birds circling high and the boobies circling low, until suddenly both were winging arrow-straight for their nesting grounds. In the same way that the Aborigines of Australia have for millennia been following the pardalote to their desert water-holes, so the Polynesians of the Pacific must have followed the frigate-birds and boobies to their islands. A catalogue of such skills would be endless. Their knowledge of swell patterns would have helped them hold course in the open sea and judge the proximity of land. Their ability to interpret cloud patterns would have helped them make landfalls by day, and their knowledge of *te lapa* (underwater phosphorescence) would have helped them by night. They knew where to look for and how to interpret the loom columns of white-sand and lagoon refracted up on to the horizon. By understanding signs which would have been unintelligible to landsmen, they could have survived where other races would have perished.

They would have made a more than competent deep-water crew.

Provisioning a *pahi* would have been no problem, for most of the larger islands contained all the foods needed for a long voyage, dried and salted fish, fresh meat in the shape of pigs, dogs and chickens, and a plethora of vegetables; the most commonly taken being fermented breadfruit, taro, sweet potatoes, pandanus and yam. For drinking there would have been the milk of coconuts, and water stored in bamboos or gourds. All this might have been supplemented during the voyage by catching the occasional fish, flying-fish, sea-bird or dolphin, although these extras would usually have been found only near land and therefore at the time they were least needed. Such a diet was far healthier than the mixture of bread, biscuits, salt beef and peas which, before Cook introduced sauerkraut, was the staple fare of a European ship's company. In particular it contained vegetables rich in vitamin C, with the result that the scurvy which so often decimated European crews was unknown to the Polynesians. The quality of a *pahi's* provisions could hardly have been bettered.

The quantity that could have been carried is more open to question. Polynesian *aficienados* like Edward Dodd have hinted that *pahis* may have had a carrying-capacity of up to 40,000 lbs. This estimate, however, is based on suspect evidence: a missionary's report of 'double canoes capable of carrying 300 men' – almost certainly the 300 is an exaggeration, and almost certainly the canoes in question were war canoes. Captain Wallis was probably nearer the mark when he wrote of 'canoes about fifty feet long, which I dare say would have carried near eight tun' (17,600 lbs). From similar reports and from measurements known to be accurate it would seem reasonable to assume that one of the larger *pahis* could have carried at least 15,000 lbs. Not all this, however, would have been devoted to provisions; we have to allow for the weight of the crew and equipment. If we assume the crew numbered 25 and weighed on average 160 lbs, then their total weight would be 4,000 lbs. The weight of the equipment is more difficult to estimate; wooden paddles and fibre sails tend to be heavy, but on the other hand the Polynesians probably took few extras with them in the way of clothes, weapons or trinkets for trade. A reasonable guess would be that the equipment weighed about the same as the crew. This would leave 7,000 lbs for provisions. If we assume that each of the crew ate 3 lbs of food per day and drank 3 lbs of water (which is quite generous), then 150 lbs of provisions would be consumed daily. On this basis a *pahi* could remain at sea without reprovisioning for at least six and possibly seven weeks.

For voyages of this duration Polynesian vessels were probably more easily and better provisioned than their European counterparts.

Seaworthy ships with knowledgeable crews and a cornucopia of provisions were not, however, all that was needed for long-distance voyaging in the Pacific. As Sharp points out, if the Polynesians couldn't navigate, the only way they could have reached the more distant islands was by fortuitous drifts. Here therefore is the hub around which controversy revolves.

Could they or couldn't they navigate?

Sharp reckoned that accurate navigation was beyond the capability of *all* early seafarers. In support of this view he cited 'the great margin of error without modern aids, the fact that when the sky is overcast the navigator is robbed of his heavenly guides, and the power of the storm to turn short navigated voyages into long unnavigated ones'. This is undoubtedly true. According to European standards *none* of the early seafarers could navigate, least of all the Polynesians who lacked even an embryo compass. I suggest, however, that it is egocentric to judge everything through European eyes and by European standards. Rather than dismiss the islanders as navigators because they lacked the scientific techniques on which we rely, shouldn't we ask if they might not have had *other* techniques, *other* ways of getting from island to island? Recent research and voyaging indicates they had.

Like most early seafarers, the Polynesians navigated by the stars. 'The sun is their guide by day,' wrote Cook, 'and the stars by night.' One of the first people to understand and record how they did this was the Spaniard Andia y Varela, who wrote in 1774:

When the night is clear they steer by the stars. This is the easiest method for them because, the stars being many in number, they are able to note by them the bearings on which several islands known to them lie. They then make straight for their destination by following the rhumb of the particular star which rises or sets over the island to which they are journeying, and thus they make landfall with as much precision as the most expert navigator of civilized nations.

This technique is further explained by Ellis and Firth:

They steer by a star path. . . A star path is a succession of stars, on the same bearing as the island for which they are heading, and towards which the bow of the canoe is pointed. Each star is used as a guide when it is low in the heavens; as it rises up, it is discarded and the course is reset by the next to rise in the star path. One after another these stars rise and are followed till dawn.

This is a system of navigation totally different from our own. Our system is basically a combination of trigonometry and time, with measurements taken by scientific instruments transposed on to a grid or chart. The Polynesian system is a combination of vision and memory, with certain stars being sighted, lined-up-on and followed according to precedent. The European system, provided everything is right, is far more versatile and far more accurate; but the Polynesian system works – provided two things are known – where one is starting from, and where one is going to.

The first of these requirements explains why Polynesian voyagers were always so meticulous about their point of departure. To quote the missionary John Williams, writing in 1837:

We had still one more island to seek, and inquired of Roma-tane if he had ever heard of Rarotonga. 'Oh yes!' he replied, 'it is only a day and a night's sail from Atiu, we know the way there.' This information delighted us; but when we inquired of him the position in which it lay, he at one time pointed in one direction, and another in quite the opposite. But this was soon explained; for the natives, in making their voyages, do not leave from any part of an island as we do, but, invariably, have what may be called starting points. At these places they have certain land-marks which they line up and steer by until the stars become visible; and they generally contrive to set sail so as to get sight of their heavenly guides by the time their land-marks disappear.

It is clear from this that the basis of Polynesian navigation was alignment with land-marks by day and with stars by night. Suppose a voyager wanted to travel between two islands. He would sail from his departure-island a little before sunset aligning his canoe with two land-marks which he knew (so long as he kept them one behind the other) would enable him to start his journey on the correct course. When it became

Natives with a canoe, Santa Cruz, Solomon Islands.
Note the cabin and the length of the paddle,
photographed by John Watt Beattie, *c.* 1906.

too dark for him to line-up on his land-marks, he lined up instead on stars, pointing the bow of his canoe at the star which, he knew from experience, was emerging over the horizon immediately beyond his destination-island, and keeping the stern of his canoe in line with the star which was disappearing below the horizon immediately behind his departure-island. As Dodd explains:

All he needed to do was stand in the middle of his canoe, sight his goal-star over his bow and his departure-star over his stern. If they lined up he could be nowhere except on his direct course. If he was carried to one side or another by storm or current or leeway, he had only to scramble back to his primary path by sail or paddle; once back on it, he could safely resume his journey.

All this, however, was easier said than done. The main difficulty was that the stars were ever-moving, and no sooner had our navigator lined up with his departure and destination stars than they moved out of alignment with his island. When this happened, he had to pick other stars to steer by, the ones he chose being those which emerged over or disappeared under the horizon at the same place as his original guide stars. Dodd, again, explains this very clearly:

> *We steer by a star, but the Polynesian steers by a 'star-pit', a point on or below the rim of the horizon from which his star, or rather his procession of stars, emerges. From a practical seaman's point of view, this is an important concept to keep in mind. The pit lies right on the horizon; it does not move up into the sky as the star does. And, importantly, when one star soars too high or too obliquely, another pops up to mark the same point. And if there is not another nicely in line, there are probably a couple that indicate the pit between them. Speed this action up as you would a movie camera, and you have a font of stars spouting out of the pit ahead of you all night long and of course a cascade of stars 180° away disappearing into the complementary pit astern.*

It follows from this that a Polynesian navigator and a European navigator see the night sky through very different eyes. A European sees the stars as his stationary helpers; he is interested in them only at one particular moment in time, the split second at which he uses his instruments to take a bearing on them. A Polynesian, in contrast, sees the stars as his moving helpers; his whole system of navigation is based on the fact that the stars are constantly altering position and he has to make adjustments accordingly. The one is interested in stars, the other in star-paths.

This Polynesian technique of navigation demands considerable knowledge and considerable skill in application. It has limitations, drawbacks and dangers – those who use it and become lost are often lost beyond hope of survival. It does, nonetheless, under certain circumstances, make intentional long-distance voyaging a possibility, at least in theory.

And in recent years the star-path system has been proved, in the most conclusive way imaginable, to work not only in theory but in practice. It has been used as the sole method of navigation for several long-distance voyages.

The experiments started in 1965 when Doctor David Lewis and his wife and two small children (aged two and three) sailed their catamaran from Tahiti to New Zealand, navigating without instruments and relying entirely on the sun, stars, swell-patterns, bird-sightings, and the sort of island-to-island knowledge which would have been available to the early Polynesians. After 36 days at sea, during which they covered 2,200 miles, they made a remarkably accurate landfall. Other voyages followed.

In 1969 the ketch *Isbjorn* sailed from Puluwat in the Carolines to Saipan in the Marianas and back again. This was a shorter passage – no more than 550 miles each way – but it was made by a Polynesian navigator who relied wholly on traditional skills and denied himself all help from modern or external aids. The outward leg took seven days, the homeward six; navigation once again proved no problem, and the ketch returned to a spectacular reception by torch-carrying islanders 'happy to reaffirm their voyaging heritage'.

In 1976 a specially-built *pahi*, the *Taratai*, sailed from the Gilbert Islands to Fiji. She covered the 1,250 miles, navigating solely by the star-path system, in 47 days. And if this seems an inordinately long time it should be pointed out that for the crew of the *Taratai* socializing en route was as important as the voyage itself, and who could blame them if they did stay longer than was strictly necessary on Rotuma, 'an atoll renowned for its sweet oranges and sweeter girls'? The voyage of the *Taratai* was followed by a more publicized and more important voyage, that of the *Hokule'a*, another reconstructed *pahi*, with hull and sails based on measurements recorded by Cook. The

Hokule'a made the 2,500-mile passage from Hawaii to Tahiti. She navigated entirely by the star-path method without recourse to modern or scientific aids; she had aboard a number of plants and animals of the type which might have been carried by the early Polynesians, and every aspect of her voyage was meticulously recorded and made available for research. At the end of 35 days at sea the crew were tense and exhausted both mentally and physically; they did, however, manage to make their landfalls with surprising accuracy, and all the animals and all the plants except the taro survived.

This voyage proved in practice what had for some time been apparent in theory – that the ancient Polynesians had sufficient navigational expertise to make long intentional journeys between islands whose positions were known to them.

But did they have a motive to embark on such journeys? None of those usually put forward seems convincing.

Some writers have made much of the Polynesians' courage. 'Fired by the lust of adventure,' writes Firth, 'and the desire to see new lands, canoe after canoe set out and ranged the seas. Fear of storm and shipwreck leaves them undeterred.' This, however, is nonsense! For in the same way that those who live in the mountains would be foolish if they *didn't* fear avalanche and hyperthermia, so those who live by the sea would be foolish *not* to fear storm and shipwreck. We can therefore dismiss lust of adventure as a motive. The Polynesians knew too much about the Pacific to venture into its lonely reaches in pursuit of a chimera.

Nor is trade a convincing motive. Other seafaring nations may have made great voyages of exploration in pursuit of trade – the Phoenicians to England for tin, the Arabs to Sri Lanka for tea, emeralds and pearls, and the Portuguese, the Spaniards and the Dutch to Indonesia for spices. The Polynesians, however, did little trading. This is partly because the produce of one Pacific island is very like that of another, and partly because the islanders were not by nature acquisitive and tended to be satisfied with what they had. There was a certain amount of continuous small-scale barter between neighbouring archipelagos, and a small number of tribute-bearing voyages in the aftermath of war; but the desire for trade would never have taken the Polynesians as far afield as New Zealand, Easter Island and Hawaii.

Nor would religious zeal. It was the Chrstians who were the proselytizers. At least one great voyage in the European era of exploration – that of Quiros – was inspired by the hope of converting the Polynesians to Christianity. The Polynesians, in contrast, never wanted to convert anyone, not were their dissident sects ever driven, like the Pilgrim Fathers, to seek new lands in which to practise their faith. Religion played no part in the Polynesians' settlement of the Pacific.

A more likely reason for exploratory voyaging would have been war, either the desire to conquer new lands, or the desire to escape from would-be conquerors. Many Polynesian legends describe battles with 'raiders from the west'; the people of Papua New Guinea are known to have raided the Caroline Islands, the people of Tonga are known to have raided the Societies. The motive of these raids may have been as simple as plunder, but there is another possibility, that as people were forced off the mainland of Asia (perhaps by a population explosion, perhaps by war), so pressure was exerted on the offshore islanders to move on in their turn to remoter and less crowded archipelagos. This would have led to little ripples of migration fanning eastward across the Pacific. Such migrations would normally have been absorbed by conquest and intermarriage. However – and this could be the crux of the matter – it seems likely that there may have come a time when the economy of many of the islands would have been unable to support any substantial increase in population. On atolls and the smaller islands food always was, and probably always will be, in short supply, witness the tradition, still in force today, that a visitor will leave instantly, *no matter what the circumstances*, if there is the slightest suggestion that he or she is becoming a burden to feed. It should also be noted that although the Polynesians had, deservedly, a great reputation for hospitality, this hospitality was short-term rather than long-term; they always expressed considerable anxiety and disapproval when their European visitors showed signs of staying for more than a few days.

Here then is a *raison d'être* for intentional long-distance voyaging: over-population leading to a shortage of food, and a shortage of food leading to the need to find new lagoons to fish in and new islands to cultivate.

It is, however, one thing to say that the Polynesians had the capability for exploratory voyaging, and another to prove that they exercised it. We need here to strike a balance between the enthusiasts (like Lewis and Dodd) who would have us believe that the islanders could and did sail virtually everywhere, and the sceptics (like Andrew Sharp) who would have us believe they all arrived on their islands by accident. Taking both points of view into account, can we reconstruct how, when and by what routes the Polynesians spread throughout the Pacific?

I suggest there were four phases – obviously all overlapping and all subject to local variations. The first phase from 1500 BC to 1000 BC was an era of purposeful migration as the Polynesians spread rapidly through Melanesia and probably through Micronesia until they reached and occupied the most westerly of their archipelagos, Samoa and Tonga. The second phase from 1000 BC to AD 200 was a period of slow, largely accidental drift-voyaging, during which the Polynesians established themselves in their heartland, gradually populating all the islands and atolls which lie to the west of the Marquesas and the Tuamotus. The third phase, AD 200 to AD 1200 was an era which saw a limited number of purposeful voyages with the Polynesians fanning out from their heartland impelled by a population explosion – to discover and settle on even the most peripheral islands of the Pacific. The last phase, AD 1200 to the present day, was a time of retrenchment (some would say stagnation) when the Polynesians realized there were no more islands to be discovered, and each community withdrew into its own little world. When the Europeans reached them, their long-distance voyaging was, in some of the archipelagos, little more than a memory.

The first of these phases is well documented, although at the heart of it lies an enigma: nobody knows *exactly* where the Polynesians originated. 'Their earliest traceable homeland,' Peter Bellwood tells us, 'can be located among the Neolithic cultures of the Philippines and Indonesia'. Efforts to pinpoint a more specific heartland have not been wholly convincing, although the Moluccas are a possibility, and Dodd recently put forward the intriguing theory that they might have originated among the people who lived at the mouths of the great rivers of south-east Asia, the Irrawaddy, Salween, Mekong and Yangtze. In support of this theory Dodd points to the fact that archaeologists have found a trail of similar-shaped adzes running from these river-deltas, through Indonesia and the Philippines and deep into the Pacific. He also points out that the delta-dwellers and the Polynesians shared the same horticultural technique of propagating by root-cuttings. It strengthens Dodd's theory – although it certainly doesn't prove it – that there was a major population exodus from the mainland of Asia at much the same time as the first Polynesians filtered through to the more westerly of their islands. But wherever they may have originated, there is little doubt about how, when and by what route there arrived. Around 1400 BC the Polynesians began to migrate through Melanesia into the open reaches of the Pacific.

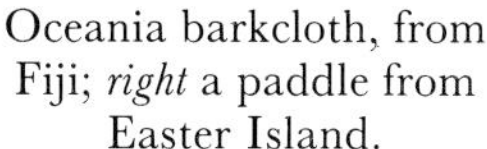

Oceania barkcloth, from Fiji; *right* a paddle from Easter Island.

The evidence of this migration is mainly archaeological. A form of pottery known as Lapita pottery – sand-tempered, fired in open bonfires and often with distinctive red-banded decoration – has been found throughout almost the whole of coastal Melanesia and as far east as Samoa. Lapita pottery appears only in this area, and can be dated to within a span of 300 to 400 years. Peter Bellwood explains the implications:

> *The Lapita Culture provides an admirable record of the rapid movement of mobile Polynesians, eastward from New Guinea to as far as Samoa, between 1500 and 1000 BC. Lapita sites in Melanesia are generally found in coastal situations or on small offshore islands, and the people who settled them were almost certainly in contact with the very different and probably much larger Melanesian populations already settled in the area. The Lapita people who settled in Melanesia became absorbed into these* (local) *populations, and only a few racial and ethnographic traces of them survive today. . . The Lapita voyagers who entered Polynesia had a very different history; they entered a huge island world devoid of men, and founded the societies which we now call Polynesia. The present Polynesians are the direct descendants of these intrepid voyagers of 3,500 years ago.*

All this adds up to deliberate and purposeful voyaging. We can picture the Polynesians coming to island after Melanesian island – Papua New Guinea, the Bismarck Archipelago, the Solomons, Santa Cruz, Banks, the New Hebrides, New Caledonia – and finding them always populated, usually forest-covered and not infrequently malarial. We can imagine them leaving behind little communities who had lost heart and given up who in turn left behind caches of Lapita pottery. And we can picture the more determined voyagers coming, eventually, around 1200 BC, to Fiji.

Fiji was a frontier post. Behind it lay skein after skein of inhabited Melanesian islands; ahead of it lay the vast reaches of the central Pacific into which no man had ventured and returned. A small number of Polynesians undoubtedly stayed in Fiji, and intermarried with and were absorbed by the local population. The majority continued to head east and discovered Tonga and Samoa. Here at last they found reasonably fertile, malaria-free and above all uninhabited territory where they could settle. By 1000 BC they were firmly established in both Tonga and Samoa.

What happened next is conjecture. With a time gap of 3,000 years and no written records it is impossible to say with certainty how much of the post-Tongan-and-Samoan settlement was deliberate and how much accidental. We have no idea how many original Polynesian settlers there were – estimates vary from 10 to 10,000 – nor do we know if they increased in number because they were augmented by further waves of settlers, or because of a natural increment of births over deaths. Sharp has produced some interesting figures to support the latter theory. If we assume a slow but steady population increase, with ten people becoming eleven people at the end of each generation of 25 years, then all the million-odd Polynesians who lived in the Pacific *circa* AD 1800, could have been descended from no more than 100 original voyagers arriving in Samoa in 1000 BC. Sharp writes:

> *A handful of people coming into Polynesia 3,000 years ago, and increasing at a moderate average rate, could easily have propagated the entire Polynesian population of historical times. In the light of this, the necessity of imagining shuttle services of Polynesian colonists in order to account for the population disappears, in the same way that it is unnecessary to imagine the British settlers brought shiploads of rabbits to New Zealand in order to account for the countless millions that arose there.*

The comparison may not be happiest, but the point is valid and proven. If there was indeed no more than a handful of the original settlers and if their numbers were not significantly increased by later migrations, this would account for the slow tempo of the second phase of settlement. In the first phase, the Polynesians pushed east for 4,000 miles in 400 years. In the second phase they pushed east for 2,000 miles over 1,100 years, half the distance in nearly thrice the time. It would therefore seem that in this second phase Sharp's theories are vindicated; that settlement was indeed slow, haphazard and largely accidental, with the benefits likely to accrue from deliberate long-distance voyaging outweighed by the disincentives and hazards. These disincentives and hazards would have been formidable indeed.

For many centuries the Polynesians would have had no motive to move from Tonga and Samoa. Tonga and Samoa consist of nearly a hundred habitable islands and atolls and today support over 100,000 people. Three thousand years ago they would have been well able to sustain all the original settlers, who would have been foolish indeed to exchange the security of their new-found homes for the insecurity of the open sea. And in any case they would surely have been too preoccupied, initially, with day-to-day survival to have had either time or inclination for long-distance voyaging. The idea that they led lives of indolence, surrounded by a cornucopia of flowers, fresh fruit and sea food owe more to legend than reality. The smaller atolls in particular were a harsh environment, with everything – animals, trees, plants and crops – having to be introduced and nurtured by man. To quote Edwin Bryan in *Geography of the Pacific*:

> *Even under best conditions man finds life difficult on low coral islands. There is little or no fresh water. Few plants will grow. During dry periods both food and drink disappear. Violent storms blow down houses and coconut palms, ruin crops, and may even cause waves to wash completely over the low surface.*

It must have taken the Polynesians many generations, if not many centuries, to adapt to an environment the like of which no people before them had attempted to live in.

This fact pinpoints another disincentive to voyaging; when the Polynesians headed into the Pacific they were entering a world which was unknown in the most exact and literal sense. Most races, when they migrated to new territory, had at some time been preceded by someone or something; they had someone or something from whom to learn. The Polynesians, in contrast, when they left Fiji, were heading into an alien environment in which no human being before them had ever attempted to live. Each time they sailed for a new island, they were taking a leap into the unknown.

The final disincentive was distance. It is difficult for people who don't live in the Pacific to appreciate the sheer size of it – if you piece all five continents together they fail to fill this one vast ocean. When the Polynesians were migrating through Melanesia, they needed to make only comparatively short voyages from island to island; in the journey from New Guinea – New Britain – the Solomon Islands – Santa Cruz – Banks to the New Hebrides, there is never much more than a 100-mile gap between islands. It was a very different story in mid-Pacific; here the gap between landfalls is often not 100 miles but 1,000 – in broad terms it is 1,000 miles from Tonga to the Cook Islands, 1,000 miles from Samoa to the Societies, and 1,000 miles from the Societies to the Marquesas. The peripheral islands (New Zealand, Hawaii and Easter Island) are even farther from the nearest meaningful landfall.

These are distances which ancient seafarers would never have attempted to sail unless they had a strong motive. Polynesians in the first millennium BC lacked such a motive. We must therefore conclude that voyaging, in this era, was basically unintentional. To quote Sharp:

> *Accidental voyagers had a hundred generations, with scores of involuntary incidents in each generation, in which to hit or miss each of the natural groupings* (of the archipelagos). *Most accidental voyagers were no doubt overwhelmed by storm or exposure, or were carried on to islands which were already populated. Of those who came on an uninhabited island, most would be men who had been carried away while fishing or while going on forays against neighbouring islands. The great events in the prehistory of the Pacific were when an isolated canoe with women aboard happened for the first time on a new island group. In the early days this would be a very infrequent event, since the population would be fragmentary. . . But when it did happen, the seed of human continuity and increase throughout that island group was sown. No doubt in the case of the bigger island groups several such canoes started separate involuntary colonies on different islands within the group, which in due course expanded and intermarried. As the population grew, other involuntary voyagers were launched into the Pacific wastes, most to die, a very occasional handful to carry their seed to a new island.*

Throughout the first millennium BC this is surely the way it was. However, when one tries to extend this concept of accidental voyaging beyond AD 200 in time, and beyond the Marquesas in distance, one runs into problems. First, the mind rather boggles at the thought of canoes drifting accidentally to the most far-flung and peripheral islands. Hawaii, New Zealand and Easter Island, for example, are all more than 1,500 miles from the nearest reasonably-sized landfall, and in the case of Easter Island in particular many hundred (if not many thousand) canoes would have been swept past this miniscule island for every one that made a landfall by chance. The death-rate in populating the peripheral islands solely by accidental voyages would have been horrendous. There is also another problem. Computer analysis of winds and currents indicates that it is virtually impossible to drift by accident from central Polynesia to Easter Island, Hawaii or New Zealand; the winds and currents are such that one has to sail there intentionally. It is of course true that computers cannot be programmed to take account of freak storms. Nonetheless, recent thinking tends to the view that although Sharp was right for most of the islands most of the time, he wasn't right for all of the islands all of the time. So here is what might be termed a codicil to his thesis.

If one looks at the dates by which the various archipelagos are thought to have become populated, one is struck by two facts – the paucity of discoveries before about AD 200 when, apart from Samoa and Tonga, virtually no new archipelagos seem to have been discovered and settled, and the sudden proliferation of discoveries immediately after AD 200 when, within a comparatively short space of time, all the central archipelagos *and* all the remote peripheral islands are believed to have been settled. The Marquesas were settled *circa* AD 200, the Societies *circa* 250, Easter Island *circa* 550, Hawaii *circa* 500, the Cook Islands *circa* 700, the Austral Islands *circa* 750 and New Zealand *circa* 900. It seems that after about AD 200 the tempo of settlement was stepped up. And if one asks why, Sharp himself has provided the answer. 'Always must it be kept in mind,' he writes, 'what magic is effected by slow population increase over a long time . . . this increase is like compound interest – slow at first, but cumulative as more population arises to beget more population.' I suggest that towards the middle of the first millennium AD the Polynesians began to have a population problem, that their numbers increased beyond the capability of their islands comfortably to support them.

Again, this is difficult to prove, but several factors point to the probability of it. The Polynesians were a virile race with an uninhibited approach to sex; given favourable circumstances, one would expect them to be prolific and for their numbers to increase at first slowly and then, in accordance with Sharp's analogy to compound interest, dramatically. They were also a healthy race; so far as we know they suffered no plagues like the Black Death which so decimated the population of Europe, and no diseases like the malaria which so debilitated the people of parts of Africa – a windswept atoll with little if any surface water is a poor breeding ground for the *Anopheles* mosquitoes which are carriers of malaria. Although they indulged in warfare, their weapons were not sophisticated enough to cause widespread carnage; wars would therefore have reduced their numbers only fractionally. They practised no artificial method of keeping their population in check, nothing like the mass human sacrifices of the Aztecs, although some writers have suggested that the Ariois' infanticide was motivated by the desire to prevent a population explosion. It has also been suggested that further evidence of too many people with too little to eat is the occasional instance of cannibalism. Cannibalism seems to have been practised only by remote and isolated communities whose supply of food was permanently limited, for instance in the lonely longhouses of the Borneo and New Guinea rain forest, and the even lonelier islands of the Pacific. And it may be significant that in the Pacific, cannibalism was only practised by those who lived in what might be called the end-of-the-line islands – New Zealand and the Marquesas, both of which are situated on the very edge of the habitable world and have no islands beyond them to which a hungry and surplus population could easily emigrate.

One last fact strengthens the theory of over-population. During the latter part of the first millennium AD the Polynesians appear to have discovered and tried to settle on just about every available scrap of land in the Pacific, no matter how unsuitable. Not only did they reach and populate the distant islands like New Zealand and Hawaii, they also settled on even the smallest and most difficult-to-find islands like Pitcairn – subsequently chosen by the mutineers from the *Bounty* as the most inaccessible haven in which they could hide. One feels that the Polynesians would not have exchanged the comfort and security of Tahiti, for example, for the discomfort and insecurity of some remote and isolated atoll without good reason.

Sharp of course takes the view that they drifted there by chance, and in the case of the islands of the mid-Pacific there is a great deal to be said for this theory. However, with regard to the peripheral islands there is some doubt. Apart from the improbability of a canoe drifting by chance for such enormous distances against both wind and current, one wonders if a New Zealand population of over 100,000 could *really* have been built up solely from the accidental arrival of two or three women in drifting canoes? Theoretically, perhaps it could; but genetically and practically there would surely have been problems. Common sense seems therefore to support the view that although islands like New Zealand and Hawaii were probably first discovered by chance, they were subsequently settled at least in part by deliberate voyaging, which may have followed a pattern something like this. . .

The first step would have been involuntary – a fishing *vaa-taie* would be caught by a storm, swept into unknown seas, and, if she were lucky, cast up on an unknown and uninhabited island. If the island had a lagoon, a reasonable supply of water and a minimum of vegetation, the crew would probably have survived. However, five or six males are not the ideal complement of castaways; they must often have yearned for their homeland, and some are quite likely to have attempted the journey back. Winds and currents would frequently have favoured them – in about five cases out of six, vessels in Polynesia tend to drift to the west – and a small percentage of the castaways would almost certainly have managed to struggle home, bringing with them the knowledge that there was land to the east. Most of the time this knowledge would have been of little interest; but occasionally it could have been of vital significance.

In time of war, for example, a tribe might well have opted for probable death searching for a distant island, rather than certain death at the hands of an all-powerful enemy – this is known to have happened in the Marquesas. Or under the stress of over-population, a tribe might well have opted to search for a new island rather than face certain death from starvation, as was the case on Rotuma, where, to quote Sharp, 'large canoes had been retained so that when population pressure arose, expeditions of voluntary exiles might go off in them'. If the Polynesians on islands like Rotuma increased in numbers at even half the rate at which Sharp estimates they increased in New Zealand, there would indeed have been a population explosion, and this, I suggest, would have led to a number of deliberate voyages of exploration-cum-migration. These voyages were probably few in number. A total of less than a dozen, carried out successfully by a total of no more that three or four dozen *pahis*, would explain how all the peripheral islands came to be populated.

And this, in the first millennium AD, is surely the way it was; a large number of accidental drift voyages spawning, under the pressure of increasing population, a small number of voyages of intentional long-distance migration, until by about AD 1200, even the smallest and most far-flung atolls of the Pacific had been discovered and settled.

One might have expected the fourth and most recent phase of Polynesian voyaging (AD 1200 to the present day) to be the easiest to reconstruct, but this is not so. Everyone agrees that during the last 1,000 years long-distance voyaging in the Pacific has declined, but no-one is certain why.

One possible explanation is that by AD 1200 the Polynesians had discovered and settled in just about every habitable speck of land. There were no more islands to be discovered; they realized this and stopped searching for them. This may be part of the truth, but I doubt it is the whole truth. Quite a few islands, at the time of the European invasion, had been settled once and subsequently abandoned. Also there was none of the trade which might have been expected between the founder-island and the founded (between, say, the Marquesas and Hawaii or the Societies and New Zealand). This underlines the truth of Sharp's contention that long-distance voyaging was always difficult and nearly always one-way. But it also underlines, I believe, something else: by AD 1200 Polynesian civilization was on the wane.

Evidence that it was waning can be found in the number of things that the Polynesians were giving up. They had once been skilful and prolific potters; by AD 500 they had ceased to make pottery altogether. They had once built huge statues and complex

Three totemic wooden carvings. *Right* Idol of Ku, the god of war, from the temple of Kawailae, Hawaii. *Above left* Ceremonial mask made for the malanggan memorial and initiation ceremonies. *Above right* Tlingit owl man made to commemorate the death of a man at Yakutat, Alaska.

temples; by 1800 most of these were in ruins. Their *pahis* had once been ubiquitous; by the time of Cook's landing they were rare. This decline didn't extend to all aspects of Polynesian life, nor was it uniform – it would obviously be nonsense to talk of a waning civilization in New Zealand, where settlement was in the vigour of youth. In some of the other islands, however, Polynesian civilization had been evolving, slowly and without interruption, for something like 2,500 years, and that in historical terms is a very long time indeed. (Both the Greek and Roman civilizations collapsed after about 750 years.) No wonder that by the time Europeans arrived in the Pacific the Polynesians were running out of steam. This is not to say that their civilization was decadent or ailing. It was simply old. And as old people tend to concentrate more and more on the few things that matter to them most, so, after about AD 1200, the Polynesians tended to withdraw more and more into little self-contained communities where they became wrapped up in what was dearest to their hearts: their horticulture, their inshore fishing, their social graces, their ancestral legends, and the physical pleasures of bathing, swimming, wrestling, dancing and making love.

On a lot of islands there tended to be too many people and too little food, and to this perennial problem the Polynesians applied a number of remedies. They did their best to improve their agricultural and horticultural techniques. In the Society Islands the Arioi practised infanticide and this eased the problem for a particular group of people in a particular area. But the most effective remedy of all was war, which Robert Louis Stevenson (who lived in Samoa) rightly described as 'the most healthful, if not the most humane, of all field sports'. A good example of the efficaciousness of war can be found in New Zealand, where the Maori built up a fine vigorous civilization while almost constantly engaged in tribal warfare.

The final phase of Polynesian voyaging would therefore seem to have been one of withdrawal rather than expansion – in some archipelagos so complete a withdrawal that by the time of the European invasion the golden age of exploration was little more than a memory.

But what a memory it was. There may be doubt as to how much Polynesian voyaging was intentional and how much was accidental; but there is no doubt that the net result was the discovery and population of just about every habitable island in the Pacific Ocean. For this great achievement the Polynesians have seldom been given sufficient credit. If we look up navigation in the *Encyclopedia Britannica*, we are told that the earliest navigators were the Phoenicians (*circa* 600 BC) and the Vikings (*circa* AD 600), yet long before the Phoenicians traversed the land-locked Mediterranean and edged up the coast of Europe, and long before the Vikings island-hopped some 300 miles at a time to Greenland and possibly to America, the Polynesians were sailing in deep water without landfall for distances of over 1,000 miles. They were the greatest seafarers the world has ever known. And it was they and not the Europeans who followed them who were the true discoverers of the Pacific.

Nor should it be forgotten that the way of life which they established in their island-kingdoms was near-idyllic. David Howarth makes this point succinctly:

> *It would be a pity to forget what the Tahitians* (in particular and the Polynesians in general) *achieved. They made a society which, in a simple way, came near perfection: nearer perhaps than any other that has been recorded. They were able to do this because they were left alone, because the place where they lived provided plenty of the needs of human life – enough food, warmth, beauty, leisure and fun – and because they had no ambition to struggle for anything more, and were generous and unselfish people happy to see that everyone else, and not only themselves, had enough.*

Comparisons may be odious, but one cannot help contrasting the behavoir of the Polynesians toward the European explorers and the behaviour of the European explorers toward the Polynesians. The Polynesians offered their guests food, drink, shelter, rest and the pleasure of sex, and expected nothing in return. Not all European explorers treated the Polynesians badly but without exception they seemed to regard them as children of a lesser god; and not infrequently they massacred them as wantonly as though they were so many head of game, killing them, to quote a Spanish soldier, 'because to kill is our pleasure and our profession, and what matter if the heathen are consigned to the fires of hell today since they will go there in any case tomorrow?'

Who, one wonders, were the true Christians, the meek who have been promised inheritance of the Earth?

THE CASTILIAN LAKE

THE VOYAGES OF THE SPANIARDS

Lord del mare, nos amarra los suenos la noche espanola
(Lord of the sea, the Spanish night binds down our dreams)
PABLO NERUDA, 'LORD COCHRANE DE CHILE'.

The Polynesians and the Spaniards could almost have been different species. Sixteenth-century Tahiti and sixteenth-century Castile could have been in different worlds.

At the beginning of the sixteenth century, Spain had emerged as a nation after an 800-year crusade against the Moors. Her people have been nicely described by Hammond Innes as 'born to the sword, and burning with a wild religious fervour', and with the freeing of their homeland from the Infidel, all their chivalry, all their military expertise and all their penchant for proselytizing were channelled into the New World which Columbus had recently discovered and laid claim to on their behalf. With this background it is not surprising that Spanish conquistadors were to blaze a trail of heroism and horror halfway around the world. At first their activities were confined to Southern and Central America. Then one of the ablest of them, Balboa, sighted the Pacific.

It was 26 September 1513. The isthmus of Panama was veiled in mist, the rivers were in spate, and the Spaniards in heavy armour were sinking up to their waists in freshet and swamp. There were 66 of the Spaniards, all that was left of the 190 who a month earlier had headed inland from the Atlantic, intent on finding, on the far side of the isthmus, the fabled sea. Here, they had been told, 'men ride camels and even the cooking-pots are made of gold'. Their route was short – not much more than 50 miles – but it had taken them through some of the most difficult terrain on Earth: steep-sided hills festooned with rain forest, rivers which rose 40 feet overnight, and swamps white with the mist which in those days was thought to harbour fever. They had suffered malaria and heat stroke. They had been harried by Indians – in one battle alone the Spaniards had killed 600 Indians in an hour and then let loose their bloodhounds to savage the bodies. They had advanced on average little more than a mile a day. But now at last their goal was in sight. From the top of the next hill, their guides told them, they would be able to see the Great Ocean which no white man had yet set eyes on. They hacked their way upwards.

At midday, as they approached the summit, Balboa ordered them to wait.

> *Then* (we are told in *De Orbe Novo*), *he went forwarde alone to the toppe. And there, prostrate upon the ground, and lifting up his eyes to heaven, he poured forth his prayers to almightie God.*

And when he had made his prayers, he beckoned to his companions, pointing out to them the great maine sea, heretofore unknown to the inhabitants of Europē, Aphrika and Asia.

It was one of the great moments in the history of exploration.

A few days later the Spaniards were standing on the shore of the new-found ocean, and that evening Balboa in full armour waded into the Pacific, in one hand an image of the Virgin and Child, in the other the banner of Aragon and Castile, and in the names of Juana and Ferdinand he 'took possession of these seas and lands and coasts and islands . . . for as long as the world shall endure'.

The conquistadors found no camels on the shore of the Pacific – the animals whose outline the Indians had drawn for them in the sand were llamas – but they did find vast quantities of gold. At the end of three months they returned laden with treasure to the Atlantic coast, and Balboa with more honesty than perspicuity sent Ferdinand of Castile that fifth-share of the plunder which was legally his. This was tantamount to signing his death warrant. For as soon as it became known in the Spanish court that a great new ocean *and* a great new source of gold lay on the far side of the isthmus, plans were set in motion to oust Balboa and gain possession of the untapped wealth he had discovered. It was not long before the conquistador was arrested, and, on trumped up charges, summarily executed – a wretched end for one of history's most colourful adventurers, and one which plunged the isthmus into an orgy of terror during which (to quote the contemporary Peter Martyr) 'no other thing was acted save to kill and be killed, to slaughter and be slaughtered' – not a happy augury for Spanish dominion over the ocean they had discovered.

At much the same time as Balboa – the first European to sight the Pacific – was beheaded, Magellan – the first European to take a ship into its waters – was petitioning the king of Spain to sponsor a voyage to the Moluccas.

Magellan's circumnavigation of the world, during which he became the first man to cross the Pacific, is arguably the greatest and most important journey ever made. It was a great journey because of its sheer length (three years and 42,000 miles), and because of the many and terrible dangers Magellan had to overcome. It was an important journey because it proved in the most practical way that the Earth was a sphere, thus ending centuries of legend and superstition. It was also important because it inaugurated three-quarters of a century of Spanish suzerainty over the new-found ocean.

Magellan's expedition has sometimes been seen as a natural follow-up to Balboa's sighting – what would seem to be more logical than that having set eyes on a new ocean the Spanish should want to explore it? This, however, is only part of the truth. The whole truth is a more complex story, a story which begins on the banks of the River Tagus one evening in the autumn of 1516.

Dom Manuel the Fortunate of Portugal was enthroned in state in his Lisbon palace on the bank of the Tagus. All day a succession of supplicants had been kneeling at the king's feet, begging in public those favours for which they lacked the influence to petition in private. By the time a herald announced the name of the last petitioner, the sun was setting and the king was tired.

'Fernão de Magalhaes.'

Ferdinand Magellan (1480-1521) and the *Victoria*, the first ship to circumnavigate the world.

A murmur of surprise ran round the court. For Ferdinand Magellan was a man of substance, not the sort of person one would expect to go down on his knees in public. Heads craned forward as the short, thickset figure limped awkwardly up to the dais. And Dom Manuel frowned. He had disliked Magellan when they had served together as boys in his aunt's court. The years had done nothing to mellow his feelings.

The mariner began his petition. He outlined his many years' service in Africa, India and Indonesia, mentioning the great battles in which he had fought and the three times he had been wounded. He ended with a plea that he might be raised in rank. Brusquely Dom Manuel refused. Magellan had half-expected this. He stayed on his knees. He was making another petition now – that he might be given command of one of the royal caravels soon to set sail for the distant Spice Islands, the Moluccas. Again Dom Manuel refused. He had, he said, no use for Magellan's services, in a caravel or anywhere else. Magellan had not expected this; his sense of justice was outraged, and his indignation all the greater because his humiliation was in open court. 'Then may I be permitted,' he cried, 'to seek service under another Lord?'

Dom Manuel rose from his throne. He was a commanding figure, towering over the crippled and insignificant Magellan. 'Serve whom you will, Clubfoot,' he said loudly. 'It is a matter of indifference to us.'

For a moment Magellan didn't move; then automatically, he bent forward to kiss the king's hand. But Dom Manuel put his hands behind his back.

It was an expensive gesture. A year later Magellan was outlining to a more sympathetic monarch, the young Charles V of Spain, his scheme for reaching the Moluccas not by sailing via the old route south-eastward along the coast of Africa, but via a completely new route south-westward across the Atlantic.

Dom Manuel's rejection of Magellan was one of the great blunders of history. It was due in part to personal antipathy, but the basic reasons go deeper. Portugal, 50 years after the death of Henry the Navigator, was exhausted. Her seamen had discovered almost three-quarters of the world, but her people were neither numerous enough nor powerful enough to hold on to what they had discovered. So throughout the sixteenth century her rulers faced a dilemma; the more discoveries their seamen made, the more men and wealth they were obliged to pour out to try and preserve them. The strain became more than a small nation could bear.

> *My country, oh my country,* lamented a contemporary chronicler, *too heavy is the task that has been laid on your shoulders. Day after day I watch the ships leaving your shores filled always with your best and bravest sons. And too many do not return. Who then is left to till the fields, to harvest the grapes, to keep the enemy on our frontiers at bay?. . . Heaven curse the man who first launched timber on to the sea or first unfurled a sail!*

We cannot forgive Dom Manuel for the manner in which he rejected Magellan, but we can understand his motives. Portugal in 1516 was sated with discoveries, and on the *Restelo*, the Beach of Tears, grizzled seamen with grandiose schemes of exploration were thick and pestilential as flies.

So Magellan emigrated to Spain. Here he became friendly with Ruy Faleiro, a fashionable astronomer, and with Duarte Barbosa, a member of the Spanish nobility whose daughter he was soon to marry. Through the patronage of these influential friends he was granted an audience with the king.

At first Charles V of Spain was suspicious. He had had dealings with Portuguese renegades before, men anxious to legitimize their maraudings against Portugal's far-flung possessions, and he questioned Magellan closely about the exact position of the

Moluccas, and his novel, indeed revolutionary, proposal how to get there. Magellan was persuasive, showing the king secret charts which had been given to him by the little-known Portuguese navigator John of Lisbon. These charts indicated a recently-discovered strait leading through the continent of America and into the ocean which had just been sighted by Balboa. It was thought that the Moluccas would be found close to the far end of this strait. This misconception was due to the fact that although sixteenth-century cartographers could calculate positions north-and-south with some accuracy, they had no way of calculating positions east-and-west; for although it was known in theory that the earth was a sphere, its circumference was unknown and much underestimated. On the strength of John of Lisbon's charts and his favourable impression of Magellan, Charles gave the voyage his support.

So the first European fleet to enter the Pacific sailed under the flag of Spain and not Portugal. And what a fleet it was. For more than a year the five ships lay moored to the Dock of Mules in Seville, being refitted, recaulked and recanvassed. They were provisioned for three years. Their armament was formidable. Their navigational equipment was comprehensive. Their crew were in good heart and the only note of discord lay in the relationship of their captains. For Magellan, in overall command, was a Portuguese of comparatively humble birth, while the other captains were aristocratic Spaniards who disliked having to take orders from 'the upstart Portuguese whom the young king has been seduced into placing above us'. Before the ships had left Spanish waters there was talk of mutiny. But on 10 August 1519, dissent was for the moment forgotten in the excitement of departure. The church bells were pealing and the mistral was moaning down from the hills, as ropes were cast off and the five ships drifted slowly away from the Dock of Mules. As they came to mid-river and the current caught them, they hoisted foresails and one by one set course for the open sea. First Magellan's flagship, the 110-ton *Trinidad*, then the *San Antonio*, then the *Concepcion*, then the *Victoria* and finally the diminutive 75-ton *Santiago* – 277 men setting out in the hope of loading a cargo of spices, little dreaming that the few of them to survive would return home three years later having sailed all the way round the world.

It took Magellan 453 days to reach the Pacific, a fact which pinpoints very clearly the most serious obstacle to the exploration of the Ocean by Europeans. It was impossibly far away. Even to reach it, let alone explore it, a ship had to voyage for more than 10,000 miles. And in the sixteenth, seventeenth and eighteenth centuries, voyages of 10,000 miles were in themselves major achievements – witness what happened to Magellan before he even set eyes on the Pacific.

At Tenerife he faced an incipient mutiny. Off Sierra Leone his ships were scattered by a succession of storms during which they rolled so steeply that, we are told, the *Trinidad*'s yardarm actually feathered the sea. In mid-Atlantic there was another mutiny; then the ships became becalmed in the Sargasso Sea. There wasn't a breath of wind in the Sargasso, and in heavy swell the five vessels spun, pitched and corkscrewed, to the groaning of timbers and the rattling of spars. Week after week the tropic sun blazed down on them, causing the tar to melt in their seams and their timbers to split; the pumps had to be manned day and night, but so stifling was the heat that after ten minutes' pumping the seamen fainted. Their meat turned putrid; the hoops on their water-casks burst. It took the armada a month to drift clear of the doldrums; then they enjoyed a respite, an idyllic run down the coast of Brazil followed by an even more idyllic saturnalia in Rio. 'The women,' wrote Magellan's diarist Pigafetta, 'wear no clothes at all except their hair, and in exchange for a knife or an axe we could obtain two or even three of these delightful daughters of Eve, so perfect and well shaped in every way.' In between a frenzy of love-making, during which even the priests had to be dragged back unwillingly to the ships, the five vessels were careened and reprovisioned.

Then they set out again, heading south in search of *el paso*, John of Lisbon's strait. And early in 1520 they thought they had found it. Rounding a headland they saw ahead a broad reach of water running west into the sunset. As they headed into it their hopes were high; however, after a couple of days mist closed around them and the water turned muddy and shallow. Magellan had just tasted the water and found it fresh, when his lookout shouted, 'I see a mountain' – hence the name Montevideo – and as the mist momentarily cleared the truth became all too apparent. Ahead lay not a strait, but the mouth of a great river, La Plata. *El paso*, it seemed, was a chimera, their shortcut to the Spiceries a myth.

Magellan, however, refused to give up. 'Though the strait is not here,' he told his ships' companies, 'we shall surely find it farther along the coast.'

Standing south, his armada now came to seas into which no European had yet ventured. And what seas they were! For eight weeks the fleet was battered by winds of hurricane velocity, bludgeoned by mountainous waves, lashed by hail and sleet, and weighed down with ice. Three times the ships were scattered; the *Victoria* ran aground, the *Santiago* was dismasted, the *San Antonio* sprang a leak and all but foundered. It was a voyage of appalling danger, heightened by Magellan's insistance that his vessels keep close inshore to examine every inlet and bay. His crew came to respect him for his endurance and fine seamanship, but his Spanish captains had little stomach for such voyaging. 'The fool is obsessed with his search for *el paso*,' one of them is reported to have cried. 'On the flame of his ambition he will crucify us all!'

The weather worsened, the coast became increasingly barren, and Magellan realized that he had to find a haven in which to winter. On the last day of March he found one, his ships scraping over a foaming sandbar and dropping anchor in the bleak but sheltered harbour of Saint Julian. Magellan must have hoped that the worst of his troubles were now over. In fact they were about to begin. For his ships had barely lost way, when the discontent of the Spanish captains flared up into mutiny.

Before the fleet had left Seville the Spanish commanders had sworn to 'follow the course ordered by their captain-general and obey him in all things'. Twice in the Atlantic they had mutinied and twice Magellan had forgiven them. On this third and more serious occasion he felt the need to assert his authority. The mutiny was crushed. Mendoza, captain of the *Victoria*, was killed in the fighting; de Quesada, captain of the *Concepcion*, was publicly executed and his body quartered and strung up on gibbets, while Cartagena, captain of the *San Antonio*, was marooned. There was no doubt now who was master.

Saint Julian was a gloomy and claustrophobic anchorage. There was, however, plenty of beech for firewood and plenty of shellfish and seafowl for food. There were also, to quote Pigafetta, 'strange animals, half-fish half-bird the like of which no Christian man had e'er set eyes on': penguins, which proved easy to kill and provided a welcome addition to their diet.

For four months the armada was forced to lie up, while winter storms of unbelievable fury lashed the Patagonian shore. Then, with the coming of spring, Magellan sent the *Santiago* south on reconnaissance. The tiny vessel, however, became trapped on a lee shore, was driven on to a sandbar, and pounded to destruction. By a near-miracle most of her crew survived and were subsequently rescued by the *Trinidad*. It was October before Magellan was again searching for the elusive strait. He was now closer to the Antarctic than any European before him. And still his course was south.

Théodore de Bry's map of the Straits of Magellan: from *Historia Americae sive Novi Orbis*, part XII 1591.

On 21 October, his armada hove-to at the approaches to what looked like a large bay. The water was light green and thought therefore to be shallow, while in the distance a line of snow-capped peaks could be seen through rifts in the cloud. It seemed a most unpromising place to search for *el paso.* Magellan, however, ordered the *San Antonio* and the *Concepcion* to explore the bay. The Spanish captains grumbled at such an obvious waste of time, but a sudden and violent storm cut short their dissent and drove them willy-nilly towards the shore. The last Magellan saw of them it looked as though they were being driven straight on to a rocky promontory and he gave them up for lost. He himself had just sufficient leeway to head for the open sea, where for two days his remaining ships rode out the storm. The moment the weather cleared, he headed back into the bay to search for survivors. As his ships neared the rocks, the lookout spotted smoke, which raised Magellan's hopes that some at least of the ships' companies had survived. For a moment all eyes were on the thin column of white. Then, as the *Trinidad* rounded the promontory, her crew saw something totally unexpected. Ahead of them lay a narrow channel, quite hidden from the open sea, running due west through the mountains as far as the eye could see.

They had barely recovered from their surprise, when the lookout shouted, 'A sail!' Running free down the strait, under a great press of canvas, came the *San Antonio* and the *Concepcion*, bedecked with flags, their crews waving and cheering. And it came to Magellan in a moment of joy almost too wonderful to be believed that not only had his missing ships been restored to him, they had discovered *el paso.*

Then, we are told, 'he fell to his knees in tears'.

Soon the exultant captains were reporting aboard the *Trinidad.* And what a story they had to tell. Here is Charles McKew Parr's account of their discovery of the Straits of Magellan.

> *After tacking frantically in the storm and exhausting every manoeuvre to escape the lee shore, the two ships had been swept round the promontory and blown helplessly towards the breakers. Suddenly they saw a narrow passage, like the mouth of a river, ahead of them in the surf, and managed to steer into it. Driven on by the wind and a flood tide, they raced through these narrows into a wide lake.*

Still driven by the storm, they were carried west for some hours across this lake and into another narrow passage, although now the current had been reversed, and what appeared to be a great ebb tide came rushing towards them. They debouched from this second strait into a broad body of water that stretched far towards the setting sun. . . Every test and check convinced the pilots that this was a genuine strait, opening westward into the Great Sea . . . and they seized upon a change of wind and raced back to Magellan with the news.

Next day the armada stood into *el paso.*

at first they enjoyed easy sailing, with the narrows opening out to form a stretch of sheltered water surrounded by hills. However, as the ships headed westward, the country became more spectacular and their voyage more hazardous. On the third day they came to a maze of tortuous channels hemmed in by towering cliffs. Their longboat was sent ahead to reconnoitre, while the four vessels, close-reefed, followed in single file. Soon they found themselves hemmed in by 2,000-foot walls of rock, rising near-sheer from the sea; powerful tides and currents threatened to sweep them to destruction; the wind shifted violently and unpredictably through every point of the compass. Sleet fell without respite out of a sodden sky, while banks of mist, dense, chill and eerie, came rolling down from the ice caps. By day there was little sign of life, but at night the darkness was pinpointed by flickering flames, the campfires of the Patagonian Indians – hence the name given to the islands to the south of the strait – *Tierra del Fuego.*

For more than 300 miles the armada groped through these dangerous waters, their survival a testimony to Magellan's skill as a navigator. Their only loss was that of the *San Antonio,* and this by design rather than accident; for the ship deserted Magellan in the hour of his triumph and headed back for Spain, taking with it more than half the fleet's already inadequate supply of food. To reprovision, Magellan put into a small inlet – the Creak of Sardines – and it was from here that his longboat discovered the Pacific.

The entry in Pigafetta's diary is brief, and has none of the sense of occasion which one might expect from so great a moment in the history of exploration. He says simply:

Soon after reaching the Creek of Sardines we sent a boat well equipped with men and provisions to search for the entrance to the other sea. They spent three days going and returning, and when they got back they told us that they had found the entrance and seen beyond it the Great and Wide Ocean. Whereat the Captain-General said that the headland at the mouth of the entrance should be known as Cape Deseado, as a thing long desired and sought for.

Magellan didn't hurry his entry into the new-found ocean. He spent more than a week in and around the Creek of Sardines, searching for the *San Antonio* and stocking up with provisions. The provisions he took aboard were ample in quantity but not in quality, for he filled his ships' holds with fish and meat – sardines which he seined by the thousand, and seafowl, rabbits and prairie hens. It never occurred to him to gather in the antiscorbutic vegetables which in the months ahead would have saved his crew from the ravages of scurvy. For scurvy, in those days, was thought to be an infectious disease, like cholera, leprosy or typhoid; it never occurred to anyone that it was due to a dietary deficiency, a lack of the vitamin C which is found in green vegetables and citrus fruit. Two and a half centuries later, Cook, passing through the Strait, loaded up with 'nutritous sea kale, wild celery as good as any I have tasted, and the sweet herb Appio'. But Magellan (like all seamen of his day) failed to realize the value of these vegetables, and in this lay the seeds of tragedy.

On 27 November his armada passed Cape Deseado and saw open water ahead.

The eruption of the volcano Anak Krakatau (the daughter of Krakatoa) in the Sunda Straits in October 1981.

The coconut palm (*Cocos nucifera*), now a symbol of the grace and beauty of the Pacific Islands, provided the early Polynesian settlers with many of the necessities of life.

In the triangle Tokyo–Djakarta–Pitcairn lie 80 per cent of the world's islands. *Top* Heron Island, Great Barrier Reef. *Above* Ulithi Atoll, Caroline Islands.

The Pacific is an ocean of spectacular contrasts. *Top* Icebergs off the coast of Antarctica. *Above Loberia floreana* on the coast of the Galapagos Islands.

Four Melanesian/Polynesian artefacts. *Top left* Ceremonial house-carving, Maprik, Papua New Guinea. *Top right* Ku, a Hawaiian god. *Bottom left* Rarotongan ironwood image of a god. *Bottom right* Figurehead from the bow of a Marquesan canoe.

During Cook's second voyage Hodges painted Vaitepiha Bay, Tahiti, on 17 August 1773.

Poedua, a Tahitian girl, painted by John Webber (1752–98), the artist aboard HMS *Resolution* on Cook's third voyage (1776–80).

They were now about to make a greater leap into the unknown than seamen had ever made before, and Magellan seems to have sensed this, for as his vessels stood into the new found ocean, crucifixes were raised, and the chanting of the *Te Deum* drowned the cries of the sea birds. Then their cannon thundered a broadside, and the lions and castles of Castile broke free from their mastheads. 'We are now standing into waters,' Magellan cried, 'where no ship has ever sailed before. May this sea be always as calm and peaceful as it is today. In this hope I name it the *Mar Pacifico*.'

They stood north-west into the unknown.

To start with, the *Mar Pacifico* must have seemed to them like the waters of Paradise. As they headed out of the sub-Antarctic storm belt, the sea became calmer and the climate balmier. With a wind from abeam and a favourable current the ships made rapid progress, their crews peering eagerly ahead, expecting any day to sight the longed-for Moluccas. So little happened during December that Pigafetta's diary contains only one entry for the whole month – the description of 'a very amusing hunt of Fishes'.

> *There are,* he wrote, *three sorts of fish in this ocean a cubit or more in length, which are named Dorades, Albacores and Bonita. These follow and hunt another kind of fish which flies and which we called Colondriny* (sea swallows), *a foot in length and very good to eat. And when the three kinds of fish find the Colondriny in the water they chase them and make them fly – and they fly for as long as their wings are wet, about the distance a man can fire a crossbolt. And while the Colondriny fly, the other fish swim after them, seeing and following their shadow; so that as soon as they re-enter the water they attempt to seize and devour them – a merry and marvellous thing to see!*

As his ships neared the 30th parallel, Magellan altered course to the west-north-west, still expecting any moment to sight the coastline of Asia. He was desperately unlucky. If his heading had been only a few degrees farther south he would have sighted the Tuamotus or the Societies, which lie scattered across some 300,000 square miles of ocean. As it was, his course carried him a shade to the north of these archipelagos and into the vast and empty reaches of the mid-Pacific.

By early January his ships' companies were becoming anxious; never in the Atlantic had they sailed so long or so far without a landfall. The monotony began to fray their nerves; day after day the same blustering wind, the same unclouded sky, the same brazen sun, and soon to add to their anxiety, hunger – for Magellan, alarmed at how fast his supplies were dwindling, ordered a cut in rations. But worse was to come. As they stood deeper into the tropics, the little food they had began to deteriorate. First to go was their penguin and seal meat. In the heat of the sun it turned putrid, breeding long white maggots which crawled everywhere and ate, with impartial voracity, supplies, clothes, leather and ship's timber. The water in their casks became coated with scum; it turned yellow and stank so overpoweringly that men retched as they tried to drink it. The crew became weak and listless; dark circles appeared under their eyes; their limbs began to ache and their gums to swell and turn blue. Six weeks out from the Straits of Magellan men began to die.

They died painfully and without dignity, their bodies emaciated and their joints grotesquely swollen, from a disease they called simply 'the plague' but which we know today was scurvy.

Scurvy was the bane of sixteenth- and seventeenth-century seamen. They could neither prevent it nor cure it. They could only suffer it. And no one has depicted their suffering more vividly than the Dutchman Roggeveen, writing of his voyage across the Pacific when more than half his ship's company died:

Top Magellan discovering the path to the Pacific, from an illustration by O. W. Briely. *Above* Christmas Sound, Tierra del Fuego, engraved by Watts from a painting by William Hodges.

No pen can describe the misery of life in our vessels. They reeked of sickness and death. The stricken wailed and lamented day and night, and their cries would have moved stones to pity. Some become so emaciated that they looked like walking corpses and death blew them out like so many candles. Others became very fat and blown up like balloons; these were so afflicted with dysentery that they passed nothing but blood except for two or three days before they died when their excrement was like grey sulphur – and this was a sure sign that their hour had come. All were overcome by a fearful melancholy . . . Even those who were not seriously ill like myself, were left weak and enfeebled. My teeth were loose in my gums, which were swollen up almost to the thickness of a thumb, and my body was covered with swellings, red yellow green and blue in colour and the size of hazelnuts.

What happened to Roggeveen and to Magellan was to happen time and time again during the exploration of the Pacific. Vessels crossing the ocean reckoned it quite usual for 40 per cent of their crew to die of scurvy, and losses of 75 per cent were not unheard of. Life for countless generations of seamen could indeed be described in those days as 'nasty, brutish and short'.

By mid-January more than a third of Magellan's crew were so weak that they needed a stick to help them walk, and only a handful had the strength to work helm and sails. On 20 January the Captain-General flung his charts into the sea. 'With the pardon of the cartographers,' he cried, 'the Moluccas are not to be found at their appointed place.' His ships' companies had been reduced to a single sip of water and a handful of weevil-infested biscuit a day when, after two months without landfall, they sighted an atoll.

The atoll which saved their lives was probably Puka-puka, the most northerly of the Tuamotus. Puka-puka has little vegetation and less water, but its lagoon and beaches provided the starving men with an abundance of fish, sea-birds and turtles' eggs, while a timely squall of rain – which they collected in their sails – provided them with water.

They convalesced on the atoll for the better part of a week. Then on 28 January they were again at sea, heading now for the Philippines, which Magellan reckoned might prove a safer landfall than the elusive Moluccas. Though the crews were still weak and debilitated they were in good spirits, for they thought they had come to the most easterly of the islands which they knew festooned the coast of Asia. They felt sure that from now on they would make frequent landfalls.

They were wrong. Far from having crossed the Pacific, they had traversed little more than a third of it.

The truth came to them slowly and painfully as they headed west-north-west day after day, week after week, and no more islands were sighted. By mid-February their anxiety had returned; so had their hunger and their scurvy. But with the wind strong from astern there could be no turning back. The fleet had no choice but to reel endlessly on, lit by an unrelenting sun by day and a haloed moon by night. The voyage became more and more terrible. They were athwart the Equator now, and the heat of the sun metamorphosed the sea-birds they had salted on Puka-puka to a turmoil of worms – worms that they were soon reduced to pounding to pulp and eating. Aboard the *Trinidad*, when the last of their biscuit had gone, they scraped the maggots out of the casks, mashed them up and served them as gruel. They made cakes out of sawdust soaked with the urine of rats – the rats themselves had long since been hunted to extinction. They unwound the leather from their masts, soaked it, boiled it and served it to those few of the crew whose teeth had not yet rotted free from their gums. Men lay curled up on deck, in the last stages of scurvy and starvation, their palates too enlarged to swallow even a spoonful of water. Each morning Father Valderrama, the senior of the priests, would hear the confessions of the dying, Pigafetta would write a last message to parent, sweetheart or wife, and at nightfall more bodies would be tipped over the stern to be fought for by the sharks now following endlessly in their wake.

On 4 March the crew of the *Trinidad* ate what were literally their last fragments of food – a few slivers of overbaked biscuit, hard as flint, which Magellan had pounded into a paste and mixed with sawdust and water. When this was gone there was nothing left, neither crumb nor bone, maggot nor shell. They could only wait for death. With increasing frequency in the next 24 hours men dragged themselves into the gunwales with cries of 'Land! Land!' as the dream-islands of their hallucinations floated tantalizing by. So when, in the early morning of 6 March, a seaman named Navarro clawed up the ratlines with a scream of 'Praise God! Land!' many of the ship's company didn't bother to look up. Then a cannon from the *Victoria* boomed out in ecstasy, and when they heard an echo from the tree-lined shore they realized that this time the island drifting by was real.

Magellan had crossed the Pacific.

His landfall was the Marianas, the island he first sighted probably being Rota, and the island where he finally struggled ashore Guam.

What happened next may have been inevitable but was nonetheless tragic. Magellan's ships had barely come to rest some 100 yards offshore when they were surrounded by an armada of canoes, manned by men with light tan skin, long brown hair and the physique of gods. One moment the deck of the flagship was empty, the next it was taken over by some 30 to 35 stalwart warriors, each armed with club, spear and oval shield – the latter decorated with tufts of human hair. The natives, who were almost certainly members of the warrior élite the Chamorros, took stock of the sickly Europeans and were obviously not impressed. Within seconds they had began a wholesale looting of whatever they fancied: knives, ropes, canvas and axes being passed quickly down to the waiting canoes. A seaman who tried to remonstrate was flung contemptuously into the scuppers. Magellan called his few able-bodied men to the poop. The islanders were then asked by signs to give back what they had taken. They refused, and in the fracas which followed two of the crew were injured. Magellan raised his hand. Six crossbows hummed. Six Chamorros fell writhing to the deck.

For a moment their companions were unable to comprehend what had happened. Then, in less time than it takes to relate, they disappeared over the side; but they had the wit, even in retreat, to cut loose and tow away the longboat, and they dropped none of the items they had looted. Magellan cried out that the wounded were to be spared; but his crew, in their weakened condition, were taking no chances, and all but one of the islanders were stabbed to death.

Magellan has sometimes been condemned for this 'massacre of the innocents', but since his overriding concern had to be for the safety of his crew it is hard to see how he could have acted otherwise. There is perhaps less justification for what happened next. The three ships stood close inshore and discharged a broadside into the Chamorros' village. The huts disintegrated, the islanders fled, and Magellan led a landing party up the deserted beach. The pillaging that followed was swift, orderly and comprehensive. The butts were filled with fresh water, and everything edible – chicken, pigs, rice, bananas, coconuts, taros and breadfruit – was loaded into captured canoes and ferried from shore to ships. By evening, when Magellan prudently weighed anchor and put to sea, the holds of his vessels were filled with better-quality provisions than they had had aboard at any time since leaving Rio.

There followed an orgy of feasting, and although it would be foolish to suggest that the nourishment of a single meal restored the crew to health, this was the turning point on their road to recovery. Soon they were heading once again for the Philippines.

The rest of Magellan's voyage was tragedy and anticlimax.

Continuing west through a maze of islands, he reached Samar on 16 March 1521. He was in familiar territory now; his Malaysian slave Enriques was able to talk to the islanders in his native tongue, and the Spice Islands in search of which he had voyaged so far were no more than a few days' sail to the south. But he was not to see them. For rather than head at once for the Moluccas, Magellan decided to stay awhile in the Philippines, exploring, trading (at an exchange-rate of 8 pieces of gold for every 14 lbs of iron) – and converting the people to Christianity. Most historians have criticized him for this, pointing out that his obsession with proselytizing was to lead to his death. There is, however, another way of looking at things.

> *Before long,* writes Stefan Zweig in his little-known biography of Magellan, *relations between Filipinos and Europeans grew so cordial that the Rajah and many of his followers expressed a desire to become Christians. . . On Sunday 14 April the Spaniards celebrated their greatest triumph. In the centre of the town a dais was erected and hung with palm fronds. Carpets were brought from the ships, together with two thrones swathed in velvet. In front of these was placed an altar. The Captain-General now made a dramatic entry: banners were unfurled, a salute was fired from the ships, and the Rajah and his family, kneeling in front of the Cross, were duly baptized. . . The news spread. And next day there came from neighbouring islands many more dignitaries to be initiated in these magical ceremonies. . . Seldom have great deeds been more splendidly accomplished. Magellan had discovered the strait leading to the other side of the world; new islands with abundant riches had been won for the Crown of Castile; countless souls had accepted the true faith – and these things had been done without shedding a drop of blood. . . What other conquistadors achieved only after many years – and then with the aid of the rack, the Inquisition and burnings at the stake – Magellan had achieved in a few days and without violence.*

We are told that in the course of the next week there were so many baptisms that 'the priests no longer had sufficient strength to raise their arms in blessing'. Zweig's interpretation may be over-roseate, but it is worth bearing in mind that Spanish culture and the Catholic faith have endured for four-and-a-half centuries in the Philippines, which are today the only nation in Asia that is predominantly Christian.

After the conversion of the Rajah, events moved swiftly to a climax which in retrospect seems almost inevitable. Several of the native chiefs refused to accept Christianity. hose who *had* been converted, begged Magellan to teach the backsliders a lesson. He became embroiled in local feuds, and was persuaded to lead a landing-party to punish a chief whose crime ostensibly was that he persisted in worshipping idols but who in fact was a lifelong enemy of the Rajah. Once ashore, Magellan was deserted by his Spanish captains and left virtually alone to be hacked to death by an army of 3,000 Filipinos.

'And thus,' lamented Pigafetta, 'they slew our mirror, our light, our comfort and our true and only guide', a tragic and wasteful death for a man who had voyaged so far and through such appalling hazards almost to within sight of his goal.

The chaos that followed Magellan's death is a testimony to his stature as a commander. For it soon became apparent that he alone had the knowledge, the force of character and the integrity to hold the diverse elements of his fleet together. With his hand no longer on the helm his once-proud armada drifted from disaster to disaster. His officers in their greed and folly walked into a trap and got themselves massacred. His ships were driven from the Philippines – they had been welcomed as gods but after Magellan's death they were rejected as thieves and murderers. The *Concepcion* was set on fire and scuttled and Magellan's papers deliberately destroyed.

The remaining ships then took to piracy. Since the slow-moving junks of the south-west Pacific were virtually unarmed, the carronades of the Spaniards were an argument to which there was no answer and for four months the *Victoria* and the *Trinidad* indulged in an orgy of destruction, plunder and murder. Ship after ship was captured, looted and sunk, and the crews massacred. More than one of the Spanish officers kept a harem of Muslim women aboard and this led to quarrelling and yet more murder. Eventually, their holds literally bursting with treasure, the ships arrived at the Spice Islands. Here they parted company. The *Trinidad*, attempting to re-cross the Pacific, was captured by the Portuguese and her crew hanged as pirates. The *Victoria* alone, manned by 19 emaciated survivors, managed after almost exactly three years to struggle back to Spain.

No journey could be more aptly called an epic, and no journey has ever added more to our knowledge of the world. Yet at the time Magellan received scant recognition. His achievements were belittled in Portugal because of Dom Manuel's hatred of him and because his ships had dealt so crippling a blow at the Portuguese oriental empire. And they were also belittled in Spain, partly because it seemed to the ruling junta intolerable that a Portuguese commoner should have dared to lop off the heads of the Spanish nobility, and partly because the route he discovered to the Spice Islands brought Spain no immediate tangible wealth. This last factor was the crux of the matter. When Columbus crossed the Atlantic the route which he discovered was used immediately and for centuries to come for trade. In his wake sailed a whole genealogy of vessels – treasure galleons, slavers, cargo-ships and sunshine cruises. When Magellan crossed both Atlantic and Pacific his voyage, as a feat of exploration, was much the greater, but the route which he discovered to the Philippines and the Moluccas was too long and too hazardous to bring Spain a great deal of immediate material benefit; in his wake few dared to follow. Indeed within a couple of generations Drake was to discover a safer way into the Pacific via Cape Horn, and a contemporary cartographer was to write, 'the Strait of Magellan no longer exists: either a landslide has blocked it, or else an island has risen out of the sea to dam up its channel'. So much for John of Lisbon's short cut to the Spiceries!

In the half-century that followed Magellan's death, the efforts of the Spaniards to explore and exploit the ocean he had discovered reflect the difficulties of his voyage. For Spain sent many well-equipped expeditions to try to establish her claim to the Philippines and the Molluccas and to foster trade. But for 40 years out of all the ships she sent to the Pacific not one returned.

In 1525 seven ships commanded by Francisco de Loaysa set sail from Spain for the Spice Islands: only four got as far as the Pacific, only two got as far as the Moluccas and neither of these managed the passage home. In 1527 three ships commanded by Alvaro de Saavedra set sail from Mexico, also bound for the Spice Islands; they made the outward journey safely, but all were lost on the way back, although the crew of two of the ships may have been the first Europeans to make contact with Japan where they are believed to have been wrecked. In 1542 six vessels commanded by Ruy de Villalobos set sail from Mexico for the Philippines; after terrible hardships their crew was captured by the Portuguese, and all their ships were either impounded or sunk. No wonder that with such losses the Spaniards preferred, during the first half of the sixteenth century, to concentrate on the comparatively easy pickings in gold to be won from the American mainland.

However, in 1565 a voyage took place which was as important as it is little-known. The diminutive 40-ton *San Lucas* managed to achieve what no European vessel had achieved before, a voyage across the Pacific from west-to-east. The *San Lucas'* captain, Alonso de Arellano, may have been an enigmatic character, and her pilot Lope Martin a highly dubious one (with a penchant for murder, mutiny and getting himself marooned), but there is no doubt about the authenticity of their voyage nor its significance. On 22 April 1565 they left the Philippines on a course not of east but of north-east. Skirting Japan, they continued on their original heading as far north as the 43rd parallel, where they saw 'porpoises as big as cows' and 'it was so cold that [their] cooking oil froze'. Here they picked up favourable currents, the Kuro Siwo and the North Pacific Drift. They also picked up the storm-belt of the westerlies, and with both wind and current in their favour they reached the coast of North America on 17 July.

The voyage of the *San Lucas* initiated an era of increased Spanish activity in the Pacific. With voyages across the ocean now possible in both directions, Manila in the Philippines became a major emporium; a sort of pumping-station which drew in silver from South America and in return dispersed the treasures of the Orient – in particular Chinese jade and silk. 'We are now at the gate of the most fortunate countries of the world and the most remote: Great China, Burnei, Siam, Japan and other rich and large provinces,' wrote a Spanish sea-captain. The Spaniards, however, were not alone at the gate. The Portuguese still controlled the Moluccas and had just set up a new base at Macao; while the waters of 'the Spanish Lake' were soon to be ruffled by the bow-waves of ships from both England and the new-found Dutch Republic.

Alvaro Mendana de Niera (1541-95), and a sixteenth-century Spanish galleon of the type which he and Quiros commanded in their voyages across the Pacific.

Not surprisingly the increasing volume of Spanish trade in the Pacific soon led to new discoveries.

In the North Pacific the trade routes to and from Manila passed through few of the major archipelagos except the Marshall and Caroline Islands, both of which the early explorers frequently sighted and sometimes landed upon. In the South Pacific, in contrast, the trade route to the Spiceries passed through a whole plethora of archipelagos, many of which were discovered in the latter part of the century by Mendana or Quiros.

Mendana and Quiros were great explorers who deserve greater recognition than they are usually accorded. The inspiration behind their voyages was the usual Spanish quest for gold and God – Mendana being chiefly concerned with finding 'that golden heaven where in an Island known as Solomon there must surely be great riches', and Quiros being chiefly concerned with the saving of souls. Their expeditions have been described by Spate as 'among the most remarkable (voyages) in the whole history of maritime discovery, alike in their geographical results and as a story of high ideals, bitter disillusions and suffering, baseness and grandeur': a judgement particularly apt in the case of the voyages of Pedro Fernandez de Quiros.

The date was 28 August, 1601, the place Saint Peter's, Rome, where a pale, slightly-built man in pilgrim's robes was kneeling at the feet of Pope Clement VIII. He was a humble man, but he pleaded his cause with eloquence. 'There is a great Countrie south of the *Mar Pacifico'*, he told His Holiness, 'a new and undiscovered world wherein lies an infinity of souls crying out to be saved.' The Pope was first sceptical then impressed. There were further audiences, and the most learned pilots and mathematicians in Rome checked the petitioner's credentials until eventually Clement VIII was won over. He not only wrote to Philip of Spain recommending that a proselytizing voyage be made, he also, as tangible evidence of his support, handed over a number of specially blessed rosaries and a piece of the True Cross. For never before had he given audience to a man so eager and apparently so well qualified to spread the Gospel to the farthest ends of the Earth.

The man in pilgrim's robes was the 36 year-old Pedro Fernandez de Queiroz – whose name by general usage has become corrupted to Quiros – an explorer whom history has dismissed as an impractical visionary, but whose achievements were in fact those of a caring man and a highly competent navigator.

Quiros's audience with the Pope and his subsequent expedition can, I think, be attributed to his passage to the Philippines in 1595 as chief pilot to Alvaro de Mendana.

Mendana's expedition had an unhappy birth from which it never recovered. The Spanish authorities in Peru didn't look with favour on voyages of exploration, and Mendana had been obliged to acquire his ships by force and provision them by trickery; he had been given deliberately falsified charts; on weighing anchor his crew were drunk and brawling, and Quiros admitted to being 'very uncertain what would be the end of the voyage, seeing that its beginning was so disorderly'. After crossing 3,500 miles of featureless ocean Mendana's ships, in mid-July, discovered the Marquesas. There followed what is usually regarded as the first substantial contact between Europeans and Polynesians. And sorry reading it makes. The Marquesas were beautiful beyond dreams: swaying palms and golden sands, waters seething with fish, and rich volcanic soil. The inhabitants were beautiful too, 'gentle and graceful creatures, almost white, lovely of leg, hand, eyes, face and figure and with much cause to praise their Creator.' But their grace and beauty were no armour against the bolts of

Mendana's arquebusiers. Initial contact, with both parties wide-eyed with mutual curiosity, seems to have been friendly; but when the islanders began to help themselves to loose gear lying about on the decks of Mendana's ship, there was triggered off an often-to-be-repeated sequence of remonstration, scuffling, shooting, reprisal and massacre. Mendana and Quiros seem to have been quite unable to restrain their ships' companies who killed (once again to quote Mendana's camp-master) 'because to kill is our pleasure and our profession . . . and what matter if the heathen are consigned to hell today since they will go there in any case tomorrow?' One soldier admitted to killing a nursing mother simply to prove his prowess as a good shot. After spending a fortnight in the Marquesas, during which it seems probable that some 250 Polynesians were killed and some 400 wounded, the fleet again stood west, leaving behind on Fatu-Hiva three mutilated Marquesan bodies and three beautifully carved wooden crosses – symbols of the tragic gulf between Spanish intention and achievement.

A month later the ships discovered Santa Cruz at the approaches to the Solomons. Events here followed much the same pattern. Once again the islanders were killed wantonly and often without provocation. Mendana, for example, swore friendship with a chief they named Malope; but his men invited Malope and his family to a meal, then murdered the lot of them on the grounds that 'they might, perhaps, have been planning treachery'. Before long the Europeans fell to quarrelling among themselves. There were mutinies, beheadings and the settling of a host of private vendettas, then, as if in retribution, they were decimated by 'the plague' – probably on this occasion not scurvy but blackwater fever. Men died by the score, among them Mendana and his second-in-command. At the end of a month there were no more than two dozen men capable of working the ships. At this nadir of the expedition's fortunes Quiros took command. He piloted Mendana's surviving vessels out of the misnamed Bay Graciosa and set course for the Philippines. As the hills of Santa Cruz disappeared below the horizon the soldiers and seamen 'gave thanks that at last [they] were leaving behind this corner of hell'.

But the hell had been of their making.

Quiros's passage from Santa Cruz to the Philippines was a fine piece of seamanship. More than half his crew lay dead around the Bay of Grace, and the survivors were debilitated by fever and hunger, his ships were literally rotting to pieces, their sails were in tatters, and much of their superstructure had been improvidently burnt as fuel. Mendana's widow, Dona Isabella, did her best to undermine Quiros's authority, countermanding his orders and washing her clothes in her private supply of water while the crew were dying of thirst. But after a three-month voyage, the remnants of Mendana's armada staggered into Manila Bay. Of the 400-odd men who had left Peru the previous year, three out of four were dead; and what a legacy of grief and sorrow they had left in their wake!

Quiros had been appalled at the violence and brutality to which the islanders had been subjected, and on his return to Peru he sought an audience with the viceroy. If he were given a ship of 70 tons and a crew of 40 he would, he said, return to the archipelagos of the south-west Pacific and bring their inhabitants peaceably into the fold of the Catholic Church. He would then push on to discover and colonize the great southern continent, *Terra Australis Incognita*, which, he argued, would surely be found to the south-west of Santa Cruz. This was an ambitious scheme, but it was far from being the scheme of an impractical visionary. As Magellan had proved, the people of the Pacific Islands were susceptible to proselytizing, and Quiros was intending to search for *Terra Australis* in exactly the right place. His proposal, however, was not well received; for Spain by the early 1600s had lost its fervour for both proselytizing and exploration. This was Quiros's tragedy: that he was born a century too late; that the people from whom he expected support had become apathetic if not antipathetic to the ideal to which he was now determined to dedicate his life. The viceroy referred him to the Court of Spain; the court of Spain referred him to the Papacy; the Papacy referred him back to Philip III; Philip recommended him to the Council of the Indies, and the Council of the Indies passed him on to the Council of State. It was seven years before he was back in South America, worn out by the machinations of politicians, and weakened by internal injuries caused when a building collapsed on him. But he had, at last, won approval for his voyage. He handed the viceroy instructions from Philip III and Clement VIII that were too explicit to be ignored, and in the autumn of 1605 a fleet began to assemble in the Peruvian port of Callao.

There is a saying that 'it is more blessed to journey than to arrive', and that autumn must have been one of the happiest periods of Quiros's life. He was given two adequate ships, the *Capitana* and the *Almiranta*, and a small 25-ton *zabra* or pinnace *Los Tres Reyes Magos*. His provisions were sufficient for a year. His crew numbered 280, and included not only the usual quota of seamen and soldiers inveigled aboard by the promise of women and gold, but also a large number of friars. On the feast of Saint Thomas, 21 December 1605, when his armada put to sea, half his ships' companies were dressed in sackcloth and on their knees in prayer. And to quote the pilot of the *Almiranta*, 'With our desire to serve God, to spread the True Faith and to enrich the Crown of Spain, all things seemed possible to us.'

Cynics may point out that Quiros's achievements turned out to be less impressive than his aspirations, but this in no way detracts from the idealism with which his expedition was conceived.

The armada's passage from Peru to Polynesia was pleasantly uneventful. They had plenty of provisions, winds and currents were favourable, the weather was equable, and in this early part of the voyage their only problem appears to have been Quiros's health. We don't know what was the matter with him but since his diary makes frequent references to his 'sickness' and since he died young, we must assume that his complaint was serious. And in this lies an explanation of the unpredictable course his expedition was to follow. For when Quiros was well things went according to plan, but when he was ill there was chaos.

For a month his three vessels stood west-south-west. At first Quiros seems to have been confined to his cabin, but by early January he was sufficiently recovered to appear on deck armed with a voluminous scroll of orders. These orders epitomize both his mastery of the technicalities of his calling and his inability to fathom the complexities of human nature. For they contained eminently sensible directives on subjects such as rationing, fire precautions, and shallow-water pilotage among atolls and reefs. But they also laid down a code of behaviour that was impossibly idealistic: 'There must be neither cursing nor blaspheming . . . no playing with dice nor with cards – all gaming tables to be thrown overboard . . . all crew each afternoon to go down on their knees before images of Christ and the Virgin Mary and pray for intercession.' A Cromwell might have been able to enforce such rules, but Quiros lacked the ruthlessness to impose on others a code he laid down for himself. Those who transgressed, he forgave.

Towards the middle of January the weather turned squally, with a bitter wind and a huge swell rolling endlessly out of the south-west. The pilots began to grumble, complaining that they were heading too close to the Pole, and Quiros was persuaded to alter course. From a long-term viewpoint this was unfortunate – if his vessels had continued on their original track they would almost certainly have sighted either New Zealand or Australia. However, the immediate result was all that could have been hoped for. On 26 January they sighted land.

It was an uninhabited atoll they saw first – 'a piece of water surrounded by coral' was their graphic description of it. To their disappointment they found no sign of life on the atoll and no water, 'only coconuts too unripe to eat'. However, in the course of the next few months they made a whole succession of landfalls and landings as their ships in squally weather, were driven through the archipelagos of the Polynesian heartland. Sharp summarizes their discoveries as follows:

> *On 26 and 29 January, Quiros discovered Ducie and Henderson respectively, a landing being made on Henderson. On 3, 4, 9, 10, 12 and 15 February respectively he discovered Marutea, the Actaeon group, and Vairaatea Hao Amanu Raroia and Tukume in the Tuamotu Archipelago, landings being made on Hao. On 21 February he discovered Caroline Island, a landing being made. On 2 March he discovered Rakahanga in the Northern Cooks, a landing being made. On 7 April he discovered the Duff Islands, landings being made. On 21 April he discovered Tikopia. On 25 April he discovered Mero-Lava Gaua and Merig in the Banks Islands, and Maewo and possibly other islands in the New Hebrides . . .*

These were important discoveries, enabling cartographers to sketch-in skein after skein of islands throughout some 4,000 miles of previously uncharted ocean. And perhaps even more significant than the extent of Quiros's discoveries was the manner in which he made them. A decade earlier Mendana's contact with the Pacific islanders had been marked by treachery and violence; hundreds if not thousands had died, and when his ships left they had been showered with stones and curses. Quiros's contact with the islanders was, in contrast, marked by fair-dealing and kindness. On island after island, when his ships left, his crew were showered with gifts and the Polynesians wept.

What happened on Taumaro in the Duff Islands was typical. About 150 Polynesians gathered on the beach to oppose the Spanish landing. Quiros ordered his men not to fire, and in due course friendly relations were established. A local chief known to the Spaniards as Tumai was invited aboard, given presents and dressed in fine silk. The Spaniards promised neither to harm Tumai's people nor pilfer their possessions, and in return the islanders promised to provide the supplies their visitors needed. Both parties kept faith; and there followed a ten-day idyll all too rare in the history of Pacific exploration. There was no bloodshed and no thieving, but 'good fellowship abounded, and gifts and names were freely exchanged'. The islanders, working in shifts, ferried water, wood and food to the waiting ships, and in return were given mirrors, fish-hooks and bells. The Spaniards then made a thorough exploration of the island, marvelling at the white beaches, the heavily-laden fruit trees, the clean airy houses and the magnificent outrigger canoes – some of them 40 feet long, beautifully carved and with their prows inlaid with mother-of-pearl. Soon they were wandering about singly or in pairs, unarmed; and to quote Quiros's Diary, 'if any of our belongings such as clothes or cooking pots were missing one knew for certain they were not stolen but were only being washed by the natives in a nearby stream.'

Those who dismiss Quiros as an impractical visionary might bear in mind that few other Pacific explorers were able to establish such an immediate and unflawed *rapport* with the islanders. And when, at the end of ten days, the Spanish ships put to sea, not only were their holds full of water, fresh food and fuel, but their pilots had been given directions on how to reach 'a very large land called Manicolo', which lay to the south-west. This, Quiros was convinced, would turn out to be the Great Southern Continent of his dreams.

For several days his armada coasted through chain after chain of atolls, exchanging greetings and gifts with the inhabitants; then a violent storm obliged them to heave-to. When the weather cleared and the pilots asked Quiros for a course, he told them to 'let the ships run free. God will guide them'. And it must have seemed to the Spaniards that their course was indeed divinely inspired, for during the next few days they sighted no less than eight beautiful and fertile islands (the Banks Group). Here again they made friendly contact with the inhabitants, offering them knives, plumed-hats and mirrors in exchange for figs, fruit and sugar-cane. On 27 April yet more land appeared over the horizon, until at every point of the compass, between south-east and south-west there seemed to be islands, while in the distance rose 'a massive and exceeding lofty chain of mountains, their peaks wreathed in cloud'.

This, to Quiros, was 'the most joyful day of our whole voyage'. For he felt certain that he was at last approaching *Terra Australis*, 'that great and undiscovered continent, wherein lie countless millions of heathen awaiting saviour from perdition'.

On 3 May his ships dropped anchor in a sheltered bay. An advance party rowed ashore, marvelling at the exotic woods, the rich soil, the dark fast-flowing rivers and the abundance of wild life. A few days later Quiros himself landed to supervise the building of those symbols of Spanish suzerainty, a church and a fort. There followed a series of ceremonies which can be seen in retrospect to have an air of magnificent futility. Ministries were set up, religious orders were inaugurated and the foundations of a great city (the New Jerusalem) were dug literally out of the sand. There were processions, Masses and a ceremony of taking-possession as grandiloquent at it was ineffective. Quiros, who appears to have been overfond of making speeches, knelt and kissed the earth, 'sought for so long by so many and so much desired by me' and in the names of the Trinity, the Catholic Church, St Francis, the Order of the Holy Ghost and Philip III of Spain, he took possession not only of the land on which he now stood but also 'of all the lands which I have sighted and am going to sight, and of all this region of the South as far as the Pole, which from this time forth shall be called Austrialia del Espirito Santo, with all its dependencies and belongings'. The ships fired their guns and the soldiers their arquebuses; there were rockets and fireworks and dancing and feasting; banners and crosses were paraded around the bay, while the Melanesians from their primordial forest peered in wonder at a scene beyond their comprehension.

Alas for Quiros's dreams! He had discovered not a great continent but a small island, Espiritu Santo. To those approaching Espiritu Santo from the north-west, its coastline and that of the overlapping islands of Pentecost, Ambrim and Aurora appear to be a mass of high continuous land. Probably less than one person in a thousand today could place Espiritu Santo accurately on a map, and it belongs not to Spain, but to Great Britain and France. Indeed Spanish tenure of the island was confined to a few weeks, for during Quiros's brief visit just about everything went wrong.

It was the islanders who were the stumbling block. They didn't want to be saved. And it is unfortunate for Quiros's reputation that his mistaken landfall coincided with his one and only failure to win the friendship of the local inhabitants. It isn't hard to visualize what happened. The islanders were not easy-going Polynesians but the more warlike and aggressive Melanesians. Quiros's men were bored with inaction and had had their fill of piety; most of them were seamen or soldiers, not missionaries, men who had come in search of El Dorado rather than the New Jerusalem. Now after six months of proselytizing with never a sign of gold, they were looking for trouble. There is no reason to doubt Quiros's account of what happened next:

> *The Captain ordered a party of soldiers to go ashore and try to catch some of the natives, so as to establish peace and friendship, based on the good work we intended to do for them. The landing party ran their boat high up on the beach, and quickly deployed; for the natives were coming, and it was not known with what purpose. Approaching, the natives made signs and spoke, but were not understood. Our people called out to them in return. The natives then drew a line in the sand; seemingly to indicate that we were not to pass beyond it; though it seemed there was no one in either party who could really make himself intelligible. Soon natives were seen in the woods, and to frighten them muskets were fired into the air. But one of the soldiers fired low and killed a native, whereat the others, with loud cries, fled. Then another soldier cut off the head and one foot of the dead native, and hung his body from the branches of a tree. It so happened that three native chiefs came to the place where our people were; and we, instead of showing them kindness and bringing them on board, showed them instead their comrade without a head and streaming blood. The chiefs showed great sorrow. They went back to their people, and after awhile the sound of instruments blowing with great force was heard among the trees. Then the natives began shooting arrows and darts, while our people fired back on them.*
>
> *The Captain saw all this from his ship, and great was his sorrow that peace was turned to war. . . Soon a tall, elderly native advanced by himself, blowing a shell. He seemed to be indicating that his people would defend their country against the invaders who came and slew the inhabitants. And eight of our musketeers lay in ambush; and one of them – as he said afterwards by mistake – shot and killed this man. Whereat the others raised him up on their shoulders and went inland, leaving their villages deserted. Such was the end of the peace that the Captain had hoped for and sought, and the great good that he had intended was now but a hollow sound.*

There followed three weeks of alternate overture and skirmish. Quiros made every possible effort to win back the islanders' confidence. Alone and unarmed he went on a penitential walkabout through the villages, sowing Peruvian calabashes, melons and potatoes; he ordered the pigs that his soldiers had stolen to be returned; he conducted an endless succession of Masses. But the evil that had been done could not be undone, and at the end of May Quiros decided to leave the anchorage where his achievements had fallen so tragically short of his expectations, and 'visit the lands to windward'.

Historians have condemned this decision. 'So,' writes Beaglehole, 'on the pinnacle of glory, Quiros turned his back, and there began that melancholy retreat the truth of which is so hard to disentangle.' However, it seems to me that there is a simple enough explanation of Quiros's behaviour: he had begun to suspect that Espiritu Santo might not, after all, be the continent of his dreams, and to check on this he had decided to explore the mountains which had been sighted to the south. His Diary is explicit on this point – 'the Captain resolved to weigh anchor in order to obtain a near view of the great and high chain of mountains'. In other words Quiros was planning an advance rather than a retreat, but unluckily for him, at this critical moment, he again fell victim to his recurrent ill-health.

Again his Diary gives the sequence of events. When it was decided to leave Espiritu Santo, Quiros's second in command Luis de Torres suggested that they spend their last day in harbour fishing and taking aboard provisions. Quiros agreed. But as ill-luck would have it, the fish they netted included a number of the highly poisonous *fargos*. All who ate the *fargos* were violently ill, with nausea, vomiting and high fever. Among those most seriously affected was Quiros, whose health was never robust and who seems for several days to have been close to death. Departure was postponed; but even so Quiros was far from fit when, on 8 June, his ships put to sea.

What happened next was by no means unusual in the days of sail. Quiros wanted to head south-east; this, however, was directly into the wind, and the wind was fresh and freshening. Peruvian-built vessels were difficult to handle under little sail, and notoriously inept at heading into wind. Quiros's fleet therefore made little progress; indeed towards evening, as the wind strengthened, they began to be blown literally backwards. There was a conference of pilots, and it was decided to return to harbour. This, however, proved easier said than done. All night the three vessels beat to and fro, trying to claw their way back in the teeth of a rising gale. The *Almiranta* and the *Tres Reyes Magos* made it. The *Capitana* didn't. Quiros ordered his pilot to hoist more sail, but was told that wind and sea were too high, and that if the ship was driven harder her timbers would split. We have no way of knowing if the pilot was giving a reason or making an excuse, but the outcome was the same – the *Capitana* was driven farther and farther from the shore, until 'with great sorrow' Quiros saw Espiritu Santo vanish beneath the horizon.

So far events have been clear enough, but what happened next is an enigma. It is easy to understand that Quiros might have been temporarily thwarted by wind and wave; however, when the storm blew itself out, one would have expected him to return to Espiritu Santo. He didn't. He headed back to Peru. His Diary doesn't tell us why. It is full of 'lamentations,' 'sorrowful discourses' and explanations which fail to explain. There is, however, a hint of mutiny, and the scene isn't difficult to visualize: the men bored with proselytizing and frustrated by the lack of women and gold, the commander ill in his cabin and with his congenital lack of firmness accentuated by the aftermath of food poisoning. I don't think they tried very hard to beat back to Espiritu Santo. This, at any rate, was the opinion of Torres who wrote, 'the *Capitana* departed without signal, and although next morning we went in search of them we could not find them, for they did not sail on the proper course or with good intention'. Torres, incidentally, went on to make discoveries almost as important as those of his erstwhile commander. After exploring the New Hebrides, he discovered the southern coast of Papua-New Guinea, then stood into the unknown and dangerous strait between that island and Australia. And during his passage of this strait he almost certainly sighted the tip of Australia's north-east coast some 160 years before its generally accepted 'discovery' by Cook.

Quiros, meanwhile, was having a difficult journey back. His crew suffered thirst, slaked by a timely cloudburst; hunger, alleviated by a fortuitous shoal of albacore and bonito; an earthquake, followed by a tidal wave; and an eclipse of the moon, followed by a violent storm off the Gulf of California in which the *Capitana* came close to foundering. But at last, on 23 November 1606, he dropped anchor off Acapulco.

He had been away for nearly a year. He had voyaged for more than 25,000 miles (some three times the distance covered by Columbus during his crossing and recrossing of the Atlantic). He had discovered skein after skein of islands in the south-west Pacific. He had established friendly relations with the people of all but one of these islands; and of his ship's company only one man, the aged Commissary of the Friars, had died. This was a major feat of exploration, and Quiros deserved a

Two Pacific ports used by the Spanish explorers: *top* Manila in the Philippines, from *Le Voyage autour du Monde* by Guillaume de Dampierre and *above* Fort de Penco, Chile.

better welcome than he was accorded; for the rest of his life was anticlimax.

Back in Peru, his claim to have discovered a 'Whole New World' aroused little enthusiasm, especially when he failed to produce evidence of its wealth; when he sought funds for another expedition, he was quickly referred to Spain. By the time he reached Cadiz he was once again in poor health, and, since he had received no payment for his expedition, virtually destitute – forced not only to pawn his clothes, but to sell his fragment of the True Cross and the flags he had unfurled at the New Jerusalem. What happened next shows very clearly the quandary in which the Spanish hierarchy found themselves. Quiros was an embarrassment to them. For Spain in the early seventeenth century was in exactly the same position as Portugal had been in during the early sixteenth century – satiated with discoveries. She was having such difficulty keeping control of the territory she already laid claim to, that the last thing she wanted was to accumulate more. Which is why Spanish seamen made so many remarkable discoveries in the south-west Pacific (including the discovery of Australia) only for Spanish politicians to play down their achievements and hush them up.

So for seven frustrating years Quiros was passed to and fro between courts and councils, the victim of never-ending procrastination and intrigue. It has to be said that he didn't help his own cause, for his petitions were as grandiloquent as they were interminable. 'He is not a reliable man,' noted a member of the Council with some justification. 'He has got it into his head that he is a second Columbus, and this is his affliction.' Even the arrival of Torres's dispatches, confirming the existence of great new lands in the south-west Pacific, failed to arouse official enthusiasm. Faced with such disinterest, a lesser man would have given up. But Quiros had the tenacity and the nervous energy of a fanatic. Though he became so poor that he several times fainted in the street from hunger and had to kneel awkwardly at Mass for fear men saw the holes in his shoes, his flood of petitions didn't diminish with the years; if anything it increased, and in 1614 he reckoned he saw a ray of hope. A new viceroy was appointed to Peru, and Quiros was given permission to accompany him. 'Seeing', he wrote, 'that my health and patience were by now quite worn out, I decided to put into this man's hands all my life's work. "Trust me," the viceroy said, "and I will do my best to help you".' They sailed for Calloa.

It was as well for Quiros that he died *en route*. For death spared him the last betrayal. He never knew that among the viceroy's papers was an order expressly forbidding him ever again to search for the continent of his dreams.

It has been said with some truth that Quiros was the last of the conquistadors and that with him died the heroic age of Spain. Certainly in the Pacific his death marked the end of an era. Throughout most of the sixteenth century the Pacific had been, to all intents and purposes, a Spanish lake. Only gradually had it become apparent that the lake was too large, too diverse and too rich in resources to be held under the suzerainty of any single nation. The Spaniards did their best to envelop the new-found ocean in a cocoon of mystery. Their discoveries they hushed-up; their maps they falsified; their treasure-ships they sailed in secret; they pursued a tight protectionist policy in trade and a strict exclusive attitude in religion.

This, it can be seen in retrospect, was too negative an approach. Spain was unable herself to supply her colonies with all their material needs, yet she forbade them to get what they needed elsewhere – trade was permitted only with the mother country. This condemned colonies like New Spain (Mexico), Peru, Chile and the Philippines to poverty; it also encouraged widespread smuggling and peculation. As for religion, sixteenth-century Spain was the bastion of the Catholic faith, and successive Spanish monarchs regarded it as their principal mission in life to uproot heresy both from their homeland and their dominions. *Auto-da-fés* and the Inquisition stamped out all traces of the Protestant Reformation in Spain itself, but it was a different story overseas, where religious antagonism gave a cutting edge to British and Dutch forays against Spain's far-flung possessions.

As the century drew to its close these forays became increasingly frequent and effective – especially those of the Dutch.

CORNUCOPIA

THE VOYAGES OF THE DUTCH

Some men of noble stock are made: some glory in the murder blade:
Some praise a Science or an Art, but I like honourable Trade.
JAMES ELROY FLECKER: *The Gates of Damascus.*

In the sixteenth century, the exploration of the Pacific had been almost entirely in the hands of the Spaniards; not without reason had Magellan's *Mar Pacifico* been dubbed the 'Castilian Lake'. The early years of the seventeenth century, however, saw the arrival of a new and totally unexpected nation who were soon to play a leading role in the ocean's westernization – the Dutch.

The Low Countries were originally part of the Spanish-Habsburg empire; but towards the end of the sixteenth century – for reasons partly religious and partly economic – they renounced their allegiance to Philip II of Spain, and after 25 years of bitter warfare wrung from their former overlords an acknowledgement of independence. It was, on the face of it, an unlikely triumph, a conglomeration of tiny provinces defying and indeed defeating the most powerful and best-led armies in Europe. The Dutch, however, had one big advantage over their adversaries – they controlled the sea.

Few nations are more at home on the sea than the Dutch. It is ever on their doorstep, much of their land has been reclaimed from it, and water – in the form of the North Sea, the Zuider Zee or some river or canal – is for many Hollanders an everyday ingredient of their lives. In their struggle for independence it was this that saved them. Unable to defeat the Spaniards on land, the better part of the Dutch nation took to the sea. They became known as 'The Sea Beggars', tough mobile privateers, adept at intercepting supplies and treasure-ships, ever evacuating a port that seemed likely to fall or reinforcing a port that seemed likely to make a stand. Nor were the activities of the Sea Beggars confined to the coasts of Europe. Because the Spaniards denied them the right to trade with the great emporia of the Iberian peninsula, they were forced to trade elsewhere, to go farther afield and to seek the gold, silver, silks and spices which were their lifeblood at source. It was in quest of trade that, at the turn of the century, the Dutch captain, Barents, became the first explorer to winter in the Arctic ice, a Dutch fleet visited Thailand and China, and the Dutch East India Company, the first and arguably the greatest of the chartered conglomerates, was founded. If so much could be done in time of war, how much more could be done in time of peace. It was not long before the Dutch could boast over 10,000 warships and merchantmen in service, and soon their *jachts* (small fully-rigged pinnaces) and *fluyts* (flat-bottomed trading vessels) were penetrating to the most far-flung corners of the known world – including the Pacific.

The *jachts* and *fluyts* brought a new breed of Europeans to the *Mar Pacifico, Europeans who were interested in one thing only – trade. This led to a change in the leitmotiv* of Pacific voyaging, with the old-fashioned proselytizing ventures of the

Spaniards giving way to the more modern and more mundane trading ventures of the Dutch. It was of course all to the good that Spanish intolerance and restrictive practices should be superseded by Dutch tolerance and expansionism. However, the Dutch treated the people of the Pacific only marginally better than the Spaniards had done, and they were only in favour of expansion when it was their profits which were expanding – they were not averse to burning the islanders' clove and nutmeg bushes in order to create a shortage to keep up prices.

This preoccupation of the Dutch with trade explains why Pacific voyaging in the seventeenth century tends to be less heroic than it had been in the sixteenth. Instead of one or two dramatic and quixotic leaps into the unknown, we have a multitude of small and carefully thought-out probes into selected (profitable) areas. Areas that were not profitable, the Dutch neglected. Their failure to explore Australia is the classic example of this. On more than a dozen occasions in the early years of the seventeenth century the Dutch sighted and landed on the northern and western shores of Australia. But because they considered the land to be 'worthless' and its inhabitants 'the most miserable creatures on Earth', they failed to follow-up their discoveries. The only use they had for Australia was as a 'marker-buoy' on their voyages to Batavia. In areas that promised to be profitable, on the other hand, the Dutch proved themselves skilled and assiduous explorers, spreading octopus-like from their emporium of Batavia throughout Indonesia and the Philippines and even managing to establish themselves in the forbidden islands of Japan. As the Pacific had once been a Spanish Lake, so Indonesia soon became a Dutch archipelago, its rich and fertile islands providing Europe with a continuous supply of spices (pepper in particular), silks, precious woods, pharmaceutical drugs, tea, coffee, sugar, copper and saltpetre.

This trade was nurtured by men and ships whose names are almost unknown outside the ledgers of the *Vereenigde Oost-Indische Compagnie* (the Dutch East India Company). Their voyages individually were for the most part unremarkable, but *in toto* they added up to a considerable achievement. Dutch exploration was careful, cumulative and corporate. Individual expertise was rare, and when it did occur it tended to be frowned on – as Le Maire and Schouten were to discover to their cost.

Isaac Le Maire was an entrepreneur, a man blessed with vision, boundless energy and perennial optimism. In 1614, resenting the stranglehold that the VOC were exerting over trade with the Pacific, he decided to defy the Company and launch an expedition of his own. He was shrewd enough to find legal justification for his voyage in a loophole in the Company charter – anyone discovering a *new* sea-route to the Pacific was to be allowed to use it for three subsequent voyages. Isaac was convinced such a route existed and that he knew where to find it...

The ships had been at anchor for several months off the well-sheltered port of Hoorn. Everyone could see that they were being refitted and provisioned for some great venture, but no one knew where they were going – 'such secrecy was observed that some fancyed they were bound to one place and some to another. The common people called them 'gold-finders'; the merchants, being better informed, called them the "Austral Companie".' And it was indeed the lonely reaches of the Southern (or Austral) Ocean towards which the ships were soon heading; for this was the unknown seaway by which Le Maire was convinced that he would find his new *entrée* into the Pacific. The ships were the 220-ton *Eendracht* (*Concord*) and the 100-ton *Hoorn*. Their crews were comparatively few in number, with 65 in the larger vessel and 22 in the smaller. Walter Raleigh noted in a memorandum to Queen Elizabeth that whereas an English ship of some 100 tons needed a crew of 30, a better-rigged Dutch ship of corresponding tonnage could

make do with no more than 15. The men had been hand-picked, and although they were not told where they were going there had been no shortage of volunteers – a fact which emphasizes how unusually well-planned and efficiently conducted the expedition of Le Maire and Schouten was.

The ships left Holland on 14 June 1615 and put into Dover where they took aboard a gunner; a couple of days later they put into Plymouth where they took aboard a carpenter. The fact that they came to England to sign-on these specialists confirmed Raleigh's boast that English gunners and carpenters were 'esteemed the best in Europe'. The first part of their voyage was unremarkable. However, in mid-August Le Maire made an interesting decision.

> *From August 2–19,* he wrote in his Diary, *we had variable and contrary winds; and as our crew were beginning to contract scurvy, we resolved to set course for Sierra Liona to reprovision.* In Sierra Leone they found *crocodiles, marmosets, buffalos, birds which barked like dogs, the footprints of wild beasts . . . and eight or nine lemon trees, which, when shaken, yielded about 750 lemons almost ripe.* A few days later Le Maire himself managed to find and bring back

about 1,400 lemons, and shortly after that they *made contact with the blacks, and got our casks filled with water and obtained by barter almost 25,000 lemons, all for a few beads and some poor-quality Nuremberg knives. We could* (Le Maire adds) *have got 100,000 lemons, had we desired them, for there were whole forests full of them.*

The inference from this preoccupation with lemons is obvious. As early as 1615 the Dutch knew that lemons cured scurvy.

This makes nonsense of the generally-held view that the two people who found a cure for scurvy were Lind and Cook. Many text books, including the *Encyclopaedia Britannica*, would have us believe that 'it was the Scottish physician James Lind (1716–1794) who discovered the vitality of orange and lemon juice in sailors' diet, as a result of which scurvy disappeared from the Navy'; and the majority of Cook's biographers express the view that it was he who proved in practice in naval ships what Lind had proved in theory in naval hospitals. The truth would seem to be more disturbing: that it was realized as early as the second decade of the seventeenth century that lemons would cure scurvy, but that the lives of seamen were held so cheap that little effort was made to carry the antiscorbutic vegetables which would have saved them. It has been estimated that during the seventeenth and the eighteenth centuries more seamen died from scurvy than from the combined toll of enemy action, fire, shipwreck, foundering and accident. In 1722, for example, the disease accounted for 140 men out of Roggeveen's 233, a couple of decades later for 621 men out of Anson's 960. It is a sobering thought that a century-and-a-half passed and tens of thousands of lives were lost before the lesson taught by Schouten and Le Maire was taken to heart.

The *Eendracht* and *Hoorn* left Sierra Leone in mid-September, some 30,000 lemons in their holds, their course south-west for Port Desire, about 250 miles to the north of the Straits of Magellan. Not till they were deep into the South Atlantic did the crews learn where they were bound. 'Then Jacob Le Maire (one of Isaac's many sons) read out to us the aim of our voyage: to get by a way other than the Straits of Magellanes into the South Sea, and there discover New Countries wherein might lie great wealth . . . whereat there was much rejoicing.'

Early in December the *Eendracht*'s lookout reported 'pale water, with much rock-weed and many seabirds and whales'. They sighted land on 6 December and next morning edged cautiously into Port Desire. Here their adventures started.

It was a gauntly beautiful coast off which they dropped anchor, 'cliffs not very high and whiteish, and an ebb tide running south with as much force as off the coast of Flushing'. They sent their pinnace inshore to reconnoitre, then followed her about a mile-and-a-half up the Deseado River. However, they had barely dropped anchor in what seemed a sheltered haven when the wind swung through 180° and increased to gale-force, driving the helpless vessels on to a lee shore. Their anchors were useless – 'nay, twenty-five would not have held us', and both the *Eendracht* and the *Hoorn* piled up on the rocks. Here, as the tide dropped, they were held fast, kept upright only by the force of the wind. 'At low tide,' writes Le Maire, 'it was possible to walk right under the keel of the *Eendracht* without wetting one's feet: a sight terrible to behold.' When the wind eventually dropped, the hapless vessel toppled on to its side, 'whereat we were all terrified, thinking her quite lost; but the tide rising and the weather falling calm, she floated off the rocks, at which we were not a little glad'.

Worse was to come. A week later they beached their vessels for careening. This was standard practice, to enable the ships' carpenters to clean the keels of weed and barnacles and recaulk the seams. They found the keel of the *Hoorn* was particularly foul, and decided to bream her, in other words to get rid of the weed by burning. Dry grass was collected and set alight. However, the Dutch hadn't reckoned on the dryness of the air and another violent increase in the wind. The flames got out of control, and 'unexpectedly and very quickly flew up the rigging and took hold of the whole ship, so that in an instant there was no chance of putting them out, especially as the vessel was beached some 50 feet above water. We were compelled to see her totally burned before our eyes without being able to do a thing to save her'. Laconic words that give little idea of how the Dutch must have felt as they were left on the edge of the known world with one ship instead of two.

The loss of the *Hoorn* gave added importance to the reprovisioning of the *Eendracht*, and Schouten and Le Maire spent several weeks in and around Port Desire taking aboard fresh water and food. For all its bleakness the Argentine coast was teeming with wildlife. In the sea were penguins, seals and vast numbers of fish; on the tideline were sea-lions, mussels and birds' eggs – one rocky island on which they landed 'was so covered with eggs that a man standing still could touch 54 nests' – while farther inland there were rheas and guanacos. It was while hunting the latter that they came across evidence of the giants.

The Patagonian giants are one of the mysteries of history. It seems they really did exist. Magellan (who was not given to disseminating tall stories) left a matter-of-fact account of his meeting with them and a convincing description of their appearance and habits. He says they were 'ten spans high' – or about 7 feet 6 inches, and confirms this by adding that 'even the tallest among us reached only to midway between their waist and shoulder'. Drake also reported them as 'more than four-and-a-half cubits high' (more than 7 feet 4 inches). Several other early explorers claimed to have made contact with them. Le Maire's account is tantalisingly brief.

11 December 1615. We proceeded downriver, where we saw some animals which looked like deer, only with long necks (guanacos) *which were very shy of us. On the summit of a small mountain*

Jacob Le Maire (1585-1616), who in his ships *Eendracht* and *Hoorn* discovered a new seaway into the Pacific via Cape Horn – named after his ship.

we found some heaps of stones, and, not knowing what they signified, turned the stones over and found under them the bones of human beings very nearly 9 foot in stature. It seems that the giants bury their dead thus to protect them from beasts and birds.

Yet the present-day inhabitants of south Argentina are small-boned and seldom taller than 5 feet 8 inches. The giants have vanished; the only traces that remain of them are some half-dozen reports from early explorers, and the name of their country – Patagonia, the land of the big feet.

The *Eendracht* left Cape Desire on 13 January 1616, and a few days later sighted the entrance to the Straits of Magellan. All previous vessels on their way from Atlantic to Pacific had stood west through this entrance. Le Maire, however, continued to head south; for he was convinced that the land beyond Magellan's Strait was an island.

What made him so certain of this was that he had made a careful study of Drake's voyage of 1578. Drake had entered the east Pacific, like everyone else, via the Straits of Magellan. On emerging from the narrows his fleet had been scattered by a succession of violent storms. One ship, the *Marigold*, had sunk with all hands; another, the *Elizabeth*, had been forced back into the Straits, while Drake himself in the *Pelican* was driven as it were backwards around Cape Horn. 'Beyond this Cape,' he wrote, 'there is no main (land) nor island to be seen to the southward, but here the Atlanticke Ocean and the South Sea meet in a most large and free scope.'

These waters to the south of Cape Horn were the new route by which Le Maire hoped to reach the Pacific.

It is easy for us today to glance at the map and see that Drake was right, that there is indeed a seaway south of the Horn; but for Le Maire to accept the Englishman's word for this in 1615 was an act of faith and a very considerable gamble which no one previously had been prepared to take. So as the *Eendracht* ran south that summer down the coast of Tierra del Fuego she was in seas no vessel before had ventured into.

The Horn was kind to Le Maire. He tells us 'it blew very hard on a rough sea'; but reading between the lines it is clear that the weather that January was almost benign. Nevertheless it must have been an anxious passage as, with neither chart nor hearsay to guide them, the Dutch headed for what they hoped was the confluence of the Atlantic and Pacific Oceans. Everything aboard the *Eendracht* was double-lashed; the watch was doubled, and there were four men instead of two at the tiller. Occasional squalls of sleet whitened the deck, rime glazed the rigging and the sea was alive with whales, seals and penguins.

At dawn on 24 January they sighted land both to starboard and to port. The land to starboard, they guessed correctly, was the southern tip of the American continent. The land to port, they assumed incorrectly, must be the tip of *Terra Australis Incognita*, the Great Southern Continent which, it was thought, must exist in the southern hemisphere to counterbalance the bulk of Eurasia in the northern hemisphere. If Drake was to be believed, there had to be a seaway between the continents.

The two land masses, Le Maire wrote in his Diary, *seemed to be about 8 miles apart, and there appeared to be a good channel between them with a strong current running south. . . We made for this channel, passing through huge numbers of penguins; also whales by the thousand, so that we had to be constantly on guard with a drag-sail set, to avoid running into them. The land to the east looked high and perilous, extending as far as the eye could see; we gave it the name of Staten-landt* (in honour of the Dutch parliament, The States General). *The land to the west was rugged, with fine sandy beaches but no trees. . . Next day we ran south through the channel, with a heavy sea from the west and very blue water which made us think we had the Great South Sea* (the Pacific) *on the weatherside, whereat we were glad, holding that a way had been discovered by us hitherto unknown to man – as we afterwards found to be the truth.*

Soon, on their starboard bow, they sighted a dramatic headland, dark cliffs backed by snow-capped mountains falling near-sheer for a thousand feet into the sea. It appeared to be the most southerly point in the land mass of the Americas, and they named it Cape Hoorn, after the ship they had lost and the town they had come from.

Their log, over the next few days, records 'a strong current, a very heavy swell from the west and blue water . . . much sleet and hail, so that we were forced often to lie-to under trysails . . . we suffered much cold and hardship'. But by 1 February the *Eendracht* was clear of land and heading into the open reaches of the Pacific.

The Dutch had made an important discovery; they had found a seaway which avoided the slow, tortuous and dangerous Straits of Magellan. And indeed their discovery turned out to be even more significant than they at first suspected. For subsequent voyages were to prove that their Staten-landt was not the tip of a great continent but the coast of a small island, beyond which lay an even more open and navigable seaway, a seaway soon to become one of the great trade arteries of the world.

Le Maire's mistake over the size of Staten Island, which is no more than 50 miles long, highlights a fallibility common to many of the early explorers: they tended to overestimate the extent of their discoveries. It was an easy thing to do. From the deck of a sailing ship their field of vision was limited to about 10 miles – less in bad weather – and although it is true this could be increased by climbing mast or rigging, the increase was only marginal. So again and again seamen in the days of sail were to discover some unknown and dramatic coast, see its outline disappear in rain or cloud, be unable because of the set of the wind to investigate their discovery more closely, and mistake an island for part of a continent. Columbus mistook Cuba for Asia; Quiros mistook Espiritu Santo for Australia; as late as the middle of the eighteenth century the French explorers Bouvet and Kerguelen mistook the islands that bear their names for the land mass of Antarctica. Le Maire was neither the first explorer nor the last to exaggerate, in all innocence, the extent of his discovery.

And soon after entering the Pacific he became involved in an incident which highlights another perennial problem of the early explorers. He made a landfall, only to find that he couldn't land.

Almost exactly a century separates Le Maire's voyage (1615-16) from Magellan's (1519-20), and in the intervening years Europeans had learned a great deal about the Pacific. Le Maire was knowledgeable enough to keep close to the coast of Chile, a route which enabled him firstly to make use of the north-flowing Humboldt Current, and secondly to make a landfall at the islands of Juan Fernandez, where he hoped to top up with fresh food and water. He sighted Juan Fernandez on the morning of 1 March. It was a pleasant day, no cloud, bright sunlight and a steady wind from the south-east. The *Eendracht* ran up the coast of the more westerly of the main islands and soon found she had a problem. The hills of the island cut off the wind, and while her sails flapped idly the Humboldt Current carried her slowly past the land. Le Maire describes their predicament:

Since we were unable to get close enough to the shore to anchor, we sent out our boat towards the land. In the evening she came back with the news that the shore was fit for an anchorage and that the land was verdant and full of green trees and fresh water. The men had caught a great quantity of fish: no sooner had they dropped a hook in the water than a fish was upon it, so they had nothing to do but draw up fish without stopping. These tidings made the crew very glad, especially those who had scurvy. In the night the wind fell altogether, so that we drifted north with the current. 2 March: We were again close to the land, but try as we might we could not get near enough to anchor. We sent the boat ashore, and whilst some men were getting water the others caught close on two ton of fish. They then had to leave this fine island, without enjoying it further. 3 March: We had by this time drifted about four miles past the islands, notwithstanding that we had for 48 hours done our best to reach them under sail, which vexed us exceedingly, seeing it was impossible to make them. It was therefore agreed by the Council that we should leave the islands and pursue our voyage – to the very great sorrow of the sick who saw all their hopes lost; but God gives relief. These islands lie in latitude 33°40′.

Few incidents demonstrate more clearly the degree to which explorers, in the days of sail, were at the mercy of wind and current.

The *Eendracht* now headed into the heart of the Pacific. For a month no land was sighted, and Le Maire's Diary reads simply, 'with a south-east wind and on a nor'westerly course, from 12 March to 9 April we made good progress'. It isn't hard to visualize the monotony, as hour after hour, day after day, week after week the ship ran before a following wind over a seemingly limitless ocean. Then at last, on the morning of 10 April, they sighted land, 'a low island, not large, with an internal lagoon . . . we shaped our course towards it, intending to get refreshments there, but our ship could not land as the sea was too rough'. This was probably Puka-puka, the atoll sighted by Magellan, and it cannot therefore be termed a discovery. In the course of the next few days, however, Le Maire *did* discover new islands – Takapoto, which he called Bottomless Island because it had no anchorage; Ahe, which he called Water-land because a well was found on the beach; and Rangiroa, which he called Fly Island because here his crew 'were entirely covered with flies to such a degree that we could recognize no part of them'. These were useful if not dramatic discoveries, enabling cartographers to add more details of the Tuamotus to the map of the Pacific.

One would have thought that the tolerant Dutch might be more successful than the proselytizing Spaniards in establishing a rapport with the islanders. This, however, was not so.

What might be called distant relations were established on the evening of 14 April when a canoe approached the *Eendracht* as she neared Takapoto. There were four men in the canoe 'quite naked, of a reddish colour, and with very long very black hair'. The islanders made signs that the Europeans should come ashore and the Europeans made signs that the islanders should come aboard, but neither party, yet, was willing to take the plunge. Next day the *Eendracht* stood-in as close as she could to the island, and again a canoe, this time with three rowers, approached her. Here is Le Maire's account of what happened next:

The Indians would not at first come aboard. However, they did approach our shallop and came alongside it. Our men showed them every kindness, giving them beads and knives; and eventually they came close to the ship. We threw them a line. For awhile they held back; then one of them clambered on to the gallery and started to pull out the nails from the port-hole of the skipper's cabin, concealing them – as he thought – in his hair. Soon all three came aboard. They were naked except for a small strip of matting over their privy parts; and their skin was marked with designs such as snakes, dragons and monsters, which stood out in blue as though burnt on with gunpowder. They were very greedy for iron, even trying to pull out the bolts from our timbers. We would have liked to keep one aboard, and send ashore in exchange a member of our crew to try and make friends with them; but this they would not have. We offered them wine which they liked greatly, and would not give us back our pannikin. Eventually we sent our shallop ashore, with 8 musketeers and 6 men with swords, in order to see what there was on the island and to make friends with them. But as soon as the shallop was beached and our men ran up through the breakers, fully 30 Indians, armed with great clubs, came out of the bush and tried to deprive our men of their arms and to drag away the shallop; they also seized two of our crew as if to carry them into the bush. However, the musketeers whose guns were still dry fired into the midst of them, so that not a few were shot dead or mortally wounded. Thank God they harmed none of our people. There were women among the Indians who fell upon the men's necks and shrieked, though our people did not know what this meant. . . Seeing there was nothing to be gained here, we decided to leave. This island lies in latitude 15 °S.

A sad little episode which encapsulates in miniature the story of the exploration of the Pacific. For what happened that day in Takapoto was to be repeated again and again in centuries to come; misunderstanding was to lead to bloodshed. As always we can reconstruct what happened only through the eyes of the Europeans, and as is often the case events are shrouded in uncertainty. Some uncertainties are trivial – did the Polynesians refuse to give back the pannikin because they wanted more wine, or because it was metal and they wanted to keep it? But others are crucial – when the shallop was beached, did the islanders *really* attack the landing-party, or did they simply crowd round them wanting to look at their swords and guns; did they *really* try to steal the shallop, or were they simply dragging it clear of the waves? And what are we to make of the ambiguities in Le Maire's account? He implies that the islanders' attack was premeditated; but if this had been so, would they have had women with them? He implies that they actually attacked the landing-party, yet he admits that no European was hurt. And what are we to make of his remark that when the women fell on the dead men's necks and shrieked, 'our people did not know what this meant'; it must surely have been obvious that the women were giving vent to their grief? Finally there is his penultimate sentence, 'seeing there was nothing to be gained here, we decided to leave'. This remark unwittingly sums up the attitude of the Dutch. They were neither cruel nor evil; but they were only interested in the islanders for what they could get out of them. They did make an effort to be friendly, but when their effort failed and blood was spilt, this was something over which they weren't going to lose any sleep. It was as though they felt that the Polynesians were children of some lesser god, and that it didn't greatly matter what happened to them, an attitude which was to linger-on for centuries – indeed some people, pointing to the atomic tests on Mururoa, say it still lingers-on today.

The *Eendracht* headed west and a few weeks later sighted more islands, the outliers of the Tonga group. This was another useful discovery, but here again the Dutch visit was marred by bloodshed.

The trouble seems to have started when Le Maire decided to capture a large 'canoe' (probably a *vaa-taie*) which was sighted off the island of Tafahi:

At noon we saw a sail coming out of the south. We headed towards her, and when we were close fired a warning shot to get her to haul down, but she would not. We therefore fired another shot, but still she refused to haul down – it seems never to have occurred to the Dutch that the maritime code had not yet reached Oceania! – *We therefore launched our shallop (pinnace) with ten musketeers to take her, and again sent a shot abaft her, without seeking to damage her, but still she would not lie to, seeking rather to outsail us. Eventually the shallop overtook her and fired four times with a musket. Some of her crew leapt overboard in fright; others were wounded. Our men sprang on board and brought the vessel alongside us without the least resistance from her crew, all of whom were unarmed. The shallop then went back to rescue the men who had jumped overboard, but got only two who indicated that the others had drowned.*

Having captured the *vaa-taie*, the Dutch made a careful study of it, marvelling at the skill with which it was built, the bright colours of its paintwork and the complexity of its fishing tackle. The survivors – who included nursing mothers and young children – were well treated; they were offered food, knives and beads, and in the evening were given back their *vaa-taie* and allowed to head for home.

If Le Maire felt any remorse at having drowned an unspecified number of Tongans his Diary gives no hint of it, and as his ship now moved from island to island he seems to have been genuinely aggrieved that his reception was at times less than ecstatic. It is true there was a fair amount of barter and at times almost an atmosphere of carnival as the *Eendracht* played host to those islanders whose curiosity got the better of their timidity. But always not far below the surface was an undercurrent of fear, and the line between horseplay and violence was razor-sharp. Off Nivatobatabu, which the Dutch named Traitors' Island, their ship was attacked by stone-throwing warriors. In reply the explorers discharged a broadside, their guns loaded with musket-balls and nails. 'They got some brave wounds,' Le Maire writes, adding facetiously, 'we reckoned that some of them would forget to go home at all'. The contemporary print from *The East and West Indian Mirror*, together with its captions, says everything that needs to be said – it all looks rather fun, until a closer inspection reveals that the *vaa-taie* is being fired at, the canoes are being rammed, the Tongans are being killed.

A week after leaving Tonga the *Eendracht* made another and this time a happier landfall in the Horne Islands. Here, it is pleasant to record, on the atolls of Futuna and Alofi the Dutch 'entered into friendship with the inhabitants', and there followed a near-idyllic fortnight of festivities – though it is perhaps worth pointing out that the islanders' friendship was based wholly on fear. Le Maire is the first to admit this.

> *These people were very frightened of our weapons. If we fired a musket they fled in fear and trembling, and we made them even more afraid by firing our cannon. When we discharged a broadside they were so panic-stricken that, notwithstanding all the assurances they had been given, they fled in terror into the woods. . . After this, great respect was shown to us whenever we went ashore; crowns were placed on our heads, and we had to walk everywhere on mats laid out before us.*

Presents were exchanged. When the Dutch had first asked for pigs they were told there was so little food on the island that the people were reluctant to part with their animals; however, after the firing of the broadside not only coconuts, taros and bananas but also chickens and pigs were brought forward in profusion. In return the islanders were given copper buckets, nails, knives and beads, 'wherewith they were well-pleased'. There were endless ceremonies. The Polynesians have a penchant for hospitality – provided their guests don't stay too long – and the people of Futuna and Alofi outdid one another in the lavishness of their feasts and the eroticism of their entertainment. There was music from the islanders' horns – 'pieces of hollow wood shaped like a pump', and from the Europeans' trumpets and drums. 'Young maidens danced naked before the king, performing very prettily and entertainingly and with much grace to the tempo of the music . . . while in the evening our men danced with the savages.' The Dutch were offered *kava*; but having seen how it was prepared, 'green herbs being chewed small in the mouth, then spat out into a big wooden trough and stirred and kneaded with water', they hastily declined.

It would seem that a good time was had by all; although Le Maire rather lets the cat out of the bag when he tells us:

> *As we sat at table we made the savages understand that we would be leaving in two days' time,*

whereat the king was so pleased that he at once leapt to his feet and shouted to his people that we would soon be going. At this there was much rejoicing. For these people were sore afraid of us, and were in constant fear that we would kill them and take their land.

By mid-June the *Eendracht* was again heading west into unknown waters.

During the next few weeks the Dutch made a number of valuable discoveries. On 20 June they sighted Nokumanu. Between 24 June and 2 July they sighted a number of islands in the Bismarck Archipelago, landing on Green, Feni and New Ireland. On 4 July they sighted the Admiralty Islands, and towards the end of the month they came to New Guinea.

It was thought in those days that New Guinea was part of a great land mass extending far into the tropics. By following the island's north coast right round to the approaches to the Moluccas, Le Maire proved otherwise. This was an important piece

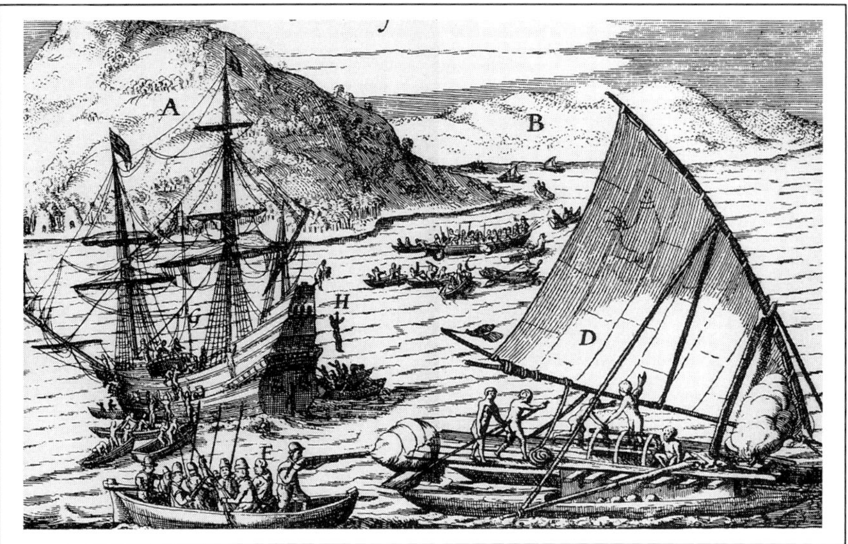

The Dutch vessel *Eendracht* engaged in 'a skirmish with the savages in which some were killed', in the Tuamotus. From *The East and West Indian Mirror,* Hakluyt Society. The key to the original is as follows: A Is Cocos Island, so called on account of the quantities of cokernuts that grow there. B Is Verraders Island, so called because they mostly came from that island who tried to betray us. C Is a skirmish withe the savages, in which some were killed. D Is one of the ships of the savages, which they well know how to manage. E Is our shallop, capturing the vessel from the savages. G Is our ship, round about which the savages swarmed in numbers, in order to exchange their wares with us. H In this manner, the savages sprang down into the sea after they had stolen something or other.

of exploration, marred only by continual skirmishing with 'the savages' – although to be fair to the Dutch it would seem that during this last part of their voyage it was generally the islanders who were the aggressors. For Le Maire soon found, as Quiros had found before him, that the warlike Melanesians were far more inclined to defend themselves than the peace-loving Polynesians. Here is his account of a typical encounter:

Top A seventeenth-century engraving of Batavia (present-day Djakarta), centre of the Dutch spice trade; *above* a contemporary illustration of pepper harvesting – pepper was the cornerstone of the spice trade – from *Le Livre des Merveilles* in the Bibliothèque Nationale.

25 July: We continued to sail along the coast, but could find no anchorage: we therefore sent out our shallop to take soundings. As the shallop approached the shore, 2 or 3 canoes filled with very black people put out to meet it. They were quite naked, wearing nothing over their privy parts, and pelted our men fiercely with slings: but when we fired at them they quickly fled. . . That evening we anchored in a bay with a bad uneven bottom. During the night the savages kept watch on us, lighting fires along the coast; and there being a bright moon and an offshore breeze, their canoes soon approached us. We threw them beads and showed them every sign of kindness; but they circled us for the better part of the night, shouting and yelling. They were most uncivilized. At dawn there were eight canoes moving round and round us. Again we showed them every kindness, giving them beads and other trifles, and making signs for them to fetch us pigs and coker-nuts. But it seemed they had something quite different in mind. For they began suddenly to pelt us with slings and assagays, thinking to overpower us. We, however, being on guard, fired at them with our muskets and cannon, so that some 10 or 12 were killed, and four canoes abandoned, their occupants leaping overboard and swimming for the shore. We launched our shallop and set out among the swimming savages, killing a few more. We also captured three prisoners and brought them aboard; all were badly wounded, and one died.

It is hard to blame the Dutch for defending themselves, and equally hard not to blame them for over-reacting.

A month later the *Eendracht* was among the Moluccas and a month after that she was anchored in apparent safety in Batavia. Her voyage had lasted nearly 18 months and covered nearly 40,000 miles. Le Maire had discovered an important new route into the Pacific and a number of archipelagos and islands previously unknown to Europeans. His navigation had been exemplary and he had kept his crew in good heart and excellent health – amazingly, out of his ships' company of 87 only three had died, none of them from scurvy. This was a fine feat of seamanship, and one wonders why Le Maire isn't better known.

The reason would seem to be that he was desperately unlucky. For the arrival of the *Eendracht* in Batavia coincided with the arrival of a new president of the Dutch East India Company, Jan Pieterszoon Coen. Coen was a strict, indeed a fanatical, upholder of the Company's monopoly. He flatly refused to believe that Schouten and Le Maire had discovered a new route into the Pacific. The recently-arrived sea-captains were, he contended, no more than freebooters; he seized the *Eendracht*, disbanded her crew, confiscated her cargo and papers, and shipped Schouten and Le Maire back to Holland in disgrace. On the voyage home Le Maire died – it is said of a broken heart – 'to the great sorrow of all his shipmates'. It was left to his father, the indomitable Isaac, to resuscitate his son's reputation. He took the mighty Company to court and after years of litigation, managed to win back, with costs, his ship, his cargo, and his son's papers and good name.

It would seem, however, that recognition won in retrospect carries less kudos than recognition won spontaneously. Few people today have heard of Le Maire, could place the strait that bears his name on a map or realize that Cape Horn is named after the ship that he lost. He lacked just one of the attributes of a successful explorer – luck.

The fate of Le Maire was a cautionary tale, a warning to toe the Company line. Not surprisingly, subsequent voyages were carried out in Company ships by Company men under Company orders.

Abel Janszoon Tasman was a Company man. He spent virtually the whole of his life in the service of the *Vereenigde Oost-Indische Compagnie*; and his voyage of 1642-3 reflects both the merits and shortcomings of the Company's efforts at exploration. It was well-planned, meticulous, meritorious and totally uninspired – it is not by chance that while the Spaniards describe their expeditions as quests, the Dutch describe theirs as labours.

Yet Tasman's voyage was at least conceived on a heroic scale. He was given two ships, a year of absence, a crew of 110, and told 'to find the remaining unknown part of the terrestial globe'. With the help of his able and dedicated pilot, Frans Visscher, he drew up an ambitious plan, the essence of which was to sail round the four sides of a rectangle centred on Australia. This was one of the great unknown segments of the habitable world; and it was the hope of the Company that 'the expense and trouble involved in exploring so vast an area would be rewarded with the fruits of material profit'. It was hardly Tasman's fault that in this the Company's expectations were never fulfilled.

Tasman's own account of his 'labours' is full of interesting detail but heavy going. Luckily there is a brief but more entertaining account of his voyage written by the fleet's barber (or surgeon) Hendrik Haalbos. Haalbos is no sluggard when it comes to narrative:

> *Two ships, Heemskerk and Zee-haen, under the command of Abel Tasman, were despatched to the Southland to discover further. On 12 August 1642 we weighed anchor before Batavia, and ran through the strait Sunda to Mauritius island* (in the Indian Ocean) *where in the north-west harbour we came to anchor on 5 September. Here we found a ship from Amsterdam providing the garizon with victuals and taking aboard ebony.*

Tasman spent a month in Mauritius, reprovisioning and repairing the *Zeehaen*, whose superstructure turned out to be half-rotten. He then headed on the southerly leg of his rectangle towards the Pole. By the end of October his ships were south of the 49th parallel. The weather was appalling: huge seas, a blustering wind, bitter cold and rolling banks of fog. They sighted seaweed and fragments of trees, almost certainly from Kerguelen Island. But Tasman, as he was to do so often, backed away from his

Abel Janszoon Tasman (1603-59), the Dutchman who discovered Tasmania and New Zealand, and circumnavigated – at a considerable distance – Australia; *right* Dutch ships anchored off the Swan River, western Australia, from Valentin's *Old and New East Indies.*

discovery, saying 'the weather was too bad to survey a known shore, let alone discover unknown land'. Bearing in mind the hazards that sailing-ships had to face in the sub-Antarctic, this was probably a wise decision. He altered course to the east, only to be hit by a succession of violent storms, with hail and heavy falls of snow. His men suffered terribly from cold and exhaustion, but for several weeks they could do little but run before the wind under shortened sail. Then they sighted land.

> *Discovered on 25 November a barren coast,* writes Haalbos, *against which the sea beat boisterously. We followed the land and found a safe bay, but then because of bad weather had to stand out to sea. Later we again approached the shore, where we found thick trees, hollow inside.* Tasman in his account adds, *with notches up the trunks five feet apart so it seems a race of giants must climb them. Round about lay mussel-shells. From the woods rose a shrill noise of people singing, whereat through fear we came back on board, and saw smoke rising through the trees. Having returned next day* (our carpenter) *swam ashore, and set up the flag of the House of Orange* (sometimes rather ineptly translated as an orange flag) *tying it to a stake in which was cut the mark of the East India Company. We named this inlet Frederik Henrik in honour of the carpenter, and the whole coast we named Antonius van Dieman in honour of the Governor-General of our Company. We then stood seaward and continued on an Easterly course.*

It was Tasmania the Dutch had discovered, a country not unlike Holland in appearance and climate, and one wonders why they didn't explore it more thoroughly. Tasman's Diary says simply, 'the wind being dead ahead further progress was impossible'. One cannot help feeling, however, that a more determined effort by the Dutch would have led to a substantial discovery rather than a brief sighting.

Much the same was to happen in New Zealand.

A week after leaving Tasmania land was again sighted, 'a large elevated country . . . because of thick cloud we could not see the tops of the mountains'. What happened next was a tragic variation of the theme of misunderstanding and massacre.

The *Heemskerk* and *Zeehaen* dropped anchor about half-a-mile offshore. During the night they were approached by two canoes.

> *We could see little,* says Haalbos, *on account of the darkness, but could hear the horrid noise of harsh voices and a shrill sound, not unlike a trumpet. We called out to them, blew on our trumpets and finally fired a cannon. At this the Southlanders began to rave terribly, blew on a horn and returned to land. Tasman called out the watch, arming them with pikes, swords and guns. Next day the Southlanders rowed out in several canoes, which were bound two-and-two-together with planks. They approached our ships as they swung on their bow-anchors. The gunner of the Heemskerk had put out in the ship's boat with 6 men, to check the ordnance of the Zee-haen. But midway between the two ships he was attacked from all sides by the Southlanders, who approaching made a fearful noise, rammed the boat and treated the seven sailors in such a way that they beat four to death with long staves – the other three managed to swim away. After committing this murder, they rowed with incredible skilfulness to the shore, so that before we could use our guns they were out of range. Tasman, noting that he could do nothing here except risk his men's lives against these savage people, named the place Murderers'-bay and set sail.*

Tasman insists that there was no provocation by his crew, yet aggression by the Maori *without* provocation is almost unheard of. Whatever the rights and wrongs of this sad affair, it is greatly to the credit of the Dutch that there were no reprisals. Tasman simply sailed away, which underlines the fact that his attitude to the people of the Pacific was, by the standards of his day, unusually enlightened. In this he was reflecting instructions set out in meticulous detail by the Company:

A page from the journal of Abel Janszoon Tasman,
showing the *Heemskerk* and *Zeehaen.*

You shall make contact amicably with the people of the Southland, and small affronts such as thieving you shall let pass unpunished. You shall carefully prevent all insolence and hostility of your crew towards the discovered peoples, and take care no harm is done to them in their houses, gardens, property or women; no inhabitants are to be brought away from their land against their will.

It is ironic that one of the least bellicose of European expeditions should have suffered what seems to have been one of the few acts of wanton aggression by the Pacific islanders.

The Dutch headed north along the coast of New Zealand, which they called Staten Landt, 'since we deemed it possible it was part of that great continent discovered by Le Maire . . . certainly it seems to be a fine country'. Surprisingly they failed to find Cook Strait, which runs between the North Island and the South. Even more surprisingly they failed to make a single landing, and after spending little more than a fortnight following the coast at a respectful distance, they hauled away to the north-east and set course for the Solomon Islands.

Tasman has been much criticized for not following-up his sighting with a more determined attempt at exploration. Senior officials of the Company were to accuse him of being over-cautious, and not bringing back as much information as he should have about the lands and peoples he discovered. This is fair comment. One can't imagine a truly great explorer – say Columbus, Magellan, Quiros or Cook – so readily quitting a newly-discovered land without setting foot on it. On the other hand the west coast of New Zealand is a lee shore (the wind blows directly on to it from the sea) and such shores were a graveyard for sailing ships. Also Tasman seems to have had an obsessive fear of giants. He reported signs of them in Tasmania. And now, on about the only occasion he did try to send a boat ashore, he reported '30 or 35 men of enormous stature, armed with great clubs; they took giant strides and shouted loudly with rough voices'. One gets the impression that when it came to landing, he didn't try very hard.

A fortnight after leaving New Zealand his ships again sighted land, 'an island

Top Queen Charlotte Sound, New Zealand. Tasman sighted the sound but failed to discover the strait separating the North and South Islands. *Above* Inhabitants and monuments of Easter Island, discovered in 1722 by Jacob Roggeveen.

shaped like 2 woman's breasts'. This was Atu, the most southerly of the Tonga group, and it is good to record that here the Dutch managed to establish friendly relations with the islanders:

> *'From the shore,'* writes Haalbos: *came a small vessel, sharply tapered fore and aft and with a wooden wing* (an outrigger) *projecting to port so it would not capsize. Three men sat in it, one behind the other, and rowed with uncommon skill to the Heemskerk. Tasman ordered us to leave the deck, so that the Southlanders should not be frightened, and himself lowered a piece of cloth into the water, which one of the men fished up and as a sign of thanks laid it on his head. Reassured they came close under the rudder, and took a knife which we had lashed to a piece of wood, and gave us in return a mother-of-pearl fishhook. . . One man ventured on board: a stately man with a broad black beard. He sat down, his legs tucked under his body, and bowed his head several times to the deck. Tasman did likewise, and took him by the hand and led him to his cabin with the intention of giving him a good reception; but because a dog began to bark, the man became frightened and leapt back into his vessel.*
>
> This, however, proved only a temporary setback; and soon a veritable armada of canoes was crowding round the *Heemskerk* and *Zeehaen, bringing pigs, poultry, coconuts and bananas, all wrapped in white cloth as gifts.* The chief of the island came aboard, *and we dressed him in shirt, trousers, jacket and hat, whereat he stood quite still for a long time astonished at himself. The mate and the boatswain's boy blew on trumpets, another of the crew played the flute and another the fiddle, while the ship's company danced, whereat the Southlanders were so astonished that they forgot to shut their mouths.* One thing led to another.
>
> *With the men came many women aboard; some were uncommonly big, and among them were two fearful giantesses, one of whom had a moustache. They fell in love with the wound-healer* (Haalbos himself) *and grasped him round the neck, each desiring fleshly intercourse. . . Some women took off their clothes and bartered them for nails. Others felt the sailors shamelessly in the trouser-front, and indicated that they wished to have intercourse, while the men of the island incited our ships' company to such transgressions.*

It was all too much for the Puritanical Dutch. 'Truly,' wrote Tasman, 'they are a good and peaceful people, but excessively lascivious and wanton.'

Next day the fun and games continued ashore, where the Dutch were 'most cordially entertained . . . the Southlanders indicating that we should go with the women, though when we did not treat them as they desired, they danced around us with strange gestures and ditties.' Tasman was more impressed with the Tongans' homes than with their morals. 'We found houses tastefully decorated with reed-shoots, and saw numbers of plots or gardens, with the beds neatly dug in squares and planted with all manner of earth-fruits, such as bananas, all standing so straight that it was a pleasure to behold, and gave forth the most lovely and pleasant aroma.'

The Dutch spent several weeks in this demi-paradise, which, for obvious reasons, was soon to become known as the Friendly Islands. Then, with their water-casks full and their stores replenished, they again stood north.

After less than a week they came to another cluster of islands which had never before been sighted by Europeans: the northern outliers of the Fiji group (the Ringgolds, Taveuni, Vanua Levu and Thikombia). This is a dangerous area for sailing ships, and the *Heemskerk* and *Zeehaen* soon found themselves 'surrounded by many reefs, with huge breakers where we could not sail, and only in one place was there egress, a small opening about the width of 2 ships, through which we passed with Great Anxiety. . . The shoals here are Very many and Dangerous'. Tasman noted that the Fijians had blacker skins than the Tongans and were more warlike; they were armed with bows and arrows.

For once, however, the islanders had no need of their weapons. For in Fiji as in Tonga not a shot was fired in anger, a state of affairs which was to continue as Tasman worked his way slowly homeward via the northern outliers of the Solomons and the islands of the Bismarck Archipelago. Indeed on this final leg of his voyage his discoveries were probably less significant than the spirit in which they were made, and the rapport he managed to establish with the Melanesians. There was no bloodshed. No recriminations, not even against 'those who pulled the nails out of our ships' timbers and offered in exchange nothing but a single mouldering coconut'.

On 15 May 1643, after a voyage of exactly nine months, the *Heemskerk* and *Zeehaen* again dropped anchor off Batavia, and Tasman wrote the last words in his Diary. 'At daybreak was rowed ashore in the pinnace. God be praised and thanked for this most happy voyage. Amen.'

Tasman was not a great leader. He lacked that inquisitiveness, that 'lust of knowing what should not be known', which is the hallmark of all the truly great explorers. He was, however, a careful and highly competent seaman, and he treated the people of the Pacific as human beings. Let that be his epitaph.

Tasman's expedition was a watershed in Dutch voyaging. It was not the last of the great projects to be initiated by the Company – indeed the very next year Tasman commanded another expedition which skirted, albeit at a distance, the entire north coast of Australia. However, the commercial benefits gained from these voyages were so disappointing for the Company that for the next 75 years they concentrated on exploitation rather than exploration. It was not until 1722 that they launched another major expedition whose objective was discovery rather than trade. Then a fleet commanded by Jacob Roggeveen, crossing the Pacific from east to west, discovered that *Ultima Thule* of lonely outposts, Easter Island. This was a major achievement, but Roggeveen paid for it dearly. In one of the most harrowing of Pacific voyages he suffered shipwreck, desertion and the death of more than 50 per cent of his crew from scurvy.

In between these expeditions the Dutch methodically built up their well organized trading empire, which for many centuries was to supply Europe with a seemingly endless cornucopia of silks and spices. It is perhaps unfair to condemn the Dutch for the fact that the trade they instigated was almost entirely one way. It was generally accepted in the seventeenth century that Europeans should take what they wanted and give little if anything in return, and the simple truth is that the Dutch did this more efficiently than anyone else.

It was left to other nations in the next century to delineate the Pacific with accuracy and to realize that its inhabitants were something more then 'mere savages' awaiting exploitation.

TO GO AS FAR AS IT IS POSSIBLE FOR MAN TO GO

THE VOYAGES OF THE BRITISH

'I have now done with this . . . PACIFIC OCEAN,' and flatter myself that no one will think I have left it unexplor'd.'
JAMES COOK

The British were late arrivers in the Pacific. In the 200 years that followed the first crossing of the ocean by Magellan, almost the only British ships to venture into its waters were privateers – or to tag them with a more romantic label, buccaneers. Of these the first and the most successful was Drake.

Most people today think of Francis Drake as a swashbuckling scourge of the Spaniards; he is best remembered for 'singeing the beard' of the king of Spain and for finishing his game of bowls before defeating the Armada. Yet he was also the first man in history to command a successful circumnavigation of the world (Magellan of course died en route), and the discoveries he made, especially off Cape Horn and along the Pacific seaboard of America, were far from negligible. Perhaps one reason why Drake-the-explorer has taken second place to Drake-the-buccaneer is that the latter is so entertaining. He seems to have been the very *beau idéal* of a Kingsley hero. 'Always', we are told, 'he robbed with a courtly air, dining and wining his involuntary guests well – on their own stores – and making elaborate presentations – but never losing out in the exchange'. He also robbed with outstanding success, and when, at the end of a three-year voyage, his ship the *Golden Hind* returned to England after sailing – with remarkably few casualties – around the world, her hold was filled to overflowing with gold and silver, pearls and jewels, silks and spices. It has been estimated that those who invested in Drake's expedition got a return of more than 4,700 per cent on their money, and that the Crown's share of the plunder alone was worth more than the Exchequer's revenue for an entire year. In the words of the monetarist J.M. Keynes:

> *The booty brought back by Drake may fairly be considered the fountain and origin of British foreign investment. Elizabeth paid off, out of the proceeds, the whole of her foreign debt and invested part of the balance in the Levant Company; largely out of the profits of the Levant Company was formed the East India Company, the profits of which during the seventeenth and eighteenth centuries were the main foundations of England's foreign connections.*

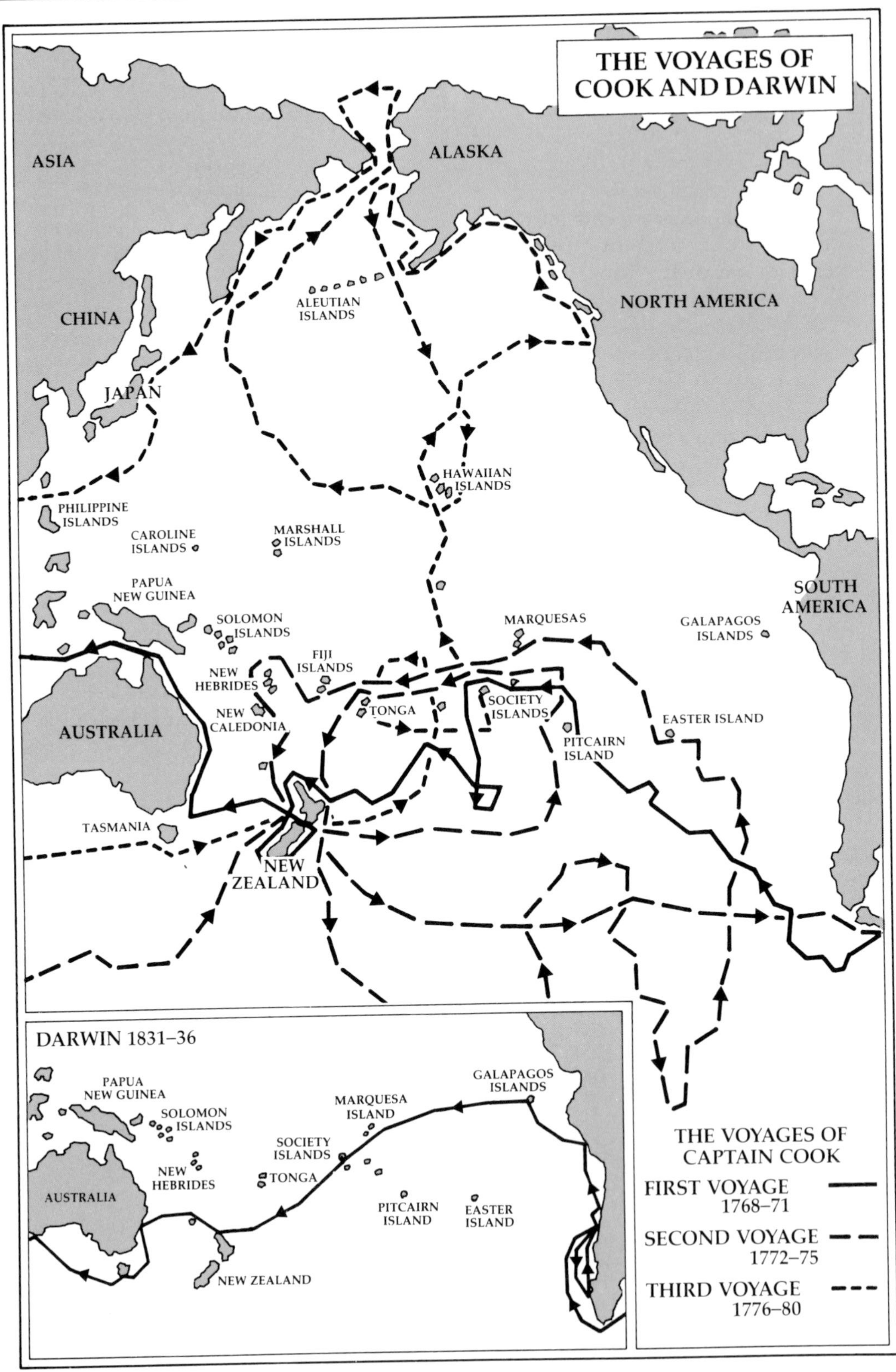
THE VOYAGES OF
COOK AND DARWIN
ASIA
ALASKA
CHINA
JAPAN
ALEUTIAN
ISLANDS
NORTH AMERICA
HAWAIIAN
ISLANDS
PHILIPPINE
ISLANDS
CAROLINE
ISLANDS
MARSHALL
ISLANDS
PAPUA
NEW GUINEA
SOLOMON
ISLANDS
SOUTH
AMERICA
MARQUESAS
GALAPAGOS
ISLANDS
FIJI
ISLANDS
NEW
HEBRIDES
NEW
CALEDONIA
TONGA
SOCIETY
ISLANDS
EASTER ISLAND
AUSTRALIA
PITCAIRN
ISLAND
TASMANIA
NEW
ZEALAND
DARWIN 1831–36
PAPUA
NEW GUINEA
SOLOMON
ISLANDS
MARQUESA
ISLAND
GALAPAGOS
ISLANDS
SOCIETY
ISLANDS
NEW
HEBRIDES
TONGA
AUSTRALIA
PITCAIRN
ISLAND
EASTER
ISLAND
NEW ZEALAND
THE VOYAGES OF
CAPTAIN COOK
FIRST VOYAGE
1768–71
SECOND VOYAGE
1772–75
THIRD VOYAGE
1776–80

No wonder Drake had a host of emulators, most, though not all of them, British; and it wasn't long before a motley rabble of adventurers were roaming the Pacific in search of easy pickings. Some were loners; others coalesced into highly volatile task-forces of anything up to a dozen ships and a thousand men. Not many were as successful as Drake, for generally speaking they lacked his flair, discipline and patience. Also, as the Spaniards gradually tightened control over their 'lake', their treasure ships became increasingly difficult to locate let alone to capture, and although Spanish ports on the mainland were often relatively easy to sack, they seldom yielded a great deal in the way of treasure – even after Morgan's rape of Panama there was 'much grumbling among the men at the smallness of their purchase' (their booty). The truth would seem to be that although Charles Kingsley's novels and Errol Flynn's films have given buccaneering a romantic and often patriotic gloss, it was in fact a gruesome and frequently a profitless calling; witness François Grogniet's casual aside that 'with some reluctance we sent the heads of 20 of our prisoners to Panama, to hasten the ransoming of the rest – in truth a little violent, but the only way to bring the Spaniards to reason'. Life was cheap. Torture was commonplace. Rape was officially frowned on but often unofficially indulged in. Drunkenness was the norm.

One might have felt more inclined to turn a blind eye to some of the buccaneers' excesses if, like those other bloodsoaked adventurers, the sealers, they had performed heroic feats of exploration. But they didn't. It is true that the most personable and persuasive of them, William Dampier, made important discoveries off the coasts of Australia, New Britain and New Ireland, but this was when he was sailing under the aegis of the Admiralty. The sum total of the other privateers' discoveries was their report of 'a low sandy flat island, without any guard of rocks' (almost certainly Sala y Gomez to the north-east of Easter Island) 'backed by a high range of land' (almost certainly a bank of cloud). Though romantics may wish it had been otherwise, the British and French

Sir Francis Drake (1545-96), the first commander to complete a successful circumnavigation of the world, and his ship the *Golden Hind* – from Hondius's map of Drake's voyages.

buccaneers who throughout the seventeenth century harried the Spaniards in the Pacific were a tatterdemalion rabble. There was, however, one totally unexpected field in which they were to achieve a sort of immortality – the field of English literature.

Towards the end of the seventeenth century improvements in the technique of printing and a rise in the standard of education led to a growing demand for books. Theology was, by tradition, the most popular subject, but it was about to be challenged by a rival – the literature of travel. In the seventeenth century educated people were beginning to realize that beyond the close-knit world of Europe-and-the-Mediterranean lay another totally different world: a world, to quote Shakespeare, 'of the Cannibals that each other eat, the Anthropophagi, and men whose heads do grow beneath their shoulders'. In this new world there were, it seemed, strange people to be saved, terrible hazards to be overcome, fabulous riches to be gained; and people got a vicarious thrill out of reading about it. However, until the last years of the seventeenth century there wasn't a great deal for them to read. There was always, it is true, Hakluyt; but even his contemporaries reckoned his massive works were heavy going – more esoteric than entertaining. Then some of the buccaneers started publishing their memoirs, and these, to a thirsting public, were like manna from heaven.

It all started in 1697 with Dampier's *A New Voyage Round the World*, and if ever there was a trend-setter this was it. The book reprinted five times in six years – unheard of in those days – and sparked off a spate of best-selling derivatives. Some of these were pure fact like Wafer's account of his life with the Cuna Indians, some were pure fantasy like Defoe's *Robinson Crusoe*, and some were fact and fantasy combined like Chetwood's

The island of Juan Fernandez, off the coast of South America, often used as a watering place by explorers, buccaneers and whalers, and the home of Daniel Defoe's Robinson Crusoe.

theatrical production *The Voyages and Adventures of Captain Robert Boyle*. These works were often more than potboilers; many were serious literate evocations of a world that people wanted to know about, full of interesting scientific facts. They marked the birth of both the travel book and the adventure novel. And how many great literary works stem directly from the writings of the buccaneers. Eight of Defoe's stories have their origin in works by Dampier. Swift's *Gulliver's Travels* is a parody of Dampier's voyages – in the very first sentence of the book Captain Gulliver refers to 'my cousin Dampier'. The plot of Coleridge's *Rime of the Ancient Mariner* is lifted straight from the journals of the privateer Shelvocke. The deeds of the buccaneers may often have been dark, but they shed light on a world hitherto undreamed of.

Apart from buccaneers, few British vessels entered the Pacific until the second half of the eighteenth century and when British expeditions *did* appear, their discoveries to start with were on a very minor scale. In 1765 John Byron (grandfather of the poet) made discoveries in the Tuamotus and Gilbert Islands. In 1767 Philip Carteret sighted Pitcairn and a number of atolls in the Solomons. And in the same year Samuel Wallis landed on Tahiti in the Society Islands – a discovery seldom given the attention it deserves, partly because his stay was brief and he was ill during much of it, and partly because it was soon to be overshadowed by the more important landings of Bougainville and Cook.

The arrival on the scene of Cook marks the dawn of a new era, for never before or since has so able a man devoted himself so singlemindedly to finding out the truth about our planet. Cook elevated exploration from a pastime to a science. And he reserved his greatest work for the greatest ocean.

He was born at Marton in Yorkshire on 27 October 1728, the second child of a Scottish farm labourer. He probably never saw the sea until he was 17, when his parents took him to the fishing village of Staithes and apprenticed him to a grocer-cum-haberdasher. For a year and a half Cook sold potatoes and lengths of cloth in a cramped little shop – an unlikely upbringing for the man who was to become arguably the greatest explorer the world has ever known. However, in 1746 he signed-on as deckhand aboard the *Freelove*, a brig carrying coal from Newcastle to London. And it was then he first displayed the trait which was to take him to the farthest ends of the Earth – determination. There is no evidence that he had a particularly quick or clever brain, but he was hard-working and gifted with 'God's good common-sense that's more than any knowledge'. In the course of the next ten years he taught himself pilotage, navigation, surveying and astronomy while working his way up the lower-deck hierarchy from deckhand to mate. In 1755 he was offered a ship of his own, a brig in trade with the Baltic. Then, it seemed to his friends, he threw it all away. He enlisted as an ordinary seaman in the Royal Navy.

To give up a master's cabin for the 14 inches of deck-space allotted to men below decks in a frigate must have seemed at the time a step backward rather than forward, and certainly life aboard Cook's first ship, the *Eagle*, was unbelievably squalid.

> *The only ventilation,* Admiral Muir tells us, *was by way of the gun-ports and hatches, which had to be closed in bad weather. The ship leaked badly, the bilge water stank with a nauseating odour which permeated the whole vessel, whilst suffocation from falling into the well was a common accident. The sanitary arrangements consisted of an open space about the heel of the bowsprit, where men were exposed to showers of spray, and excrement stuck to the bows until washed off in heavy weather. No wonder that cruising, even in home waters, was invariably accompanied by a shocking mortality. . . Put ashore today to hospital,* wrote the *Eagle*'s captain, *130 men most of which are extremely ill; buried the last month 22. The surgeon and another four died yesterday.*

Such conditions in the early eighteenth century were not the exception but the rule and the fact that Cook had to endure them helps, I think, to explain the almost fanatical measures he took to safeguard the health of his own crew. Not many naval captains in his day had enjoyed first-hand experience of life on the lower-deck.

It soon became apparent to his officers that their new seaman had a great deal more potential than the usual press-ganged landlubber, and Cook's promotions came steadily – to petty officer, to master's mate, to warrant officer, and, on his 29th birthday, he was appointed master of the *Pembroke*, a 60-gun ship-of-the-line. A few days later the *Pembroke* was ordered to the Saint Lawrence, and here Cook discovered his métier – surveying.

His first piece of survey work led to Wolfe's capture of Quebec. The French defences of Quebec were based on the fact that part of the Saint Lawrence River known as The Traverse was thought to be impassable to warships – and those who know The Traverse can understand why, for a wilder, more rock-strewn race of water it would be difficult to imagine. However, in the weeks prior to the British assault on Quebec, Cook surveyed and sounded The Traverse and marked it so effectively with buoys that one night the entire British fleet was able to edge through without the loss of a single man. The Heights of Abraham were scaled, and the French had no option but to surrender – the ceremony being carried out by Louis Antoine de Bougainville, whose path was soon to cross again with Cook's, under happier circumstances, in the Pacific.

Cook's role in the capture of Quebec raised him from obscurity to limelight. He was appointed Master-Surveyor of the British North American fleet, and during the next few years delineated the east Canadian and Newfoundland coasts with such accuracy that his charts today are still the basis for local pilotage. He also observed an eclipse of the sun, and sent his findings to the Royal Society.

This had important results; for in 1768, when the Society were anxious to send an observer into the southern hemisphere to observe the transit of the planet Venus, Cook was a candidate acceptable to both scientists and the Navy. He was given command of a Whitby-built collier, the *Endeavour*, and ordered 'from a place southward of the Equinoctial Line . . . to observe the passage of the Planet Venus over the disk of the sun on 3 June 1769'. It would, however, be naive to believe that this was the sole objective of his voyage. He also had secret orders to 'search for the Great Southern Continent, to

Captain James Cook (1728), a portrait by Bernard Direx from a French engraving, and his ship HMS *Endeavour* entering Botany Bay, Australia, in 1770.

observe with accuracy the situation of this and other lands you may discover, to make surveys of such of them as appear of consequence and to take possession of them in the name of His Majesty'. The fact that the Great Southern Continent and the islands of the Pacific might already belong to others was of no more consequence to the Admiralty in the 1760s than it had been of consequence 250 years earlier to Balboa; although it is perhaps only fair to add that Cook was adjured to 'endeavour by all proper means to cultivate a friendship with the Natives, presenting them such Trifles as may be acceptable to them in exchange for Provisions . . . and shewing them every Civility and regard'.

On 26 August 1768 the *Endeavour* stood south out of Plymouth. The first of Cook's three great voyages of exploration was under way.

Two hundred-and-fifty years had passed since Magellan first crossed the Pacific, yet the ocean was still an enigma, its extent only vaguely appreciated, its mysteries still largely unsolved. It was widely believed that a Great Continent lay awaiting discovery in the south. To the north, it was widely believed that among the ice and mist lay a seaway linking it to the Atlantic. Several explorers had managed to cross the ocean yet none could be said to have explored it, for all had kept basically to the same route. Further exploration had been frustrated partly by the enormous distances, and partly by the problems of health and navigation.

Cook's expertise in the field of both health and navigation were to make him master of the Pacific whereas all previous explorers had been its servants.

The early stages of Cook's first voyage are usually described as uneventful; and it is true that as the *Endeavour* headed for Cape Horn, via Madeira and Rio, there were no spectacular occurrences. However, uneventful is about the last word that the crew themselves would have used to describe their passage. They had barely cleared the Channel when Cook initiated a daily routine that was nothing short of a revolution. His aim was to safeguard his men's health, particularly against scurvy, and to this end he supervised their diet and their hygiene with unprecedented – many thought fanatical – strictness.

Some writers have suggested that Cook managed to conquer scurvy because he had aboard two near-magical antidotes – sauerkraut and lemon preserve – which provided his crew with a continuous source of vitamin C. This, however, is an over-simplification. It is true that there were in the *Endeavour*'s hold '8,000 lbs of cabbage cut fine and cured in brine . . . [also] much wort and lemon conserve'. But Cook unwittingly nullified much of the value of his sauerkraut by boiling it and serving it as soup – thus reducing its vitamin content, while due to an error by a victualling-yard clerk his wort and lemon conserve was made not with African lemons, which are rich in vitamin C, but with West Indian limes, which contain almost no vitamin C at all. This suggests that the *Endeavour's* clean bill of health must have been due in large part to the improvements Cook initiated in hygiene. To ensure that his men had plenty of sleep he allowed them to keep three watches instead of the usual two. He insisted that every man had at least one cold bath a day, even in the Antarctic. Hammocks, clothing and bedding were brought on deck every three days for airing. Once a week *Endeavour* was either 'cured with fires', or 'smoked clean with a mixture of vinnegar and gun-powder'. The well was regularly fumigated. Water-butts were scoured daily, while Cook himself made frequent inspections of every part of his ship and every member of his crew. There was some discontent at first at so overpowering a routine. 'Every day is a Sunday (a captain's rounds day) with Mr Cook,' complained one of the crew. But events were to prove in no uncertain manner that Cook's precautions were justified.

By early December *Endeavour* was at the approaches to Cape Horn, and Cook put ashore near the tip of Tierra del Fuego, partly to stock up with wild celery, a traditional antidote to scurvy, and partly to give his botanists the opportunity to collect plants. The seas were high, the wind a near-continuous gale, the cold 'past belief'. A landing party who set out to climb a nearby mountain underestimated the lethal combination of wind and cold, and two froze to death – one of the very few occasions on which Cook lost a member of his ship's company through what might be termed carelessness.

The approaches to the Horn were, for the first time, charted with accuracy; then *Endeavour* was on course for Tahiti, where Cook planned to set up his observation post to record the transit of Venus. Tahiti had been discovered only a few years earlier, and the fact that Cook now chose to set course straight for the island rather than head for it by the traditional route – first north to Juan Fernandez and then west along the Tropic of Capricorn – is proof that he had confidence in both the health of his crew and the accuracy of his navigation. A confidence well founded, for after an uneventful passage of eight weeks he made an exact landfall off Matavai Bay, and – almost unprecedented for a ship that had crossed the greater part of the Pacific – his crew were in good health and free from scurvy.

Cook was the first European to stay long enough in one of the mid-Pacific islands to get to know the Polynesians with any degree of intimacy. He spent three months in Tahiti, and his *Journal*, supplemented by data collected by his scientists and sketches made by his much underrated artist Sydney Parkinson, give us a fair picture of Eden before the Fall.

The British didn't eulogize over the Polynesians with quite the same fervour as the French, and Cook's appraisal of them is factual and level-headed, recording not only the beauty of their island but also the heat, the flies, the restrictive taboos, the promiscuity and the thieving. It was the thieving to which Cook took particular exception; it was an endless irritant, a poison in the blood which in the end was to bring about his death.

No sooner had *Endeavour* dropped anchor in Matavai Bay than Cook was writing in his Diary:

> *It was a hard matter to keep the Natives out of the Ship as they clime like Munkeys, and it was harder still to keep them from Stealing every thing that came within their reach; in this they are prodiges expert.* Next afternoon the British went ashore, and the thieving continued. *The Natives Flock'd about us in great Numbers and in as friendly a Manner as we could wish, only that they shew'd a great inclination to pick our pockets. . . Notwithstanding the care we took, Dr Solander and Dr Munkhouse had each of them their pockets pick'd, the one of his spy-glass and the other of his snuff Box.*

This infuriated Cook's naturalist, Joseph Banks, who up to this point had been generously distributing presents, including his handkerchief and tie. Banks had just managed to persuade a pretty girl 'with fire in her eyes' to come and sit beside him; but on hearing about the thieving he became angry, making a threatening gesture with his gun and demanding the return of the stolen items. There was instant panic. Most of the crowd fled in terror and the chief took the Englishmen to one of his huts and indicated by signs that they could take whatever they wished. Banks, however, insisted on the return of the spy-glass and snuff-box. Eventually both were brought back, and harmony was restored.

A few days later, however, there was a more serious incident. The British had begun to build their observation post, Fort Venus, and while Cook was visiting another

Two very different ceremonies attended by Cook. *Top* An initiation ceremony for the son of a chief in Tonga, from a drawing by John Webber; *below* a human sacrifice taking place in a *morai* (temple), in Tahiti.

part of the island he left a guard on the building under the command of a young midshipman. The islanders, it seems, jostled one of the guards, pushed him over and stole his musket. There is no reason to doubt Sydney Parkinson's account of what happened next:

> *The Midshipman giving the orders to fire* (at the culprits) *the men obeyed with the greatest glee imaginable, as though they had been shooting at wild duck. They killed one man and wounded many others. What a pity that such brutality should be exercised by civilized people upon unarmed Indians! . . . They fled into the woods like frightened fawns, terrified to the last degree.*

For several days there was tension; then the islanders came out to *Endeavour* with green branches, their symbol of peace, and a present of pigs and breadfruit. Friendship was reaffirmed, and it wasn't long before the British were wandering about the island unarmed, and spending the nights ashore 'snug and unafraid'.

But still the thieving continued, often compounded by the pilfering of the crew themselves – nails, the usual currency for sexual favours, were in particular demand. Soon almost the whole of Cook's ship's company found themselves sleeping on deck because they had traded-in the screws from which their hammocks were hung! Then, only a few weeks before the transit of Venus, there occurred another serious theft. An astronomical quadrant – a heavy instrument in a box about 18 inches square – had been placed in a specially guarded tent inside Fort Venus. The night-guard had neither seen nor heard anything suspicious, but by morning the quadrant had disappeared. Cook was furious. There was much beating of drums and barking of orders; some Polynesians were brought in for questioning, some were brought in as hostages; canoes were forbidden to leave harbour, and a perspiring search-party set out for the hills where, it was said, the culprit had fled. The chase was both long and exhausting.

> *At every house we passed,* writes Banks, (we) *inquired after the thief, and the people readily told us which way he had gone, and how long it was since he passed by, a circumstance which gave us great hopes of coming up with him. The weather was excessively hot, the thermometer before we left the tents being ninety-one degrees. At times we walked, at times we ran. . . When we arrived at the top of one hill, we were shown another hill about three miles off and made to understand we were not to expect the instrument till we got there.*

One has the impression that the Tahitians were enjoying the chase rather more than the British. At last, part of the quadrant was brought back, together with sundry glasses, pistol cases and items of clothing, although of the instrument itself there was still no sign. However, the arrival of a contingent of marines, in full uniform and fully armed, had the desired effect. The quadrant was returned; and a procession at once formed up in high spirits to escort it back to Fort Venus. Next day the atmosphere was a bit apprehensive, but it was not in the Polynesians' nature to remain subdued for long. That evening they invited the British to a banquet and Cook gratefully accepted. The banquet was a great success – and the occasion of much pickpocketing.

One wonders why the Polynesians never learned to stop stealing? And why the British never learned to live with it? Alan Moorehead puts it this way:

> *A point of principle, or if you like taboo, was involved. It was no more possible for the islanders to keep their hands off the Europeans' belongings than it was for the Europeans to abandon their rule that private property was sacred. Like small boys the Tahitians wanted to rob the orchard, felt, in fact, that they HAD to rob the orchard, almost as a matter of personal pride. Only the force of firearms could stop them, and when firearms were inevitably used, they were hurt, bewildered*

and reduced to crying for forgiveness.

All that is true. There was an enormous gulf between the possessive property-conscious Europeans, and the happy-go-lucky Polynesians who cheerfully shared the few belongings they had. And this gulf is, I think, an indication of a fundamental difference between the two races' attitude to life. The British, as Christians, were steeped in an awareness of heaven and hell, right and wrong. To them stealing was wrong, and must therefore be punished. The Polynesians, on the other hand, although they were a deeply religious people, had no concept of hell. Retribution and punishment were alien to them – there were no prisons or executions in the pre-European islands – and when commanders like Cook and Bougainville punished their own seamen for crimes against the islanders, the islanders were horrified, they burst into tears and begged them to stop. It has often been said that the Polynesians' attitude and behaviour in these matters were naive – writer after writer has compared them to children. This is a fair comparison – provided always we remember that it was *our* God and the Polynesians who said, 'Suffer the little children to come unto me; . . . for of such is the kingdom of heaven'.

If the British considered the Polynesians' least-attractive trait to be thieving, there is no doubt about what they considered their most-attractive – their attitude to sex.

As Beaglehole points out, Cook and his men considered themselves 'imparadised' in Tahiti, for the island offered few vexations (apart from thieving) and a cornucopia of delights. The diaries of naval officers and scientists alike are full of references to the scenic beauty, the clean airy homes, the well-tended fields and gardens, the wonderful food and the pleasures of bathing and surfing. The diarists are also mostly agreed that the Polynesian men were handsome, agile and virile, and the Polynesian women beautiful, graceful and nubile. From the moment *Endeavour* dropped anchor to the moment three months later she sailed, the younger Tahitian women made it abundantly plain to the seamen that they wished to have sexual intercourse with them. This, it seemed to them, was the most natural thing in the world, and nothing to be secretive about or ashamed of. Cook gives us a description of the way some of them made their wishes known:

> *FRIDAY 12* (May 1769) *Clowdy weather with Showers of Rain. This morning two young women with some others came to the Fort. . . Mr Banks was as usual at the gate of the Fort trading with the people, when he was told that strangers were coming, and stood to receive them. The Company had with them about a Dozn young Plantain Trees (bananas); these they laid down about 20 feet from Mr Banks, the People then made a lane between him and them; when this was done a Man (who appear'd to be a Servant of the 2 Women) brought the young Plantains Singley and gave them to Mr Banks, and at the delivery of each pronounce'd a Short sentence, which we understood not. After he had thus dispose'd of all his Plantain trees he took several pieces of Cloth and spread them on the ground; one of the Young Women then step'd upon the Cloth and with as much Innocency as one could possibly conceve, expose'd herself intirely naked from the waist downwards; in this manner she turn'd her Self once or twice round, then step'd of*(f) *the Cloth and drop'd down her clothes; more Cloth was then spread upon the Former and she again perform'd the same ceremony: the Cloth was then rowled up and given to Mr Banks, and the two young women went and embraced him, which ended the Ceremony.*

There is no doubt about the meaning of all this. The banana as a phallic symbol was ritually presented; the dowry in the form of cloth was formally offered; the sexual parts and the tattooed thighs and buttocks were invitingly displayed, and to make their meaning clear beyond all possible doubt the two girls came up to Banks and embraced him.

Cook's attitude to these goings-on was surprisingly laid back. He was clearly charmed by the Tahitians' warmth and spontaneity, and more amused than shocked by their amorality. It was the prudish Victorians of the next century who were to cover the islanders' nakedness in cast-off European clothes and forbid them to dance or sing. Cook allowed his men to spend as much of their off-duty time ashore as they pleased and even permitted girls to remain aboard the *Endeavour* at night. His feeling seems to have been: why should such innocence be destroyed? Where there is no thought of evil, it is surely hypocritical to talk of immodesty? It would seem that he himself was about the only man aboard the *Endeavour not* to take a mistress, much to the chagrin of the Tahitian girls who teased him for being old and impotent – a reputation which he accepted with good humour, and probably some amusement seeing that his wife bore him six children.

At the end of three months the transit of Venus had been observed, a mass of scientific data had been collected, the *Endeavour* had been repaired and reprovisioned, and Cook was ready to leave. His visit had, on the whole, been successful and happy, and both parties felt genuine grief that it was about to end. Several of the ship's company deserted, took to the hills with their loved ones and had to be ferreted out and dragged back by the marines. The Polynesians wept copiously and many tried to stow-away aboard the *Endeavour*. In the end Cook agreed to take two of them with him – Tupia, a member of the Arioi, and a young boy named Tayato.

As the *Endeavour*, on 13 July, stood slowly out of Matavai Bay, she was surrounded by canoes 'fill'd with lamenting men and women'. All afternoon the canoes followed her seaward; only with the approach of darkness did they one by one turn for home. Many of the British were equally saddened by the parting of the ways, and as the moon rose Banks and a handful of others stayed on deck staring back, we are told, towards Tahiti long after the time the island had disappeared.

Cook had fulfilled the first part of his orders, to record the transit of Venus. The second and more difficult part – to search for the Great Southern continent – was to occupy him for the next two years.

There was no sign of the supposed continent in the sea lanes south of Tahiti; and as *Endeavour* headed south, week after week, towards the Antarctic Circle, with a great swell and a blustering wind on her beam, Cook became increasingly convinced that the continent was a myth. Round about the 40th parallel the weather became so bad that he decided to alter course and head for New Zealand, which no one had visited since Tasman's brief sighting more than 100 years earlier. It is an indication of the accuracy of his navigation, that after beating for almost a month into continuous and violent headwinds, he made a landfall off the east coast.

Up to this point Cook's achievements had been considerable but perhaps not remarkable. However, in the course of the next year he was to establish himself as one of the greatest surveyors the world has ever known. His first feat was to chart, with pin-point accuracy, the whole of the North Island of New Zealand, and with only slightly less accuracy the whole of the South Island. Never before had a newly discovered land been placed on the map so instantly, so correctly and in such detail. And by proving New Zealand to be insular, Cook took another step towards disproving the existence, at least in this part of the Pacific, of a Great Southern Continent. His circumnavigation took him the better part of six months, with only two short breaks ashore, the first in the Bay of Plenty to observe the transit of Mercury, the second in Queen Charlotte Sound to reprovision. The reason why he didn't spend longer ashore can be summed up in two words – the Maori.

Captain Cook landing at Mallicolo (Malekula, New Hebrides).

The people of New Zealand were a great deal more warlike than the people of the mid-Pacific islands. When Cook tried to land, they defended their territory with vigour; when he tried to capture a canoe, the rowers resisted so stoutly that it was the British whose lives were in danger. However, on the few occasions when an understanding *was* reached, the Maori proved trustworthy, honest and intelligent friends – Cook describes them as 'strong, rawboned and well-proportioned, of a very dark brown colour . . . alert vigorous and in all they did most dextrous'. A Maori chief has left us this delightful account of his visit as a child to the *Endeavour*:

> *We three children sat on the deck of the ship where we were looked at by the goblins, who with their hands stroked the hair on our heads, and made much gabbling noise as they spoke. There was one supreme man in the ship. He seldom spoke, but handled our mats and weapons carefully, patted our cheeks and very gently touched our heads. . . We had not been long aboard before this chief made a speech, and took some charcoal and made marks upon the deck of the ship, pointing to the shore and then looking at our warriors. One of our old men said, 'He is asking for an outline of our land', and he took the charcoal and marked the outline of Ika-a-Maui (the North Island). . . After awhile the chief goblin came to where I and my two companions were sitting, and held out a nail. My companions were afraid; but I laughed, and he gave the nail to me, and I said 'Ka pai' (That is good). At this the elders nodded and said, 'This man is fond of children, and you can tell he is a chief by his kindness. For is it not written, "E hore te tino tangata e ngaro i roto i tokomuho".' (A good and noble man can not be lost in a crowd.)*

By the time Cook had completed his survey of New Zealand, *Endeavour's* voyage had already lasted 21 months. He had made important astronomical observations; he had taken possession of the Society Islands and New Zealand and had placed the latter accurately on the map; he had exploded, at least in part, the myth of a Great Southern

Continent. It might be thought he had done all that could be expected of him. Yet his longing 'to go as far as it is possible for man to go' was not yet slaked, and after consulting his crew he decided to return home by a route which held promise of yet more discoveries. No European as yet had definitely sighted the east coast of what was then known as New Holland or discovered whether or not it formed a continuous land mass with New Guinea. Here, Cook realized, was an opportunity to explore an unknown segment of the world. The *Endeavour* stood west.

The Tasman Sea was kind that autumn. 'Gentle breezes,' wrote Cook, 'with very pleasant weather'; and after a passage of exactly three weeks he had the satisfaction of sighting an unknown coastline, the eastern seaboard of Australia, where he made a landfall roughly midway between Sydney and Melbourne.

His first impression was 'of an agreeable and pleasant land, with hills covered in parts with trees and bushes and interspersed with tracts of sand'. He followed the coast north, searching for somewhere to land, but being thwarted for several days by 'a large hollow sea from ye SE rowling in upon the land and beating everywhere very high'. Then he came to Botany Bay. His problem here was not the surf but the Aborigines. There were only two of them – naked except for their spears – but they vigorously opposed the landing of the 30 or 40 well-armed Europeans, and refused to give way even when they were shot at – when one was wounded, he simply ran back to his hut to fetch a shield. At last, however, the spirited defenders were driven away, and Cook's nephew jumped ashore, the first European to set foot on the east coast of Australia.

Cook spent a week in Botany Bay. He was impressed with the country, noting with the eye of a farmer's son that the soil looked particularly suitable for sheep. Banks was even more impressed. 'The place,' he wrote, 'is completely fascinating, and a veritable treasure trove of strange plants and insects.' He and his fellow scientists collected more than 200 species unknown to Europe, and were the first people to appreciate that Australia enjoys a range of flora and fauna quite different from that found elsewhere in the world.

Leaving Botany Bay, *Endeavour* again stood north. The weather was fine, the country pleasant, the sea, to Cook's surprise, grew progressively calmer. The calm, however, was deceptive; for *Endeavour* was now heading into one of the most treacherous seaways on Earth. The north-east coast of Australia is flanked by what is arguably the greatest natural wonder of the world – a 1,250-mile (2,000-km) chain of coral reefs, their ocean face rising sheer from the seabed, their landward face a maze of islands, rocks and ever-shifting sandbars. As Cook edged into these hazardous waters he had a leadsman constantly taking soundings and a pinnace constantly reconnoitring ahead. But on the night of 11 June, while searching for somewhere to anchor, *Endeavour* received what to many ships would have been a death blow.

'One moment,' Cook writes, 'we had 17 fathom, but before the man at the lead could heave another cast, the ship struck and stuck fast. We had got upon the SE edge of a reef of coral.' Soon *Endeavour* was being pounded so violently by the waves that her crew could hardly keep their feet. Looking over the side they saw that part of their keel had been ripped clean away and ship's timbers were being tossed about in the surf. 'No crew,' Cook tells us, 'ever behaved better. Every man had a sence of the danger we were in and exerted himself to the utmost.' They lightened the ship by throwing overboard ballast, guns and food. As the tide rose they managed to tow *Endeavour* off the reef, only to find that she instantly sprang so terrible a leak that the combined efforts of officers, scientists and seamen at the pumps couldn't stem the inrush of water. So they fothered her.

The manner this was done, writes Cook, *was thus: we mix oakum and wool together and chop it up small and stick it loosely by handfulls all over a sail and throw over it sheeps' dung or other filth* (*Endeavour* had sheep aboard.) *The sail thus prepared is hauld under the Ship's bottom by ropes, and if the place of the leak is uncertain it must be hauld from one part of her bottom to another untill the place is found where it takes effect; while the sail is under the Ship the oakum etc. is washed off and carried along with the water into the leaks and in part stops up the hole. Mr Munkhouse, one of my midshipmen, was once in a Merchant ship which sprang a leak and made 48 inches water per hour, but by this means was brought home from Virginia to London; to him I gave the direction of this operation, and he exicuted it very much to my satisfaction.*

The fothering kept the water at bay long enough to enable *Endeavour* to limp to the shore. When they beached her, they discovered what had been their salvation. A great wedge of coral, sheered off from the reef, had jammed tight in the hole in her hull. But for this she would have foundered instantly, and those of her crew to survive would have been marooned beyond hope of rescue on an unknown shore. It was this incident which made Cook insist, on subsequent expeditions, that he was given not one ship but two.

Repairs took a couple of months – their false keel had been badly damaged and five of their main-planks 'sheared through as though by an instrument' – and in this time Cook was able to do a fair amount of exploring and to make contact with the Aborigines.

The land, he wrote, *is well diversified with Hills and Plains. The soil of the Hills is dry and stoney, yet it produceth thin grass and a little wood. The soil of the Plains is sandy and friable, and produceth long grasses and shrubs etc. It is indifferently well watered with many small Brooks but no great Rivers. The Climate is warm and fine and the air wholsom.* His description of the Aborigines is even more discerning – *They are an inoffensive race, in no way inclined to cruelty. They have no fix'd habitation, but move from place to place. They may appear to some to be wretched; but in reality they are happier than we Europeans. For they live in Tranquillity. The Earth and the Sea furnish them with all things necessary.*

What a difference there is between the British view of Australia and the Dutch view! This is partly explained by the fact that the British landed in a more fertile part of the continent. But it is also true that beauty lies in the eye of the beholder – the Dutch were looking for quick trading profits, found none and were damning; the British were looking for bases and scientific information, found both and were enthusiastic.

By early August *Endeavour* had been repaired and reprovisioned and was again heading north. However, among the inshore shoals her progress was snail-like. Cook himself climbed to the masthead and saw 'that (they) were surrounded on every side with such dangers that (he) was quite at a loss which way to steer'. So not surprisingly when a rare gap appeared in the Reef, he edged out into the open sea. His first reaction was relief to have once again deep water under his keel; but he soon found that he had jumped out of the frying pan into the fire.

Cook realized that the seaward edge of the Barrier Reef was a place of extreme danger, yet he was obliged to stay close to it in order to keep within sight of the new-found coast which he was following. For a few days all was well; but on 16 August his ship's company missed death by no more than the width of a single wave:

Soon we saw breakers between us and the land extending to the Southward farther than we could see, and a little later we saw the Reef also extend away to the Northward; we therefore hauld close upon a wind which was at ESE. We had hardly trimmed our sails before the wind came E by N, which was right upon the Reef and made our clearing of it doubtfull. (There follows a highly technical account of their efforts to tack out of trouble.) *But before long it fell quite calm. We sounded both now and several times in the night, but had no ground with 140 fathoms of line. A little after 4 o'clock the roaring of the surf was plainly heard* (a couple of years earlier Bougainville had heard this same roaring, had recognized it as 'the voice of God and turned obediently back') *and at daybreak the vast foaming breakers were too plainly to be seen not a mile from us, toward which we found the Ship was carried by the waves surprisingly fast. We had at this time not an air of wind, and the depth of water was unfathomable so there was not a possibility of Anchoring. In this distressed situation we had nothing but Providence and the small Assistance of our boats to trust to. The Yawl and the Longboat were hoisted out and sent ahead to tow, which together with the help of sweeps abaft got the ship's head round to the northward which seemed to be the only way to keep her off the reef or at least delay her. Before this was effected it was six o'clock and we were not above eighty yards from the breakers, the same sea that washed the sides of the ship rising in a breaker prodigiously high the very next time it did rise, so that between us and distruction was only a dismal valley the breadth of one wave; and even now no ground could be felt with 120 fathoms. We had hardly any hopes of saving the Ship and full as little our lives, yet in this truly terrible situation not one man ceased to do his utmost and that with as much calmness as if no danger had been near. All the dangers we had escaped so far were little in comparison of being thrown upon this Reef, where the Ship must be dashed to pieces in a Moment. A Reef such as is here spoke of is scarcely known in Europe; it is a wall of Coral Rock rising almost perpendicular out of the unfathomable Ocean, and the waves meeting with so sudden a resistance make a most terrible surf breaking great mountains high, especially as in our case where the trade wind blows directly upon it. At this critical juncture when all our endeavours seem'd too little, a small air of wind sprung up, but so small that at any other time we should not have observed it, and with this and the assistance of our boats the Ship began to move off the Reef in a slanting direction; but in less than 10 Minutes we had as flat a Calm as ever. . . Then a small opening was seen in the Reef.* (This was their salvation; with the boats towing and helped by a favourable current, *Endeavour* was swept through the opening) *till we were quite within the Reef where we anchored in 19 fathom, a corally and shelly bottom, happy once more to incounter those shoals which but a few days ago our wishes were crowned by getting clear of.*

Cook had learned his lesson. For the rest of his voyage along the eastern seaboard of Australia he hugged the coast, preferring the obvious dangers of the inshore shallows to the less obvious but greater dangers of the open sea. At the end of August he rounded the most northerly point of the continent, Cape York Peninsula, and deduced from the steady wind and swell from the west that he was at the approaches to another great ocean, the Indian, 'which gave me no small satisfaction, not only because the danger and fatigues of the voyage were drawing to an end, but by being able to prove that New Holland and New Guinea are 2 separate Lands or Islands, which until this day hath been a doubtful point with geographers'.

The rest of his voyage was anti-climax. And tragedy.

On 10 October 1770 *Endeavour* dropped anchor off Batavia, her first civilized port-of-call since leaving Rio nearly two years previously. Her crew were in good health and high spirits, glad to be on their way home. Yet before the end of the year a third of them were dead. They had survived the perils of scurvy in the Pacific only to fall victim to diseases for which Cook had no panacea – the fever, dysentery and malaria of the Dutch East Indies – a sad finale to an otherwise happy and successful expedition.

The voyage of the *Endeavour* was a milestone in the exploration of the Pacific. As a cartographer Cook defined the coast of New Zealand and proved the islands were not part of a continent. He discovered and defined the eastern limits of Australia – and hence the western limits of the Pacific Ocean. And he confirmed the existence of a seaway between Australia and New Guinea. As an ethnographer he was the first person to spend long enough among the Polynesians to bring back a well-informed account of them. As a physician he was the first person to prove that scurvy could be eradicated in long-distance voyaging. And this was by no means the end of his achievements; for he was to lead two other expeditions into the Pacific, both at least as important as the voyage of the *Endeavour*.

He had been back in England less than a year when he was given command of two ships, the *Resolution* and the *Adventure*, and handed simple-sounding but impossible orders 'to discover and take possession of convenient stations in the Great South Land'.

This myth of a South Land was based on the popular and long-lived fallacy that there had to be a land mass in the southern hemisphere to counterbalance the land mass of Eurasia in the north. While commanding the *Endeavour* Cook had proved that no such land mass existed in the vicinity of New Zealand. There were, however, plenty of other places where it was confidently assumed the continent would be found, and it was to take possession of this mythical land mass that the *Resolution* and *Adventure* sailed from Plymouth on 13 July 1772.

Cook's second voyage is regarded by many practical seamen as the greatest ever made – myself, I would place it second only to Magellan's. It was a long voyage, both in the time it took (1,114 days) and the distance it covered (roughly 68,000 miles). It was a difficult and hazardous voyage because much of it took place in the high latitudes of the Southern Ocean, a seaway of huge waves, frenetic winds and swirling banks of mist; at the approaches to Antarctica, the sea is choked by icebergs and ice-floes which it is almost certain death to brush against. And it was an important voyage because it added enormously to our knowledge of the world.

Between 1772 and 1775 Cook made what have been described by Beaglehole as 'three great summer ice-edge cruises' – wintering in between in the islands of the Pacific – three forays deep into the Southern Ocean in search of the elusive continent. On his first cruise he proved that a continent didn't exist in the Indian Ocean; on his second that it didn't exist in the Pacific; and on his third that it didn't exist in the Atlantic. The most hazardous of these cruises – in which Cook twice crossed the Antarctic Circle, reaching farther south than any man at that time – was the voyage into the Pacific.

In November 1773, after being parted from her consort by a violent storm, *Resolution* headed south from New Zealand towards what we now know as the Ross Sea. The weather was appalling and each day grew worse – high winds, heavy seas, fog and, before long, ice. It was the ice which caused Cook most anxiety. Soon it became the common denominator of his tribulations, mentioned virtually every day in his Diary:

> *THURSDAY 16 DECEMBER. Weather dark, gloomy and very cold; our sails and rigging hung with ice and icicles. . . SATURDAY 18 DECEMBER. A strong gale attended with a thick fog sleet and rain which constitutes the worst of weather; our Rigging so loaded with ice that we could scarce get our top-sails down to double reef. . . FRIDAY 24 DECEMBER. Wind northerly, a strong gale attended with a thick fogg, sleet and Snow, which froze to the Rigging as it fell and decorated the whole Ship with icicles. Our ropes were like wire, our sails like plates of metal, the sheaves froze fast in the blocks. I have never seen so much ice.*

Such conditions would be unpleasant for the crew of a twentieth-century freighter. How much more unpleasant they must have been for the crew of the *Resolution* who in all weather had to be continually aloft working their ship. Alan Villiers, himself a practical seaman, paints a vivid picture of conditions just about as terrible as seamen have ever had to face:

Ships like the 'Resolution' and 'Adventure', as square-rigged ships, could be sailed only from their exposed deck and rigging. Their sails were planes, set and trimmed to catch the wind and convert its force to forward speed; and to set them, reef them and 'hand' them it was essential for men to go aloft often in large numbers. The rigging froze, with snow and sleet coagulated into its fibres. The sails froze into stiffened statues touched to marble. It was as easy to 'hand' them as to furl pressed steel. To touch the rigging was to risk frostburn which seared like flame; and to fight the iron-hard sails aloft meant bloodied hands, minced fingers and nails torn out by the roots.

Even more dangerous than the ice in the rigging was the ice in the sea: sometimes tabular icebergs, sometimes pack ice. Cook makes light of the icebergs: 'Great as the dangers from them are, they are now become so familiar to us that our apprehensions are never of long duration, and are compencated by the Curious and Romantick Views these ice-islands frequently exhibit.' It is nonetheless true that a collision with a tabular berg would almost certainly have been fatal, and the fact that *Resolution* was able to sail among them month after month without being damaged is a tribute to the fine seamanship of both her crew and her commander. Equally dangerous was the pack ice. Cook's Diary is full of descriptions of it, perhaps the most evocative being that of 30 January 1774, the day he achieved his farthest south:

At 4 o'clock the Fogg having somewhat lifted we perceived the Clouds over the Horizon in the South to be of an unusual brightness, which we knew denounced our approach to field (or pack) *ice. Soon it was seen from the Topmast-head, and by 8 o'clock we were close to the edge of it. It extended east and west far beyond our sight, while the southern half of the horizon was illuminated by rays of light reflected from the Ice to a considerable height. Ninty-seven ice-hills were seen within this field, many of them very large and looking like a ridge of Mountains rising one above another till they were lost in the Clouds. The outer edge of this immense field was composed of broken ice, so packed together that it was not possible for any thing to enter it: this was about a mile broad; and inside was solid ice in one continual compact body. Such mountains of Ice as these were never seen in the Greenland Seas.* (And) *it is my opinion that the Ice extends quite to the Pole, or perhaps joins to some land to which it has been fix'd since the creation. Even I who had Ambition not only to go farther than any one had done before but as far as it was possible for man to go, was not sorry at meeting this interruption, since it shortened the hardships of our Navigation. Seeing therefore that we could not proceed one Inch to the South, no other reason need be assigned to my Standing back to the North, being at this time in Latitude 71° 10′ S, Longitude 106° 54′ W.*

Cook continued his cruise at lower latitudes, reaching Cape Horn towards the end of the year, having proved beyond any possible doubt that no Great Southern Continent (apart from Australia) exists in the Pacific. By midsummer 1775 he was back in England.

In this second expedition it could be said that Cook failed to carry out his orders. He took possession of no 'convenient stations in the South Land'; indeed in three years' voyaging about the only fragment of *terra incognita* he sighted, let alone took possession of, was the ice-bound island of South Georgia. Yet his expedition was certainly not a failure. Its discoveries and conclusions were almost entirely negative, but it is doubtful if any other single voyage ever added so much to our knowledge of the world. For in his three-year circumnavigation of the Antarctic Cook demolished once and for all the theory that there had to be a great land mass in the southern hemisphere to

Top Anchorage at Nootka Sound (Vancouver Island), a drawing by John Webber; *above* Sandwich Sound, now Prince William Sound, Alaska, a drawing by John Webber.

counterbalance Eurasia. In terms of the exploration of the Pacific, he removed from the southern half of the ocean a whole plethora of 'Lands of Brazil wood, Elephants and Gold', and put in their place an uncluttered expanse of sea bordered by an impenetrable field of ice.

He replaced myth with reality.

Within six months of his return to England Cook was preparing once again to put to sea, this time in search of another chimera – the navigable seaway which, it was believed, linked the Pacific with the Atlantic via the northern shores of Canada. Much to his satisfaction he was given his old ship, *Resolution*, although this satisfaction soon gave way to a very justifiable anger when it became obvious during the course of the voyage that due to chicanery in the dockyard, *Resolution*'s contractors had lined their pockets more effectively than the ship's seams. He was also given another Whitby-built collier, the *Diligence*, renamed *Discovery*. He left Plymouth on 12 July 1776, armed with an Eskimo dictionary and a guarantee that although Great Britain was at war with France, Spain and the newly formed United States of America, he and his crews would be immune from interference or capture – an unprecedented exemption, which shows the high esteem in which Cook's work was regarded throughout the world.

Cook's third expedition was his longest, over four years at sea; it was also his most extensive, taking him to all five continents and all five oceans. The highlights of the first eighteen months of the expedition were his survey of Kerguélen (in the Indian Ocean at the approaches to Antarctica), his fifth visit to New Zealand, his stay in Tonga, and his return of the Tahitian Omai to his homeland. All this formed an idyllic prelude to the sterner events to come, when, in January 1778, his ships stood into the North Pacific, searching once again for coasts and seaways no man from Europe had yet set eyes on.

The North Pacific, and especially the north-east Pacific, was still basically unexplored, and it wasn't long before Cook made a major discovery. On 18 January he sighted the widely scattered archipelago of Hawaii. This was almost certainly a new discovery, for the claim that the islands were visited by Spanish treasure galleons on passage between Manila and Acapulco is now generally regarded as non-proven. The islands Cook came to first (Oahu, Kauai, Niihau, Kaula and Lehua) had few harbours. Their coastlines consisted almost entirely of sheer cliffs pounded by majestic waves. And how majestic the waves were – the great rollers of the North Pacific which today make Hawaii the Mecca of surfers throughout the world. Cook was hard-pressed to find anywhere to land, and when he did at last discover an anchorage it was little more than an exposed beach. Visits ashore had therefore to be brief. What little contact there was with the islanders, however, augured well. The Hawaiians seemed to think that Cook was a god. Everywhere he went they prostrated themselves and showered him with gifts. Soon a brisk and amicable trade was in progress – 'and no people,' wrote Cook, 'could trade with more honesty than these people . . . they even abandoned their efforts to steal'. There was no hint, during this first visit, of the tragedy to come, and Cook only left the islands because his ships dragged their anchors and were in danger of being driven ashore. Safety lay in the open sea; once this had been gained *Resolution* and *Discovery* set course for Drake's 'New Albion'.

From this moment Cook was venturing into a segment of the Pacific that was virtually unknown.

Apart from Drake and the Spaniards Perez and Hecate, almost the only Europeans who had sighted the north-east coast of America were the Russians. In their voyages of 1728 and 1741 Bering and Chirikov had found the great arc of the Aleutian Islands; they had found that Asia extended much farther to the east than had been generally supposed, and they had found the strait that today bears Bering's name. Their discoveries, however, had hardly touched the American side of this strait – which was where Cook's orders were to take him.

Cook sighted the coast of America on 7 March 1778, his landfall being not far from the mouth of the Alsea River in Oregon. For several weeks, bludgeoned by near-continuous gales, he followed the shoreline north, searching in vain for an anchorage. Because of bad weather he missed the entrance to the great strait which reaches inland to present-day Vancouver and Seattle. But on 29 March he sighted and entered Nootka Sound on the seaward shore of Vancouver Island.

> *The land,* he wrote, *consists of high hills and deep vallies, for the most part cloathed with large timber, such as Spruce fir and white Cedar. The more inland mountains were covered with Snow, and when ever it rained with us Snow fell on the Neighbouring hills; the Clemate is, however, infinitely milder than on the East coast of America under the same latitude.*

No sooner had his ships dropped anchor than they were surrounded by a great number of canoes, manned by a people who

> *shewed not the least mark of fear or distrust. We had at one time 32 Canoes about us, and a group of ten or a dozen remained alongside the Resolution most of the night. They seemed to be an inoffensive people, shewed great readiness to part with any thing they had and took whatever was offered them in exchange, but were more desireous of iron than any thing else, the use of which they knew well.*

Cook spent nearly a month in Nootka Sound, repairing his ships and getting to know the Indians. The *Resolution* in particular was in need of repair, 'very leaky in her upper works . . . her Foremast rotton, her Standing rigging much decayed . . . her Mizenmast so rotton that it dropped of(f) while in the Slings'. It was fortunate for Cook that these defects came to light while he was in a safe anchorage and surrounded by an abundance of fine-quality timber. Webber's painting evokes what must have been a commonplace scene – the ships surrounded by friendly canoes while the crew cut timber ashore.

Cook's relations with the people of Nootka Sound started well and soon he and his crew were wandering unarmed through their villages. He describes them as 'swarthy – though this procedes partly from smoke, dirt and paint – of small stature and without the least pretentions of being call'd beauties, their faces rather broad and flat with high Cheek bones . . . In disposition courteous and good natured, but quick in resenting what they looke upon as an injury.' It soon became apparent that they were keen traders and expert thieves, watering down the oil that they sold to the seamen and 'getting a greater variety of things from us than any other people we had visited'. They lived in large, rambling, wooden and incredibly dirty buildings, surrounded by gutted and drying fish, and the pelts of bear, fox, wolf, deer, sea-otter and seal. It was clear they were expert hunters and fishermen. They were also expert at making the most elaborate and fantastic masks; these often resembled the head of an animal or bird, and were used during the ritual dances and ceremonies which appeared to be part of the tribe's daily life. Cook himself may have had reservations about the attractions of the Indian women, but his crew had no such doubts – witness the Diary of the *Discovery*'s surgeon David Samwell:

> *Hitherto we had seen none of their young Women tho' we had often given the men to understand how agreeable their Company would be to us . . . in consequence of which they brought two or three Girls to the Ships. Tho' some of them had no bad faces, yet as they were exceedingly dirty their Persons at*

first sight were not very inviting. However, our young Gentlemen were not to be discouraged by such an obstacle which they found was to be removed with Soap and warm water; and this they called the Ceremony of Purification and were themselves the Officiators at it. . . This Ceremony appeared very strange to the Girls, who in order to render themselves agreeable to us had taken particular pains to daub their Hair and faces with red oaker which we took as much pains to wash off. Such are the different Ideas formed by different Nations of Beauty.

Samwell goes on to tell us that the price for a night aboard was usually 'one Pewter plate well scoured. Thus our young Gentry found means to disburthen themselves of their kitchen furniture, so that many of us after leaving this Harbour were unable to muster a plate to eat our Salt beef from.'

It was all very different from the sun-drenched islands of the mid-Pacific. In North America the girls were shy rather than provocative, the land rugged rather than gentle, the climate harsh rather than benign, the people tough rather than attractive, and their lifestyle chaotic and filthy rather than well ordered and scrupulously clean. Yet the Indians of Nootka Sound had about them a disorganized confidence and vitality; during the whole of Cook's visit not a shot had to be fired in anger, and when, on 26 April *Resolution* and *Discovery* stood seaward, they were accompanied by 'very many of our friends the Indians . . . who importuned us much to return'.

The story of the next seven months, as Cook edged his way north along the coast of present-day British Columbia and Alaska, is one of careful surveying rather than spectacular discovery. He failed of course to find the entrance to the mythical strait which, it had been hoped, would provide a link with the Atlantic. He did, however, delineate for the first time a part of the world that was to all intents and purposes unknown. It is true that the Spaniards had on one occasion voyaged as far north as the 54th parallel (Hecate Strait), and that the Russians had several times voyaged this far south (Unalaska Island). Spanish and Russian maps, however, were either non-existent or, at best, sketchy; Cook was the first person to bring back an accurate picture of this vast and bleakly beautiful shore.

And how vast the coast of Alaska turned out to be! It is not generally appreciated that the shore of this single state extends for more than 3,500 miles (roughly the width of the Atlantic). It is a shore broken in the south by a multitude of fjords and offshore islands, and backed in the north by a hinterland of almost lunar desolation. Along much of its length it is pounded by heavy seas, lashed by near-continuous rain and shrouded in banks of swirling fog. In the far north, in the Arctic Ocean, there is the added hazard of ice. Cook needed all his skill – and all his patience – to survey each indentation thoroughly enough to be sure that it wasn't the entrance to the sought-for strait. Prince William Sound and Cook Inlet looked promising but turned out to be dead-ends. Then progress was barred by the Alaska Peninsula, the great half-sunken range of the Aleutians which reaches south-eastward, like a skeletal arm, into the Pacific. For week after week *Resolution* and *Discovery* followed a seemingly endless line of barren cliffs guarded by reefs of submerged rock. The inland mountains were covered in snow, which reached down in places almost to the water's edge. It was difficult to distinguish snowfield from cloudbank, and island from mainland. 'A thick fog and a foul wind,' wrote Clerke (Cook's second-in-command) mildly, 'are disagreeable intruders to people engaged in tracing a Coast'. It is an indication of the difficulties Cook faced that in order to fix the position of one particularly obscure headland, he took no fewer than 43 bearings on it. However, on midsummer day they at last rounded the tip of the peninsula and stood into the more open waters of the Bering Sea.

For six weeks Cook pursued a zigzag course to the north, landing several times on the shore of both America and Asia. He also landed on some of the islands – St Matthew, St Lawrence and Sledge – which lie in clusters at the approaches to the Bering Strait. Although the land everywhere was barren, the sea was alive with fish, whales and walrus; and it was from the sea that the Aleuts and their northerly neighbours drew sustenance and wealth. They were, we are told, 'a sturdy independent people who always dealt fair and square with us . . . and who seemed to be of an innate good Disposition'. The only time they looked like opposing a landing, Cook 'walked up to them alone without a single thing in my hand', which altogether disarmed them. David Samwell describes a visit to one of their villages:

> *On leaving the shore and ascending a very steep Hill for about a mile and a half, we came in sight of the Indian Town lying in a Valley close to the side of a deep Bay. The great Quantity of fish hanging up to dry made it appear like a Glovers Yard; these and a few People moving about were the only Signs we had of the Place being inhabited; for the Houses were not to be seen till we came close upon them, and then we were much surprised at finding small Hillocks of earth and dirt scattered about here and there with a hole in the top of them through which we descended down a Ladder made of a thick piece of wood with steps cut in it, into a dark and dirty Cave seemingly under ground, where our Noses were saluted with a Stink of putrid fish which were scattered about the House. We were welcomed into these murky Caves by the Master of the House and his Wife and other Females sitting together in one part of the Hut. Having been used to many strange Scenes since we left England, we spent no time staring about us with vacant astonishment, but immediately made love to the handsomest woman in Company, who in order to make us welcome refused us no Favour she could grant, tho' her Husband or Father stood by. Having thus paid proper attention to the Women, we had time to look about us and admire the Structure and furniture of one of these strange Habitations.*

On the previous page of his Diary Samwell had boasted that the favours of many young women had been purchased 'with a leaf or two of tobacco'. On the following page he describes at length 'a very beautiful young Woman who complyed with all our wishes in having her picture drawn'. On almost every other page of his Diary there is some reference to his amours with the local 'nymphs'. It *could* of course all be true; but one gets the feeling that the good doctor may have been too greatly preoccupied with his macho-image for it to be wholly credible.

On 8 August *Resolution* and *Discovery* passed through the narrowest part of the Bering Strait, sighting to starboard the most westerly tip of America (Cape Prince of Wales), and to port the most easterly tip of Asia (the offshore island of Ratmanova). For a week the ships headed north-east, parallel to the coast of Alaska, still searching for the elusive passage; but on 17 August a familiar brightness appeared above the northern horizon. It was the iceblink, and Cook soon found his way blocked by a vast, solid and impenetrable field of pack ice. It was the end of his hopes – which had never been all that sanguine – of finding a navigable seaway between the Pacific and the Atlantic.

For several days his ships skirted the ice-field. Its seaward edge was no more than 10 or 12 feet high; but as it extended to the north it became gradually higher and increasingly rugged. There was no flaw in its defences, no hope of the ships making even the slightest penetration. Cook spent several days reconnoitring the ice, from the point where it abutted the coast of America to the point where it abutted the coast of Asia. He soon realized that he had no more hope of sailing through it than of sailing through the cliffs of Dover. He therefore did the only possible thing: hauled away to the south and explored the coast on either side of the Bering Strait. Then, much to the relief of his ships' companies, he headed for Hawaii, intending to winter among the islands before embarking on another assault on the ice in the spring.

It was not to be. Cook was never to see the ice-fields again; for on his second visit to Hawaii things went tragically wrong.

By the time he dropped anchor that winter in Kealakekue Bay, Cook had been at sea almost continuously for ten years. He was physically and mentally exhausted, and the strain was beginning to show in little acts of impatience and little errors of judgement; and the wonder is not that Cook now made the occasional mistake but that up to this moment he had made virtually no mistakes at all.

Once again the people of Hawaii welcomed him as the god-from-another-world, flinging themselves at his feet and showering him with gifts. It was only gradually they came to realize that he too was mortal – and vulnerable. Perhaps not surprisingly it was a theft that sparked off the tragedy. The islanders stole a pinnace. Cook decided on the well-tried countermeasure of taking a local chief as hostage and holding him until the pinnace was returned. But this time it didn't work. As the marines attempted to seize one chief, another was accidentally shot and killed. The islanders, in fury, armed themselves, and Cook and a handful of men found themselves cut off from their boats on a hostile shore. They were hacked to death.

We will never know exactly what happened in those last terrible moments. But it would seem that Cook, for a second, turned his back on his attackers to shout to his men in the approaching boats to hold their fire. It was a quixotic gesture that cost him his life. Before he could turn again, he was stabbed in the back of the neck. He fell face down in the water.

> *On seeing him fall*, Samwell tells us, *the Indians rushed forward and held him under the water; one man sat on his shoulders and beat his head with a stone, while others struck him with Clubs and Stones; they then hauled him up on the rocks where they stuck him with their Daggers and dashed his head against the rocks, taking a Savage pleasure in using every barbarity to the dead body.*

It seems likely that his remains were then carried inland, his skull beaten to pieces, his body burned, and his bones given to the priests. An ironic death for a gentle and humane man who cared deeply for the people of the ocean which he delineated with such meticulous skill.

It would be almost impossible to overstate the contribution that Cook made to the exploration of the Pacific. By his conquest of scurvy he enabled ships to traverse vast reaches of the ocean out of sight of land without reprovisioning. By his skill in the sciences of navigation and surveying he was able to make a precise record of the tracks he followed and the coastlines he discovered. By his humane approach to indigenous peoples he proved that exploration *could* be achieved without bloodshed. In the words of Charles Darwin, 'he added a hemisphere to the civilized world'.

And Darwin knew what he was talking about; for he was himself a major figure in the story of the Pacific. Indeed his work was arguably equal in importance to that of Cook, albeit in a very different field. His forte was the study not of coastlines but of flora and fauna, including that most complex of fauna, man.

Charles Darwin was only 23 when, in 1831, he was appointed naturalist to HMS *Beagle*, a 10-gun brig about to embark on a voyage of surveying around the world. He was by no means a brilliant young man; indeed at Cambridge he had managed to scrape through his exams with no more than a modest pass. He was, however, keen on natural history, and he had a pleasant personality and seems to have had the happy knack of getting on with everybody he met. 'He was,' wrote his tutor John Henslow,

Charles Darwin (1809-62), whose research work in South America and the Pacific Islands provided him with material on which to base *On the Origin of Species by Means of Natural Selection*, was appointed naturalist to HMS *Beagle*, here seen in the Straits of Magellan, from a painting by R. T. Pritchett.

'altogether free from vanity or petty feeling. I never saw a man who thought so little about himself.' Without doubt it was his personality rather than his qualifications which commended him to Robert FitzRoy, the captain of the *Beagle*, and the two men at once struck up a firm if unlikely friendship, unlikely because they were totally dissimilar. FitzRoy was an aristocratic Tory, a descendant (albeit an illegitimate one) of Charles II; he was a brilliant if unstable man who enjoyed authority; failure was not a word in his vocabulary; he was what we would call today a high-flyer. Darwin was a middle-class Whig, brought up to respect those middle-class gods of frugality, hard work and morality, to which virtues he added his passion for natural history and his engaging character; he was a likeable and well-balanced young man, but, it must have seemed, a bit of a plodder. If people had been asked that winter, as the *Beagle* headed west into the Atlantic, which of the pair was destined for fame, nine out of ten would almost cetainly have put their money on FitzRoy. Only students of Aesop who knew the fable of the tortoise and the hare might have risked a bet on Darwin.

The voyage across the Atlantic was, for Darwin, a combination of purgatory and paradise. Purgatory because he was plagued by almost continuous seasickness; paradise because of the great variety of natural phenomena he was able to observe. And what an observer he was! Nothing escaped him. The birds, the fish, the natives, the plants, the rocks, even the dust; all were studied in detail and meticulously recorded. The cabin that he shared with FitzRoy became, with each passing week, more and more like the showcase of a museum. No wonder there were times when the two men became heartily sick of one another, although their quarrels were ephemeral and not, as yet, serious.

By April 1832 *Beagle* was anchored off Rio de Janeiro, and while FitzRoy prepared to survey the adjacent coast, Darwin was put ashore and left to his own devices for a couple of months. And it was now, among the teeming life of the Brazilian forests, that his collecting became augmented by conjecturing; and conjecturing of a kind that FitzRoy didn't approve of . . . FitzRoy was a highly intelligent, deeply religious man, and like nearly all such men of his day he believed implicitly in the Bible. The Creation, the Garden of Eden and the Ark were, to him, facts beyond dispute. Darwin was also a deeply religious man – indeed if he hadn't become a naturalist he would almost certainly have entered the Church – but he now found that the more closely he observed the life of the rain forest, the less he was able to accept the Biblical version of the Creation. For there seemed to be evidence that the creatures of the rain forest were ever-changing, that different species were constantly developing different characteristics in order to survive. Into his collecting jars went the insect that camouflaged itself to look like a dead twig, the moth that disguised itself to look like a scorpion, and the beetle that radiated the colours of a poisonous fruit to save itself from being eaten by birds.He found the skeletons of creatures long extinct: the giant sloth and armadillo, and the guanaco, huge as a camel. But *why* had these creatures become extinct? Their skeletons, it seemed to Darwin, suggested that the various species were continually developing, and that animals which failed to adjust died out. If this was indeed the case, then the present-day fauna must be very different from the fauna that God had created; and it followed from this that Creation, far from taking place in a single week, was a long and continuous process.

All this to FitzRoy was heresy. We can picture the two of them arguing the point in their tiny overcrowded cabin, FitzRoy turning again and again to his Bible and Darwin to his multitudinous specimens. However, at this early stage of the voyage Darwin was not prepared to argue his case too forcibly; he was willing to admit that his new ideas could be wrong. Things were different when they came to the Pacific. For here Darwin was to find more evidence to substantiate his theories: theories which were about to revolutionize man's conception of the nature of life on Earth.

The *Beagle* had a hard time in the Straits of Magellan, and it was July 1834 before she dropped anchor off Valparaiso – the Valley of Paradise – a delightful town in a delightful setting, its white flat-topped houses reaching up towards the tremendous backdrop of the Andes. Darwin loved the Andes: the invigorating air, the physical challenge and the feeling of isolation from the rest of the world. He climbed them again and again. On one of his climbs, at 7,000 feet (2,130 metres), he came across a forest of petrified pine-trees embedded in deposits of marine rock. On another climb, at 12,000 feet (3,650 metres), he came across a stratum of fossilized seashells. The question was, how did these marine rocks and seashells arrive in the upper reaches of the Andes? For FitzRoy this was how God had created the mountains, and that was explanation enough. But it wasn't enough for Darwin, who now put forward a more scientific hypothesis. The Andes, he suggested, must have been lifted out of the sea, first as a series of islands which soon became covered in woodland (like those off the south-west coast of Chile), then as a continuous chain of mountains whose summits were stripped bare of vegetation by the cold. All this, he suggested, could have been brought about by earthquakes. And early in 1835, as though to prove his point, Chile suffered one of the most devastating earth tremors of modern times.

In the early hours of 20 February, huge formations of seabirds were seen flying inland; dogs in the coastal settlements began to take to the hills, and later that morning shock waves were felt throughout central Chile. The first shock waves were little more than a trembling, but they quickly built up to a terrifying crescendo. The ground heaved and split open. Fissures reeking with the stench of sulphur zigzagged through woodland, field and city. The sea drained out of the harbours, then, with an appalling roar, swept back in a succession of tidal waves – great moving hills of water. Ships were tossed ashore like flotsam. Whole houses were picked up, carried far inland, then sucked out to sea to disappear in a series of whirlpools. The town of Concepcion was demolished in six seconds. When, a couple of days later, FitzRoy and Darwin rode through it, not one building was standing; instead of streets there were lines of rubble. No one has ever been able to estimate how many people were killed.

All this took place not much more than 150 years ago. Yet people at the time could think of only two possible reasons for what had happened. The educated and intelligent (like FitzRoy) believed the earthquake was caused by the wrath of God, a punishment for human wickedness. The uneducated and superstitious believed it was caused by an old Indian woman, a witch, who had been insulted by the people of Concepcion and had taken her revenge by climbing the Andes and plugging up the vents of the volcanoes.

Darwin had other ideas about what caused the earthquake: 'We can scarcely avoid the conclusion,' he wrote, 'that a vast lake of melted matter is spread out beneath a mere crust of solid land. . . Nothing, not even the wind, is so unstable as the crust of the earth.' At the time he was too shaken by the devastation and the suffering to argue his point. But in retrospect, the more he came to think about the disaster the more convinced he became that it had been caused neither by God nor by the devil, but by natural forces restructuring the face of the Earth. As evidence of this he could point to measurements, taken at the time, which showed that rocks along the Chilean shore line were several feet higher after the earth tremors than they had been before them. So not only was it true that the Andes *had* been raised from the sea; they were still being raised from it, foot by foot.

This may have had little direct bearing on Darwin's theory on the origin of species; but it had a very considerable indirect bearing. For it substantiated his growing belief that the world and the creatures in it were not – as was then almost universally assumed – exactly as God had created them, but were ever-changing, ever-evolving, and that far from having been created in the Biblical six days,the world was still in the throes of creation. Of this he found living proof in the Pacific islands.

Los Encantados (the Enchanted Isles), better known today as the Galapagos, lie astride the equator about 620 miles (1,000 km) to the west of Ecuador. At first sight the islands were more bizarre than enchanting: outcrops of black lava, covered with skeletal brushwood and overrun with hideous-looking lizards and antediluvian tortoises. No one, in the conventional sense, would describe them as beautiful; that symbol of the Pacific's grace and beauty, the coconut palm, was conspicuous by its absence. Yet they had about them an aura of primordial innocence which made them somehow different from any other place in the world. It was as though, from the moment of their creation, they had been trapped in a time-warp, set apart not only geographically but temporally from all extraneous influences.

FitzRoy spent more than a month in the Galapagos, and while *Beagle* moved methodically through the archipelago, charting and surveying, Darwin was left ashore on James Island (Isla San Salvador). It was here that he found himself face to face with the evidence on which he later based his great work *On the Origin of Species by means of Natural Selection, or the preservation of favoured races in the struggle for life*.

The fauna of the Galapagos was strange in appearance and stranger still in habit: cormorants which never flew, lizards with webbed feet which spent half their lives in the sea, and giant tortoises, stone deaf, ever waddling in slow procession between the cactus-belt where they ate and the freshwater-springs where they drank. These creatures and many others, Darwin realized, had developed idiosyncratic characteristics in order to survive in their idiosyncratic environment, characteristics which made them quite different from other members of their species living in other parts of the world. And he hadn't been long in the Galapagos before he made another important discovery: even within this one archipelago a species often differed from island to island. It was, for example, possible to tell just by looking at the shell of a tortoise which island it came from; on some islands the finches had developed long thin beaks to enable them to catch insects, while on other islands they had developed short strong beaks to enable them to crack nuts. All this substantiated the theory now taking shape in Darwin's mind, a theory nicely summarized by Alan Moorehead:

> *Darwin's thesis was simply this: the world as we know it was not just 'created' in a single instant of time; it had evolved from something infinitely primitive and it was changing still. There was a wonderful illustration of what had happened here in these* (Galapagos) *islands. Quite recently they had been pushed up out of the sea by a volcanic eruption such as they had seen in Chile, and at first there was no life at all upon them. Then birds arrived, and deposited seeds from their droppings and possibly from mud clinging to their feet. Other seeds which were resistant to sea-water floated across from the South American mainland. Floating logs may have transported the first lizards across. The tortoises may have come from the sea itself and have developed into land animals. And each species as it arrived adjusted itself to the food – the plant and animal life – that it found in the islands. Those that failed to do so, and those that could not defend themselves from other species, became extinct. That is what had happened to the huge creatures whose bones they had discovered in South America; they had been set upon by enemies and destroyed. All living things had been submitted to this process. Man himself had survived and triumphed because he was more skilful and aggressive than his competitors, even though in the beginning he was a very primitive creature, more primitive than the Fuegians, more primitive even than the apes.*

All this may seem eminently reasonable, and indeed undeniable, today, but in the mid-nineteenth century it was widely regarded as blasphemous nonsense. For didn't the Bible categorically state that 'God created man in his own image . . . and every living creature according to its kind, and saw that it was good'? We can imagine the arguments which raged that summer in FitzRoy's cabin as *Beagle* worked her way across the Pacific; and the farther the voyage progressed the more the attitudes of the captain and his naturalist hardened, FitzRoy ever withdrawing into a more rigid interpretation of the Bible, Darwin ever reaching out toward a more scientific explanation of the origin of life. The wonder is not that the two men sometimes exchanged angry words, but that, on a personal level, they remained friends. Their friendship, however, was not to extend beyond the quarters they shared in the *Beagle*; and when at last, after a five-year voyage, the little vessel returned to England, they went their separate ways and hardly saw one another again.

Darwin's subsequent life was, by and large, a story of success. He enjoyed a happy marriage, and had ten children with whom he maintained an excellent relationship. Though he received no official recognition for his work (the Church saw to that!), his theories gradually won universal recognition, and towards the end of his life were described by Thomas Henry Huxley as 'providing a foundation for the entire structure of modern biology'.

FitzRoy's subsequent life was, in contrast, a story of failure. His wife and daughter, to whom he was devoted, both died in tragic circumstances. He was appointed Governor of New Zealand; but his championship of Maori rights made him unpopular with the settlers, and he was recalled. In the Navy he failed to gain the promotion which

Top A nineteenth-century engraving of Chilean country costumes, after a sketch by M. Rugendas.
Above Return of the Dutch East India fleet to Amsterdam in 1599, painted by Andries van Eertvelt (1577–1652).

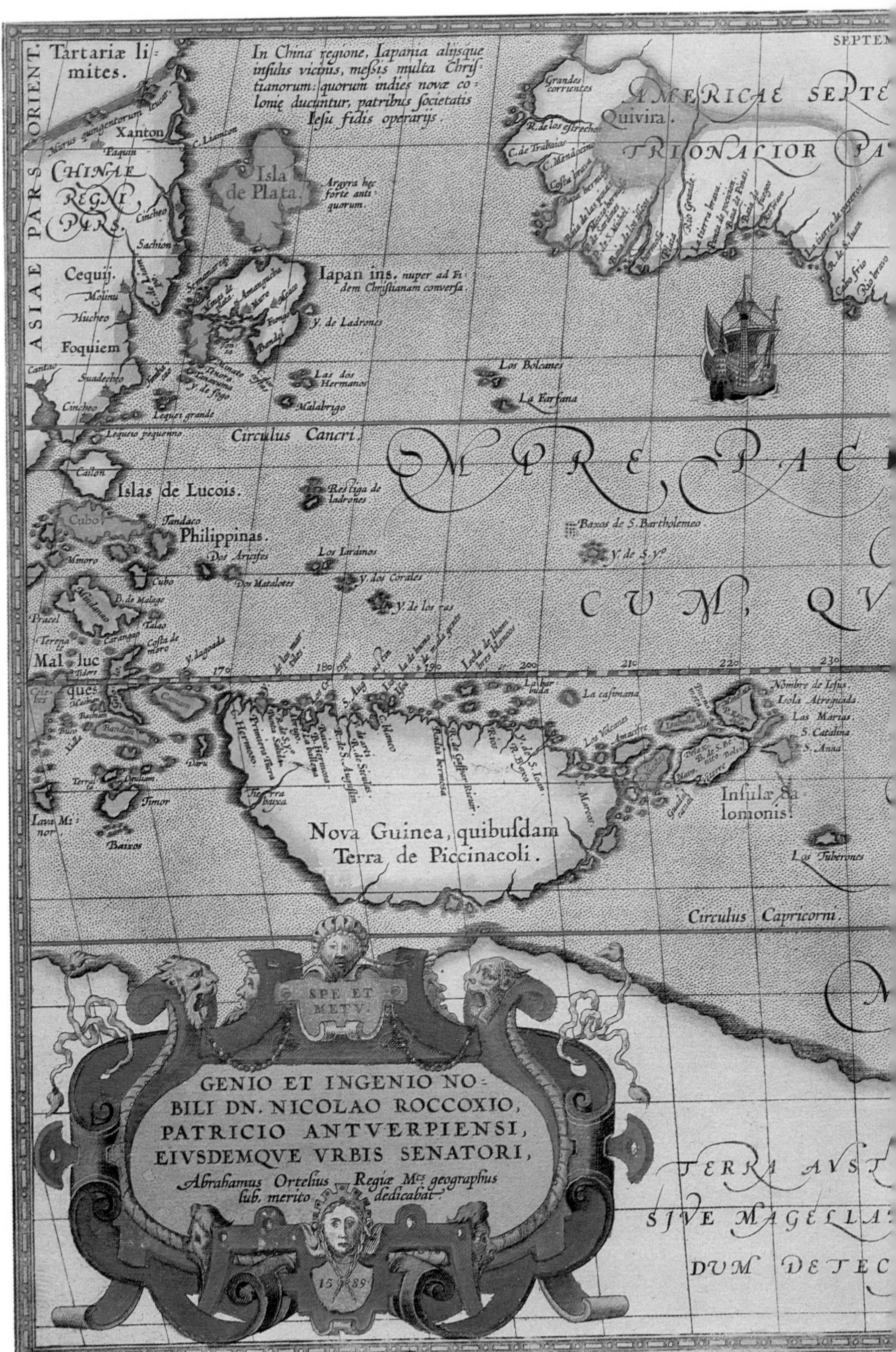

Map of the Pacific as it was known in 1589 by Abrahamus Ortelius (1527–98).

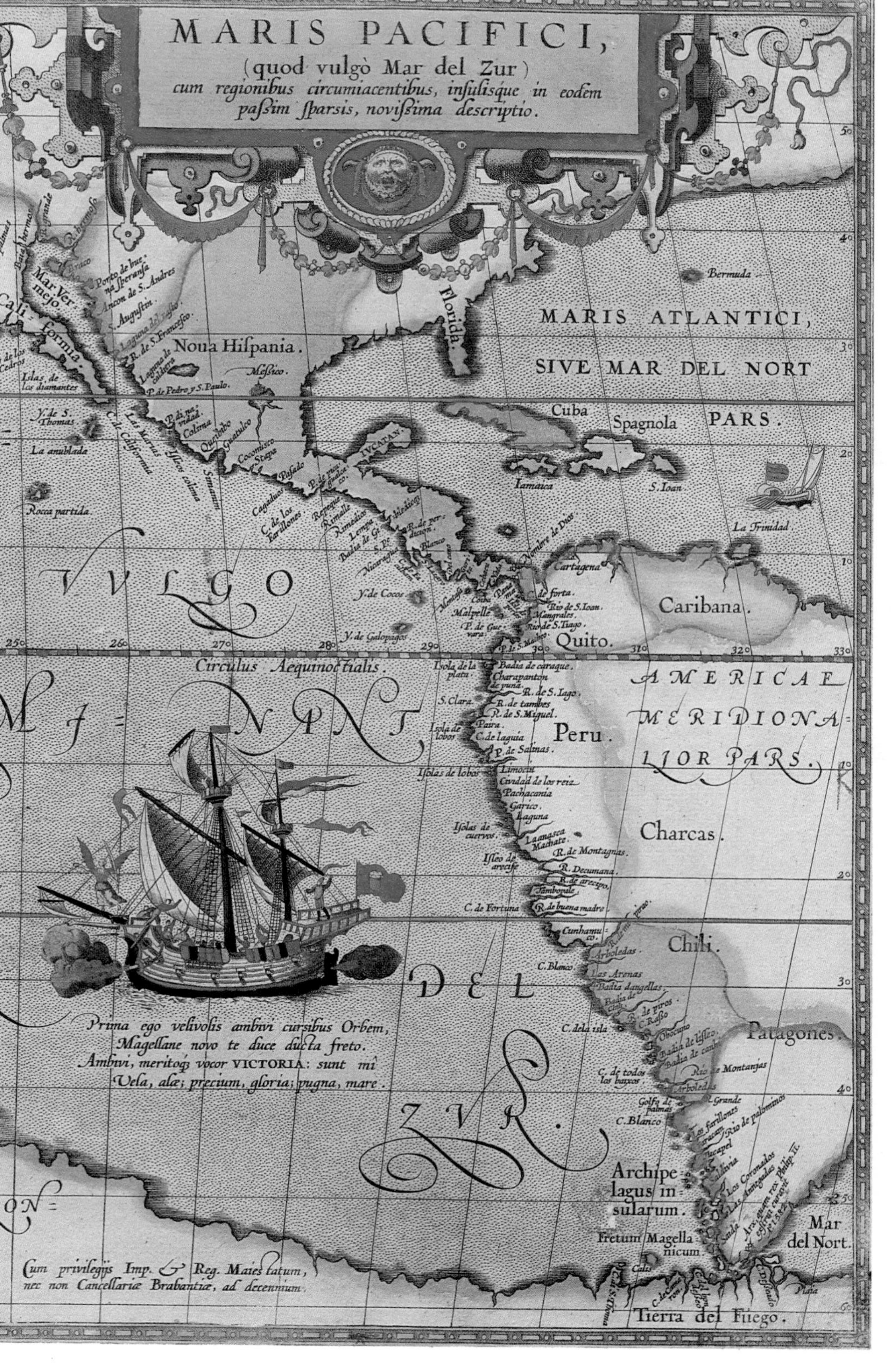
MARIS PACIFICI,
(quod vulgò Mar del Zur)
cum regionibus circumiacentibus, insulisque in eodem
passim sparsis, novissima descriptio.
MARIS ATLANTICI,
SIVE MAR DEL NORT
PARS.
Bermuda
Florida
Noua Hispania.
Mexico.
Cali-
fornia.
Mar Ver-
mejo.
Cuba
Spagnola
Iamaica
S. Ioan
La Trinidad
Cartagena
Caribana.
Quito.
Circulus Aequinoctialis.
AMERICAE
MERIDIONA-
LIOR PARS.
Peru.
Charcas.
Chili.
Patagones.
Archipe
lagus in
sularum.
Fretum Magella
nicum.
Mar
del Nort.
Tierra del Fuego.
VULGO
DEL
ZUR.
Prima ego velivolis ambivi cursibus Orbem,
Magellane novo te duce ducta freto.
Ambivi, meritoq; vocor VICTORIA: sunt mi
Vela, alæ; precium, gloria; pugna, mare.
Cum privilegijs Imp. & Reg. Maiestatum,
nec non Cancellariæ Brabantiæ, ad decennium.

Top Maori war canoe approaching Mount Egmont, painted by Nicholas Chevalier. *Above* The arrival of de Bougainville in Matavai Bay, Tahiti, 4 April 1768, painted by Gustave Alaux.

Top HMS *Endeavour* beached on the coast of Queensland after striking the Great Barrier Reef during Cook's first voyage, based on a drawing by Sydney Parkinson. *Above* Tahitian war canoes, painted in 1774 by William Hodges.

Tahitian seascape, painted by William Hodges (1744–97), the artist aboard HMS *Resolution* on Cook's second v

5).

Top Cook's ships HMS *Resolution* and *Adventure* in 61°S during Cook's second voyage, taking aboard ice for drinking water, painted in 1773 by William Hodges. *Above* Cook's ships on his third voyage, HMS *Resolution* and *Discovery*, anchored off Moorea (Society Islands) from a drawing by James Cleveley.

his ability seemed to call for. But perhaps the most bitter blow of all was the fact that with every passing year Darwin's 'heretical' theory of evolution gained credence at the expense of his own traditional and Biblical theory. Matters came to a head in the summer of 1860.

On Saturday 30 June there was a meeting of the British Association in Oxford. The subject to be debated was evolution, and both the old guard and the avant-garde assembled their big guns; the former were led by the anti-Darwin anatomist Richard Owen and by Wilberforce, Bishop of Oxford, the latter by the scientists Hooker and Huxley. The meeting started sedately, but soon livened up when Wilberforce enquired of Huxley if it was through his grandmother or his grandfather that he claimed to be descended from the apes. There was much cheering and jeering, women fainted, and in the middle of the furore a slim grey-haired figure leapt on to the rostrum brandishing a Bible. In this Book, and in this Book alone, FitzRoy shouted, was the truth to be found. Long ago, in his cabin aboard the *Beagle*, he had warned young Darwin of the dangers of heresy. . . The rest of his speech was howled down. At the end of the debate the traditionalists were routed, and Darwin's theory took another major step towards both scientific and popular acceptance.

It was not long after this that FitzRoy, in a spasm of total despair, committed suicide. A tragic end for a good, caring and able man, but one which underlined the validity of Darwin's argument: those who fail to adapt, fail to survive.

Only one other British expedition played a major role in the exploration of the Pacific. In 1872 HMS *Challenger*, stripped of her guns and loaded with scientific apparatus, embarked on a voyage round the world that was devoted to the exploration of the sea itself, an entirely new type of exploration. George Nares commanded the ship, Professor C. Wyville Thomson led the team of scientists, and during a cruise of three-and-a-half years and nearly 70,000 miles they traversed every ocean except the Arctic, trawling to take samples from the sea and dredging to take samples from the bed of the sea. No expedition before, and few since, ever amassed such a wealth of novel scientific data – 4,417 completely new species of plants and animals, 'many of them strange and beautiful things which gave us a glimpse of the edge of an unfamiliar world'. It was the dawn of a new science – oceanography.

When it came to delineating the Pacific no nation made a greater contribution than the British. But when it came to disseminating ideas about the ocean, the pre-eminent nation was the French.

A WALK THROUGH THE GARDENS OF PARADISE

THE VOYAGES OF THE FRENCH

'As we walked over the grass, dotted here and there with fine fruit trees and intersected by little streams, I thought I had been transported to paradise. Everywhere we went, we found hospitality, peace, innocent joy and every appearance of happiness.'
Louis Antoine de Bougainville

It has often been said that the French explorers of the Pacific got it all wrong: that they endowed the Polynesians not with the virtues they had, but with the virtues they thought, as Noble Savages, they *ought* to have. This criticism is most frequently levelled at the gifted and likeable Louis de Bougainville and his highly intelligent but highly-strung naturalist, Philibert Commerson.

Louis Antoine de Bougainville was born in Paris on 11 November 1729, just a few months after Cook – and the careers of the two men were to run curiously parallel. Both, in their mid-twenties, went to Canada and played a leading role in the siege of Quebec. Both, in their late-twenties, wrote learned mathematical treatises which earned them fellowships of the Royal Society. And both, in their late-thirties, led expeditions to the Pacific. It was lucky for Cook and unlucky for Bougainville that the Admiralty were better able to support a succession of costly maritime ventures than the *Ecole Navale.*

When Bougainville left Brest in 1766 in command of *La Boudeuse* and *L'Etoile* he had little experience of the sea. He had led only one other expedition, in 1763, when he had established a French colony on that most argued-over of archipelagos, the Falkland Islands. Bougainville had been astute enough to realize the strategic importance of the Falklands at the approaches to Cape Horn and had settled some 27 French Arcadians on the islands. For a few years the colony flourished, and one of its members, Father Pernety, made a fine collection of the islands' flora. Then the Arcadians fell victim to political expediency. The Falklands were also claimed by Great Britain and Spain – the former on the grounds that the islands were first discovered in 1592 by John Davis; the latter on the grounds that they were part of their territory of Argentina. The French were put under pressure to withdraw, and the unfortunate Bougainville found himself obliged for the second time within a decade to make a formal surrender to the British. On this occasion, however, his disappointment was assuaged by the fact that he had been commissioned by Louis XV to continue his voyage into the Pacific, where it was hoped he would find other islands of which he could take possession.

After the surrender, which took place on All Fools' Day 1767, *La Boudeuse* and

L'Etoile put in to Rio. Here, while the ships were being reprovisioned, the ethnologists and naturalists had a field day ashore. Bougainville gives us a good description of what is perhaps the South Americans' best-known weapon: 'The Indians are always on horseback . . . they make much use of nooses and of balls. These balls are two round stones, about the size of a two-pounder, both encased in a strap of leather and fastened to the end of a thong about six or seven feet long. When on horseback they use this weapon as a sling, and have been known to hit the animal they are pursuing at a distance of 300 yards.' While Commerson gives us an equally good description of what is perhaps the country's best-known flower: 'An admirable plant, with large blossoms of a sumptuous violet, which is often found climbing over houses . . . and which I named bougainvillea in honour of our commander.'

With such diversions it was almost a year from the time the ships left Brest to the time they entered the Straits of Magellan. And it is an indication of the lack of liaison

Louis Antoine de Bougainville (1729-1811), who loved and was loved by the Tahitians and whose glowing reports on the island gave credence to the myth of the Noble Savage, and his ship *La Bordeuse*, by Gustave Alaux.

between the nations of Europe that, more than 150 years after Le Maire's discovery of open water to the south of the Horn, Bougainville still chose to enter the Pacific through Magellan's narrow and tortuous channels.

He had a hard time of it: 52 days of battling with hurricane-force winds and driving blizzards of snow through which the campfires of the Patagonian Indians flickered as if in defiance of the elements. '*Nix, glando, glacies spiritus procellarum*', the erudite Bougainville noted in his Diary ('Fire, snow, mist and mighty winds fulfilling His word': Psalm cxlviii, 8). It was a nightmare voyage, alleviated only by their occasional meetings with the Patagonians, whom Bougainville describes as a 'good and gentle people who practice none of the cruel customs of most other savages'; probably

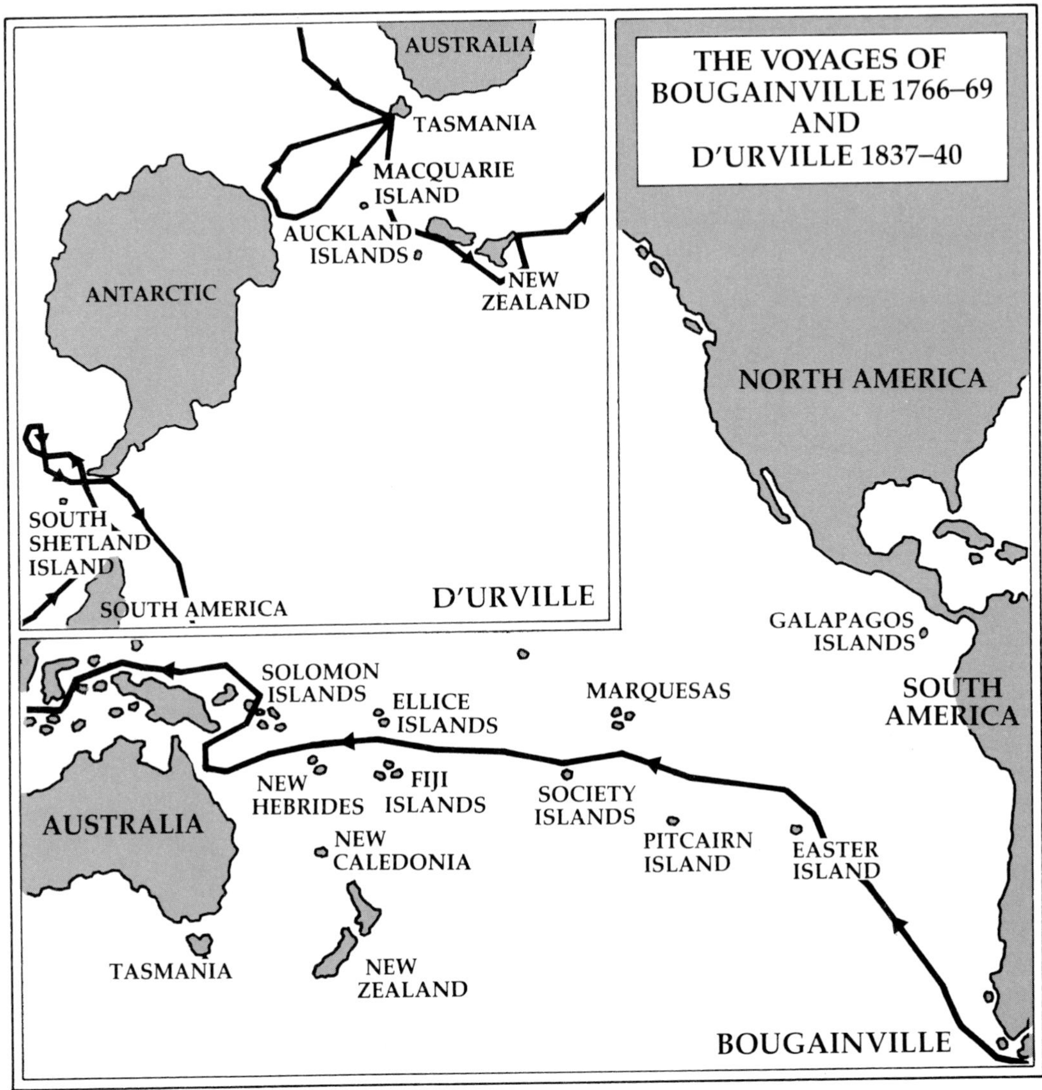

in their precarious toe-hold on the world they found simply keeping alive a full-time occupation. It was late January before *La Boudeuse* and *L'Etoile* fought through to the Pacific, their crews celebrating their achievement, as did Magellan's, by singing the *Te Deum*.

Bougainville's crossing of the Pacific was much like other crossings in the pre-Cook era. For week after week his ships ran westward before a steady wind under a cloudless sky. There were the usual near-misses on dangerous reefs, and the usual sighting of atolls where the surf made it impossible to land, and the usual scurvy. Scurvy indeed was becoming a serious problem when on 2 April they sighted the high peaks of Mehetia in the Society Islands. A couple of days later they were running parallel to the coast of Tahiti.

It was a case of love at first sight.

Bougainville spent only ten days in Tahiti. He didn't therefore have time to get to know the island or the islanders all that well. Nor did he write a great deal about them – no more than four dozen pages in his Diary. However, what he *did* write has been quoted, misquoted, paraphrased, precised, interpreted and analysed again and again. It is heady stuff. Here is his description of the island as they saw it from outside the reef:

> *The aspect of the coast offered us the most enchanting prospect. Notwithstanding the height of the mountains, they had no appearance of barrenness; every part was covered with woods. We could hardly believe our eyes when we saw a peak covered with trees right up to its summit . . . from a distance it might have been taken for a huge pyramid, which the hand of an able sculptor had adorned with garlands and foliage. The less elevated lands were interspersed with meadows and copses; and along the coast ran a strip of low and level land covered with fields, bordering on one side the sea and on the other side the mountains. Here we could see the houses of the islanders amidst banana, cocoa-nut and other trees laden with fruit.*

Bougainville hoisting French colours on a small rock in the Magellan Straits, from Moore's *Voyages and Travels.*

This would seem to be an accurate factual description. Bougainville was no starry-eyed *ingénue* who eulogized every new land he came to. Before his arrival at Tahiti he wrote some pretty uncomplimentary things about other places he visited – the Straits of Magellan for example: 'Mountains covered with eternal snow and the valleys between filled with huge masses of dirty ice . . . nothing more dreadful could be imagined.' And after his departure he was equally scathing in his description of many other places – New Ireland for instance: 'Here eternal humidity prevails. The continual rains and the suffocating heat rendered our stay unhealthy and disagreeable.' We can therefore, I think, accept his description of Tahiti as being quite simply true.

Here is what he has to say to the people:

> *As we neared the shore, the number of islanders surrounding our ships increased. Soon the canoes*

were so numerous that we had difficulty warping in amidst the crowd of boats and the noise, with all the people crying tayo which (we learned afterwards) means friend. The canoes were full of females, who for agreeable features are not inferior to European women, and who in beauty of body often surpass them. Many of these fair females were naked, and the men pressed us to choose a woman and come ashore with her; and their gestures, which were nothing less than equivocal, denoted in what manner we should form an acquaintance with her. It was difficult, in these circumstances, to keep at their work 400 young French seamen who had seen no women for six months. In spite of all our precautions, a young girl managed to climb aboard and placed herself upon the quarterdeck, near one of the hatchways which was open, to give air to those heaving at the capstan below. The girl carelessly dropped the cloth which covered her, and appeared to the eyes of all beholders as Venus showed herself to the Phrygian shepherd, having indeed the celestial form of that goddess. Never was capstan wound in with more alacrity!

On that day, we are told in almost every book recently written about the Pacific, the legend of Tahiti was born. But is that right? The Oxford Dictionary defines a legend as a myth, and a myth as a fictitious tale. Yet there was nothing in the least fictitious about the entry in Bougainville's Diary. He was simply describing what happened, a point underlined as his Diary continues:

At last our efforts succeeded in keeping our bewitched fellows under control, though it was no less difficult to keep control of ourselves! One solitary Frenchman – my cook – found means to escape, against my orders, ashore; and he soon returned more dead than alive. It seems he had hardly set foot on the beach with the fair one whom he had chosen, when he was immediately surrounded by a crowd of Indians, who undressed him from head to foot. He thought he was utterly lost, not knowing where the interest of those people would end who were tumultuously examining every part of his body. After having considered him well, they returned him his clothes, put into his pockets whatever they had taken out, and brought his girl to him desiring him now to content those desires which had brought him ashore with her. But all their persuasive arguments had no effect; they were obliged to bring the poor cook onboard; and he told me that I might reprimand him as much as I pleased, but I could never frighten him half so much as he had just been frightened on shore!

This also would seem to be an accurate account of what took place. For of all the people whom Bougainville met during his travels – the gauchos of Argentina, the Fuegians of the Magellan Strait, the Polynesians of Tahiti and the Melanesians of the Bismarck Archipelago – it is the Polynesians alone whom he praises for their physical beauty and cleanliness. The gauchos, he tells us, are 'middle-sized, very ugly, afflicted with the itch and blacken themselves with grease'. The Fuegians are 'stunted, ugly, meagre and have an insufferable stench'. The Melanesians are 'ill-proportioned, disagreeable and many of them infected with leprosy'. So here again there is no reason to suppose that Bougainville was relating anything other than the plain unvarnished truth.

All of which indicates that we should be very careful indeed when we speak of 'the legend of Tahiti' as though we were talking of some sort of fairytale. It is true that many of the stories that were later spread round about the Polynesians were fairytales – including Rousseau's concept of them as Noble Savages – but their physical beauty and their unashamed enjoyment of sex were *not* a fairytale. They were fact. And the world is a poorer place because Europeans were to take their basic physical pleasures away from them and replace them with the idea that sex was sinful.

Bougainville's favourable first impression of Tahiti was confirmed when he went ashore. There was a slight hiccup when he started to set up camp beside a river; but the

Polynesians soon waived their objections when the French promised to leave at the end of ten days. 'Soon', to quote Bougainville's Diary:

> *our people were walking about the island alone and unarmed. They were invited into the islanders' homes and offered food and young girls, the hut being quickly filled with a curious crowd who made a circle round the lovers. They seemed surprised at the confusion our people were in, not understanding that our customs do not permit these public proceedings. However, I would not say that every one of our men found it impossible to conquer his repugnance and conform to the custom of their country!*

The only major problem was the continual thieving, although Bougainville was sensible enough to take precautions against this and a relaxed attitude towards it. 'Doubtless,' he wrote, 'curiosity for new objects excites cupidity in them – besides there are rascals to be found everywhere.' He was shrewd enough to notice that theft among the islanders themselves was almost unknown – 'Nothing is shut up in their homes, and everything is left lying about, without being under any particular person's care.'

All the same, it was thieving which led to the first serious setback in relations when an islander was found shot dead. 'What a cowardly murder,' wrote Bougainville sadly. And a couple of days later there was another and even more serious incident. In an argument over the price of a pig, three Polynesians were bayonetted to death. To say that Bougainville was angry would be a considerable understatement. He set up an inquiry, and it wasn't long before the four soldiers who had been involved were arrested and put in irons. But then came a problem.The four men covered up for one another, and it was impossible to prove which of them had committed the actual murder. Bougainville, determined that justice should be seen to be done, ordered them to draw lots to decide which of them should be hanged. However, salvation came to the culprits from an unlikely source. When the islanders heard what punishment the soldiers were facing they pleaded with Bougainville to release them. None of the French had the slightest doubt about the gist of what they were saying: 'Though you kill us, we are still your friends.'

Who, one wonders, were the true Christians – those who tried to cheat a man of his pig and when he protested stabbed him to death, or those who begged that his murderers should be forgiven?

It would be wrong to suggest that this incident was responsible for Bougainville's departure from Tahiti, but it probably precipitated it. The basic reason for his leaving – apart from the promise he had given the Tahitians – was that his ships were in a highly dangerous anchorage. Trapped in a narrow reach of water between reef and shore, with little room to manoeuvre, *La Boudeuse* and *L'Etoile* were in constant danger of being driven on to the beach by the prevailing wind, while a foul bottom cost them six anchors in as many days. On more than one occasion the ships were within a dozen feet of destruction, and were only saved by their crews taking to the boats and towing them clear of danger.

On 13 April there was a final exchange of presents, with the islanders being offered turkeys and geese, also the seeds of wheat, maize, beans, lentils, peas, onions and herbs. The latter were planted in a carefully dug garden 'and I have reason to believe', wrote Bougainville, 'that they will be taken care of; for this nation love agriculture, and their soil is surely the most fertile in the universe'. There was also a ceremony of taking possession of the island in the name of Louis XV – although Bougainville must have realized he was not the first European to reach Tahiti, since there was plenty of evidence of Wallis's visit of the year before. He named the land which during his brief visit he had come to love *La Nouvelle Cythère*, after the island off the coast of the

Peloponnese where the ancient Greeks believed the goddess Venus had risen from the sea.

Next day *L'Etoile* and *La Boudeuse* edged out through the reef. *La Boudeuse* had barely reached the open sea when the wind died, and the heavy swell began to carry her towards the wall of coral where waves were breaking steeple-high and shipwreck would have been almost certain death. But at the last moment, as though in answer to their prayers, a breeze sprang up from the west. The flagship managed to struggle clear, and by midday Bougainville was ready to continue his voyage.

An engraving of Tahitians by L. Portman after J. Knyper.

Many Tahitians came aboard for a last farewell. There was much embracing and weeping, and a young man named Ahu-Toru, the son of one of the local chiefs, said that he wanted to accompany the French on the rest of their voyage. On the spur of the moment Bougainville agreed. 'Thus,' he wrote, 'we quitted this good and gentle people; and I was no less surprised at the sorrow they displayed at our departure, than I had been surprised at the joy they had displayed at our arrival.'

Although marred by two brutal murders, Bougainville's visit to Tahiti was, by and large, both happy and successful. It comes as something of a surprise to learn that on his return to France he was criticized on several counts: for not exploring the island more thoroughly, for not bringing back more scientific data, and for taking a Tahitian (albeit a willing one) from his homeland. There may be a grain of truth in each of these charges, but no more than a grain. If Bougainville had spent longer on Tahiti he would obviously have explored the interior and charted the coast. However, he hoped, very reasonably, to discover other new lands in the Pacific and was therefore unwilling to spend too much time on any one island. The scientific side of his expedition he left to Commerson; but unhappily Commerson died before he was able to publish his numerous notes and drawings. So the unfortunate naturalist is remembered today not as the man who brought back from the Pacific some 5,000 botanical specimens and more than 1,500 drawings, but as the man who smuggled his girlfriend aboard *La Boudeuse* disguised as his valet! As for bringing back Ahu-Toru, this was the sort of thing many explorers had done in the past and many were to do in the future, often more callously. Bougainville did make a genuine effort to befriend the Tahitian, and subsequently spent nearly a third of his life's savings to arrange for him to be taken home – it was hardly his fault that the luckless Polynesian died en route of smallpox. It may be that much of the criticism of Bougainville was fuelled by the fact that he was an aristocrat, and therefore, in the run-up to the Revolution, a target for the progressively minded. Also his work was inevitably compared to that of his contemporary Cook, and it is hard to measure up to someone who is acknowledged to have achieved pre-eminence.

After leaving Tahiti Bougainville's ships stood west, and at the end of a couple of weeks more islands were sighted – almost certainly Manua and Tutuila in Western Samoa. The French were very impressed by the Samoans' lateen-rigged canoes, which sailed rings round *La Boudeuse* and *L'Etoile*, even though the latter were making eight knots. They were not so impressed with the islanders themselves – 'I do not think these people are as gentle as those of Tahiti; their features are more savage, and we have to be constantly on guard against their cheating.' Bougainville now made a brave decision. Most navigators at this point in their voyage across the Pacific stood north-west and headed for New Guinea. For it was thought that directly to the west lay the unknown coast of New Holland; and with the prevailing wind blowing strongly on to this coast, the fear of being driven ashore and wrecked had inhibited exploration. Bougainville, however, had the courage boldly to hold his course. Progress was slow: 'For it should be understood that these unknown seas must be navigated with every precaution and apprehension, since one is on all sides threatened with the unexpected appearance of land and shoals.' The weather was bad, with torrential rain and lowering banks of cloud. Soon, to add to their troubles, they were afflicted by that bane of Pacific voyagers, scurvy. 'A great part of the crew and most of the officers had their gums affected and their mouths inflamed . . . and we had no refreshments [no fresh vegetables] except for the sick.' On 22 May yet more islands were sighted: the New Hebrides, which had remained unvisited since Quiros discovered them a century and a half earlier. Here Bougainville, like the Spaniard before him, found the warlike people of Melanesia a very different proposition from the Polynesians. His ships were pelted with stones and arrows, his progress along the shore was marked by the beating of drums and the lighting of bonfires, and wherever he tried to land he found himself faced by a ring of half-naked and wholly hostile islanders. He left 'this most unfriendly archipelago' on 29 May, having managed to refill his water casks, but with few of the fresh vegetables that his crew were now desperately in need of.

A few days later he almost certainly became the first European to sight the east coast of Australia.

It was the evening of 5 June 1768 – nearly a couple of years before the first sighting usually attributed to Cook – and as darkness fell his two ships were edging cautiously west under heavily reefed topsails.

> *At eleven o'clock,* Bougainville tells us, *we perceived by moonshine some breakers and a very low sandbank about half-a-league ahead. We at once went about, and signalled danger to L'Etoile. . .*

> *In the morning we resumed our former course in order to find the sandbank again. We sighted it at 8 o'clock. It is a little sandy isle which hardly rises above the water: so flat that at a distance of two leagues and with a very clear horizon it can only be seen from the masthead. It was covered with birds, and I called it la Bature de Diane.* (Bougainville then describes the rest of the day's sailing.) *During the past 24 hours several pieces of wood and some fruits which we could not identify came drifting past the ship. The sea had fallen completely calm, notwithstanding a very fresh wind from the SE, which made me believe that we had land pretty near. At half-past-one in the afternoon another sandbank appeared about three-quarters of a league ahead. This convinced me it was time to alter course. I had hardly done this when our men at the masthead saw breakers ahead, and some were of the opinion that they could see a continuous low land to the south of these breakers. . . We approached more closely in order to get a better view. The breakers were seen to extend from NNE to SSW, and we could see no end to them. The sea broke over them with a terrible roar, and here and there outcrops of rock appeared above the water.*

It would be hard to imagine a better description of the Great Barrier Reef; and Bougainville's estimated position – 15°S, 146°E, puts him just off the edge of this Reef, opposite Cape Flattery on the north-east coast of Queensland. From here, on a clear day, the shore is faintly visible.

Bougainville continues, 'This was the voice of God and we were obedient to it. Prudence not permitting us to pursue an uncertain course in these dangerous waters, I gave orders to abandon our scheme of proceeding farther to the west.' His Diary for the day ends with the very reasonable claim that 'these numerous shoals running out to sea are sure signs of the vicinity of a great land, and this land can be nothing else than the eastern coast of New Holland.'

There was a time when jingoism gave the first sighting of an unknown shore a special significance, and this led to many first-sighting claims being disputed. Explorers themselves have usually (but not always) done their best to keep aloof from such bickering. Bougainville never claimed to be the first European to sight the east coast of Australia, but I think he was.

The rest of his voyage to Batavia was a struggle with bad weather, ill health and near starvation.

A few days after probably sighting Australia, Bougainville certainly sighted Papua New Guinea. The great island was beautiful beyond dreams; beaches lined with palms, a lightly wooded coastal plain and inland, like the tiers of some magnificent amphitheatre, range after range of towering thickly forested mountains, their summits wreathed in cloud. However, with a weakened crew, a heavy swell and mist so thick that the ships had to fire guns to keep in touch, Bougainville couldn't find anywhere safe to land. Week after week, through seas thick with seaweed and silt, his ships picked their way first along the coast of the mainland, then past the interminable archipelago of islands, shoals and reefs which stream out like the tail of a comet from the south-eastern tip of Papua. Food became scarce. Rations had to be cut; soon the crew were so hungry that Bougainville was forced to issue an order forbidding the eating of leather from the mast. They started – shades of Magellan – to hunt in the bilges for rats. On 20 June, they rounded the last headland of the last island in the archipelago which had for so long blocked their way north. They saw open water ahead of them and ten days later were in the Solomons. But they found neither respite nor safety here. *La Boudeuse* was attacked by a fleet of ten canoes which were only beaten off by gunfire. Two of the canoes were captured and brought aboard. They were beautifully made, their bows carved into the likeness of a man's head, with eyes of mother-of-pearl, ears of tortoiseshell and lips dyed red. Stowed away in the canoes were skilfully made weapons, and the jaw of a man half-broiled. Not daring in their weakened condition to land, the French struggled on to New Britain. Here at last they found a sheltered and uninhabited anchorage.

Their troubles, however, were far from over. Water and wood were plentiful, but there were none of the hoped-for fruits to alleviate their scurvy, 'neither cocoanuts nor bananas, only cabbage trees in small number, and some of these we were forced to abandon by swarms of the most enormous ants'. Night after night there were violent storms, with thunder, lightning and torrential rain. On 22 July they were terrified by a series of violent earth tremors. Their rations, yet again, had to be reduced, and their tents cut up to make clothes. Scurvy was now no longer merely weakening men, it was killing them. Realizing that if they stayed where they were, they were doomed, Bougainville pressed on towards the Moluccas. What little food they had was now putrid, the ships stank 'with a disgusting cadaverous odour', and the crew were so weak that more than half of them were unable to work the sails. 'Not one of us could say,' wrote Bougainville, 'that he was free from scurvy, and if we had remained at sea for one week longer we would have lost a great number of men.' But at last, through a maze of shoals and rip-tides, they struggled through to the island of Buru (off East Sulawesi) where the Dutch had a trading post.

A month later *La Boudeuse* and *L'Etoile* were in Batavia; a couple of months after that they were in Mauritius; and in the spring of 1769, after a voyage of two years and four months, the ships dropped anchor in Saint Malo.

Bougainville's circumnavigation of the world was a great achievement in itself. It was made to seem even greater by its aftermath; for it was to resuscitate and give credence to one of the most enduring myths in history – the myth of the Noble Savage.

The explorers returned to an enthusiastic welcome. After a succession of military defeats the French public were in need of a triumph. And what a triumph Bougainville provided for them. A voyage out-voyaging the British, and as evidence of the wonders that had been met with on the far side of the world, a real live Tahitian brought back to stand among them. It is true that Ahu-Toru was to prove a less engaging representative of his people than Omai, for he seems to have been unintelligent, and was described by Commerson as 'perhaps the ugliest man of his nation'. Initially, however, his mere presence fuelled the flames of enthusiasm. This enthusiasm was further stimulated when in 1771 Bougainville published his long-awaited *Voyage autour du mond par la frégate du roi La Boudeuse et la flûte L'Etoile*. The book was an instant best-seller, and quickly became the talking point of salons and the focal point of philosophical diatribes. It was a good book, written, as one would expect from Bougainville, with style, humanity and humour, but it was a popular rather than a scientific work. It contained virtually no facts about the flora and fauna of the lands visited, and relatively few facts about the people; less than one-eighth of it was devoted to Tahiti. It was an unsubstantial basis on which to advance a concept of evolution. But this is what happened. People, and in particular avant-garde philosophers, pointed to the many passages in Bougainville's book which extolled the idyllic lifestyle of the Polynesians, and used these passages to promote the misconception that *all* primitive peoples were intrinsically happy, gentle and good.

It didn't matter that Bougainville had spent only eleven days in Tahiti and made no claim to have studied the islanders in depth. Nor did it matter that he described *other* primitive peoples as ugly, meagre, insufferable, hostile and disagreeable. He had found this one enchanted island whose inhabitants appeared to possess all those virtues philosophers thought they ought to possess. So, it was argued, here were people living in what Rousseau had eulogized as 'the real youth of the world': that idyllic stage in *homo*

Left Jean-Jacques Rousseau (1712-78) and *right* Denis Diderot (1713-84), two French philosophers who helped to create the myth of the Noble Savage.

sapiens' evolution when family-love had been added to the basic instincts of survival and reproduction, and human beings lived in small genuinely communal units, free from those sins of possessiveness, greed and envy which in recent millennia had, it was argued, led not to the advance of our species but to its decline. And having found evidence of this one apparent Eden, the intelligentsia seized on the virtues of one primitive people and attributed similar virtues to them all.

Nor was it only the intelligentsia who now became enamoured with the concept of the Noble Savage. Many ordinary people who had shown little interest in Rousseau's *Discourses* showed very considerable interest in the activities of Bougainville's seamen. And when it appeared that these seamen had actually met Noble Savages – had spoken with them, eaten with them and made love with them – it was as though legend had become suddenly transmogrified to reality. So now, in Beaglehole's vivid and much-quoted words, 'there rose up something new, something incomparably exciting, Man in the state of nature; the Noble Savage entered the study and the drawing room of Europe in naked majesty to shake the preconceptions of morals and of politics'.

Then, however, came the inevitable question. If the people Bougainville had discovered were *really* Noble Savages, and if they were *really* living such idyllic lives, had Europeans the right to disturb them? The intellectuals thought not. In 1772 Diderot published his semi-clandestine treatise, *Supplément au voyage de Bougainville ou dialogue entre A et B sur l'inconvenient d'attacher des idées morales à certaines actions physiques qui n'en comportent pas*. Diderot's argument was a great deal pithier than his title. What benefits, he demanded, could possibly be brought to these people by Christian civilization, with its overtones of guilt, its hypocrisy and its ambition? 'One day,' he warned the Tahitians, 'the missionaries will come to you with a crucifix in one hand and a dagger in the other to force you to accept their customs and opinions. One day, under their rule, you will be as unhappy as they are.' A prophecy which seemed over-dramatic at the time, but which was, in the next century, to be fulfilled with tragic accuracy.

It has been suggested that Diderot's fears were nothing more than an intellectual's heart-cry for a return to natural innocence. But there was more to them than that. They voiced the concern of a fair number of people – and indeed of the explorers themselves. Cook, for example, was appalled by the effect that even a decade of Westernization was having on the islanders. 'We debauch their morals,' he wrote, 'and introduce among them wants and diseases which they never had before, and which serve only to destroy that happy tranquility they and their fore-Fathers had enjoyed. . . I often think it would have been better for them if we had never appeared among them.'

So in the latter part of the eighteenth century many Europeans were interested in and concerned about the people of the Pacific. Why, one wonders, did the altruistic solicitude of the eighteenth century give way to the casual exploitation of the nineteenth?

I can suggest two reasons. The nineteenth century was an age which set particular store by worldly wealth, and in terms of worldly wealth the Pacific appeared to have little to offer. The great powers were too busy carving up Africa and opening up America to be greatly concerned with a few specks of coral on the far side of the world. The ocean was therefore ignored. In other words, what happened to the Polynesians happened not so much by design as by default, not so much because of wickedness as because of neglect. The islanders were never massacred for their gold, like the Incas. They were never driven from pillar to post for their land, like the North American Indians or the Australian Aboriginals. They were simply left to the none-too-tender mercies of individual whalers, copra-traders, pearlers, adventurers and missionaries. Some people, of course, genuinely cared for the islanders, and the missionaries were well-intentioned; but no effort was made to get to know or to understand the Polynesians, who were thought of as the beautiful but backward children of some lesser god. There is also the point that the Pacific, in those days, seemed to most people so far away as to be almost in another planet. People in Europe could learn of and be concerned about the African slave trade; that was on their doorstep. But they never heard of the 2,000 men, women and children of Easter Island who were torn from their homes and shipped to work on the guano islands off the coast of Peru; not one survived. That, to Europeans, must have seemed to take place in another world. And what the eye doesn't see the heart doesn't grieve over.

Another reason for loss of interest in the Pacific was the Europeans' gradual disenchantment as they came to realize that the ocean's so-called Noble Savages were not the paragons of virtue that philosophers had led them to believe. When the two races first met, they were so totally different that they regarded one another with awe. But familiarity was to breed, if not contempt, then at least a degree of disillusion. When the Hawaiians discovered that Cook's blood was as sheddable as their own, they stabbed him to death. When Captain Bligh – of the notorious *Bounty* – discovered that the Tahitians indulged in warfare and were fettered by class-distinction, he cried out in horror, 'Why, they are just like us.' And once this fact was widely appreciated, once the islanders had fallen from the impossibly high pedestal on which philosophers had placed them, then Europeans no longer regarded them with such protective wonder. If they were just like us, the feeling was, then they could fend for themselves.

The Polynesians of course were perfectly able to fend for themselves if left alone; but they had no defence against the Europeans with their firepower, technical expertise and daemonic energy. Within a century of being discovered, they and their culture had been submerged and drowned beyond hope of resuscitation before more than a handful of people realized the tragedy that was taking place.

If only the Europeans had seen in time that although the islanders were far from perfect and were technically backward, they enjoyed a lifestyle from which the rest of the world could have learned a great deal. If only they had taken them by the hand instead of trampling them underfoot. If only some of the rapport established by French explorers in the eighteenth century had lingered on into the nineteenth. If only, if only, if only. . .

One reason why all this didn't happen is that the original rapport had been engendered in the first flush of a sensuous and intellectual enthusiasm which was not altogether justified by the facts. It was an affair of the heart, subject to all the vagaries the heart is heir to. For awhile the flame of rapport flickered bravely; then, shaken by the ravages of disease, intolerance and incompatible values, it was snuffed out, and the Polynesians began their disenchanted drift in accadie into the night to join the spirits of their ancestors.

It is possible to argue that this tragedy *might* have been avoided if both the Europeans and the Polynesians had been more aware of the facts. Facts were what Bougainville's report had been short of, and it was a lack of facts which had allowed the myth of the Noble Savage to gain credence. As if in recognition of this, subsequent French explorers of the Pacific were assiduous finders and recorders of fact – none more so than Dumont D'Urville.

Jules Sébastien César Dumont D'Urville was an engaging character. It has been said (and rightly) that he was brusque, intolerant and born to trouble; but to balance this he had courage, determination, patience and a quality he shared with his compatriot Bougainville – he was, in the classical sense of the word, a profoundly cultured man. Indeed he is probably best remembered today not as the discoverer of the bleakest and most storm-lashed coastline on Earth, but as the discoverer of the Venus de Milo; for it was he who first recognized the statue when it was unearthed on Melos, and it is largely through his efforts that it stands today in the Louvre.

Jules Sébastien César Dumont D'Urville (1790-1842) and his ship the *Astrolabe* taking aboard ice for drinking water off the South Sandwich Islands, 1838, the latter from his *Voyage au pôle Sud et en l'Océanie*.

D'Urville's first command was the *Astrolabe*, a 380-ton corvette in which he sailed from Toulon in April 1826.

Exploration was now undergoing a fundamental change. In the sixteenth, seventeenth and eighteenth centuries expeditions had set out in search of new lands; by the nineteenth century, however, there were virtually no more new lands to be discovered – except at the approaches to the Poles. Expeditions therefore began to set out in search of scientific facts. To this type of exploration D'Urville was well suited, bringing a scholarly mind to the meticulous collection and classification of flora and fauna. He spent more than two years in the Pacific, visiting places as far apart as King George's Sound, Western Australia; Hobart, Tasmania; the Bay of Islands, New Zealand; Anamoka, Tonga; Ono, Fiji; New Ireland, New Britain and New Guinea; Guam, in the Marianas; and a whole plethora of islands in Sulawesi and the Moluccas. It was an arduous voyage. Of his crew of 79, ten died, thirteen deserted and twenty had to be left behind on various islands, too weak from scurvy, dysentery or fever to remain aboard. Less than half his ship's company completed the return passage to Toulon. However, he brought back a greater quantity of scientific data than had been collected by any previous expedition: over 6,000 detailed drawings, and sufficient botanical, zoological and ethnographic information to fill fourteen weighty volumes and five enormous atlases.

On his return to France, D'Urville spent several years working on an account of his expedition, *Voyage pittoresque autour du monde*. He then applied for a number of seagoing appointments, but without success. It seemed that his career was drawing to its close, and he was thinking of retiring, when he was called to an unexpected audience with King Louis-Philippe. Almost as unexpected as the audience was Louis-Philippe's proposal that D'Urville should take command of an expedition to explore the approaches to the South Pole.

This was a far-sighted and well-timed suggestion.

It had been known for some time that although the sub-Antarctic was swept by great waves and violent winds and often shrouded in mist, its seas were teeming with life. As early as 1616 Le Maire, as he rounded the Horn, reported 'seals, huge numbers of penguins, and whales by the thousand'. A century later, Cook, at several places along the Antarctic Convergence, reported 'a multitude of seals observ'd on the offshore rocks . . . penguins . . . and great numbers of whales disporting themselves around the ship.' For some time the creatures of the Southern Ocean were safeguarded by their sheer distance from man. However, the machines of the industrial revolution demanded constant lubrication; oil in those days meant whale-oil or seal-oil. By the end of the eighteenth century, whales and seals in the northern hemisphere had been hunted to near-extinction, so men's eyes were drawn to the south. It was the sealers of New England who arrived first. Sailing from ports like Boston, Nantucket, New Haven and Stonington, their small but beautifully built brigs reaped a rich harvest from the beaches of South America. When the American beaches had been worked to exhaustion, the sealers pushed farther south, first into the Scotia Sea and finally to the hitherto undiscovered mainland of Antarctica. Soon reports of a great new continent were percolating through to Europe and America. These reports were vague and unsubstantiated, because sealing was a secretive business – no skipper was likely to disclose the location of new beaches where in a few weeks of uninterrupted slaughter he could amass a fortune in blubber and pelts. At first the sightings of a new continent were confined to the area of the Scotia Sea, south of the tip of Tierra del Fuego. However, in the early 1830s reports began to come in of a great lagoon, free of ice and backed by high mountains, which had been sighted on almost the opposite side of the world, south of New Zealand.

Great Britain, America and France began to prepare expeditions.

First to get under way were the French, although it has to be said that the omens for their success were not auspicious. D'Urville was given two ships, his old corvette, the *Astrolabe*, and the equally venerable corvette, the *Zélée* (of 300 tons); neither vessel was particularly suitable for work in the ice, their hulls being neither copper-sheathed nor reinforced. D'Urville found that he was unable to persuade many of the officers he wanted to sail with him, and he himself was in poor health. '*Ah! ce bonhomme-là ne nous menera pas loin*!' ('This old boy won't get us very far') a seaman was heard to mutter as the admiral, who was approaching 50 and plagued by gout, hobbled aboard. In fact, D'Urville was to take his ships a great deal farther than anyone had a right to expect, and at the end of an important voyage was to produce one of the most erudite and beautiful books of exploration ever written.

His orders were to explore first the area south of Tierra del Fuego, then winter in the warm waters of the mid-Pacific, and finally investigate the area of the lagoon backed by high mountains to the south of New Zealand. The plan was basically sound, but was complicated by the fact that its instigator and its commander had different priorities. For reasons of national pride, Louis-Philippe was anxious for D'Urville to surpass Cook's farthest south (71° 10′); while the admiral himself had the more scientific and more laudable objective of studying terrestrial magnetism and trying to fix the position of the South Magnetic Pole.

The two ships arrived in the Straits of Magellan in December, and spent three weeks studying the flora and fauna and trawling for marine specimens. They found the waters rich in fish, krill, plankton and crustaceans, and D'Urville himself set about classifying these, 'for I had promised myself [he wrote] to encourage personally all the various aspects of our scientific programme'. Their researches were helped by the Patagonian Indians, among whom D'Urville was amazed to find a Swiss watchmaker! This man had apparently stowed-away in a ship from Europe bound for North America; arriving in the New World, he had joined the crew of a sealer, only to find himself, along with six others, deliberately marooned on the coast of Tierra del Fuego. Five of his companions in misfortune were never heard of again – almost certainly they died of starvation and exposure – but the Swiss watchmaker and an Englishman survived. They met up with a group of Indians who befriended them, and for several years shared everything with them, including their wives. What stories these two survivors must have had to tell!

The *Astrolabe* and the *Zélée* left the Straits on 8 January and headed south. After only a couple of days they sighted their first ice, 'a glistening floe that came drifting down on us like a great triangular prism under sail'. This was the advance-guard of an adversary with whom they were to do battle for the next two months. And what a hopeless battle it was. The ships had reached only 65°S when they were brought up short by a field of impenetrable ice.

> *To the very limits of the horizon,* wrote D'Urville, *from ESE to WSW there spread out an enormous plain of ice-blocks, about 12 to 15 feet in height, all piled up and jumbled together in utter confusion. It was a marvellous but at the same time a terrifying sight, both uplifting the heart and numbing it. For no other phenomenon on Earth demonstrates so clearly man's complete and utter impotence. It was indeed a new world that unfolded ahead of us; but a world that was colourless, silent and the very negation of life.*

Only a few years earlier the British sealer James Weddell had, in much the same

D'Urville befriended the Patagonian Indians of Tierra del Fuego *(above)* but burnt the towns of the people of Viti Levu, Fiji *(top)*, both from the volumes of D'Urville's *Voyage*.

area, penetrated as far south as the 74th parallel and D'Urville was bitterly disappointed to find his way blocked at only the 64th. This was evidence of how dramatically the extent of the ice varied from season to season. Weddell in 1823 had been lucky. D'Urville in 1837 was unlucky; the ice-barrier extended another 500 miles to the north. And it was a barrier that neither strength, skill, patience nor ingenuity could breach. D'Urville spent a fortnight reconnoitring and probing it. Then he hauled away to the north and began to chart the South Shetlands – about the bleakest and most uninviting islands on Earth, an arc of volcanic cones, devoid of vegetation, rising like primordial monoliths out of the near-frozen sea. Then, hoping for a late-in-the-season thaw, he again headed south.

The weather was appalling; high winds, heavy seas, and almost continuous glacial rain intermingled with flurries of snow. There was no night, only a couple of hours' sepulchral twilight, then the world would revert again to a kaleidoscope of grey and white: the grey of sea and cloud, and the white of spume and snow. As the bad weather continued week after week, the lack of sun began to have a bad effect on the health of ships' companies who were already weakened by frostbite and scurvy. But D'Urville refused to give up. By early February he was probing once again at the pack-ice, this time to the south of the South Shetland Islands. He probed it with such determination that the *Astrolabe* became frozen in.

> *9 February*, his Diary reads. *We were locked solid in the pack-ice, with heavy almost continuous snowfalls which, we feared, would bind us into the ice even more firmly. Desperate efforts were made to break free. Some men leapt on to the ice with towing-lines, others broke up the ice ahead; then heaving lustily on the towlines they edged us inch by grinding inch towards the safety of the open sea.*

Three times *Astrolabe* fought free of the ice, only three times to become yet again ensnared. On their port beam, through occasional breaks in the cloud, they could see a high continuous land – the mountains of the Antarctic Peninsula, which they named Terre Louis-Philippe – but with the ice now thickening daily they had no more hope of reaching the land than of sailing to the moon.

By early March 11 men in the *Astrolabe* and 29 in the *Zélée* were suffering from scurvy, while D'Urville himself was so weak that he could swallow nothing but water. There was clearly no hope, that autumn, of penetrating farther south; the ships therefore hauled away from the ice and headed for Chile. By the time they dropped anchor off Talcahuano nearly half the crew were so afflicted with scurvy that they could barely stand – some indeed were never to recover. D'Urville spent six weeks in Talcahuano settling the more seriously sick in hospital and giving the others a chance to recuperate ashore. Then he put to sea again, this time on a two-year cruise through the Pacific.

Up to this point it would be fair to say that although his efforts had been heroic, his results had been disappointing. His only real achievements had been to make a fine collection of the Southern Ocean's invertebrates, and an accurate chart of the South Shetlands; although in a somewhat different field, his young artist, Ernest Goupil, had painted a number of ice-scapes which – like those of Edward Wilson – combined authenticity with considerable artistic merit.

His Pacific cruise was, on the face of it, equally low-key, although the enormous amount of data he collected was later to prove of great value to scientists. In this respect his voyage was the antithesis of Bougainville's. Certainly some of the facts which he unearthed about the islanders would have been a telling antidote to the concept of the

The *Astrolabe* and *Zélée* in heavy ice off the
South Sandwich Islands, January-February 1838.
Drawings from D'Urville's *Voyage*.

Noble Savage. In Fiji, he discovered that the traditional way of dealing with people who were old and sick was to kill them. A pit was dug, the victim climbed into it and was clubbed to death. In the Solomons he discovered evidence of cannibalism.

> *Nothing,* he was told, *is more delicious than the body of an enemy killed in battle. When this occurs the people stay up all night, chanting, and at dawn the body is brought to them. The skull is opened, and the more important people push bananas into the brain and scoop it out and eat it raw . . . they then proceed to the thighs and belly. . . Finally what is left is turned over to the common people, all except the private parts which are baked in an oven, laid out on banana leaves and offered to the chiefs.*

Such macabre revelations, however, were rare. The greater part of D'Urville's cruise was taken up with the meticulous collecting of information interspersed with the occasional ceremonial visit, feast or dance. Some of the dances in particular must have helped to cement Franco-Polynesian relations – especially the occasion when one of the midshipmen, after a spirited rendering of the *Marseillaise*, tore off his clothes, 'and could be seen by all dancing *in naturalibus* among the savages'. And everywhere that D'Urville went he collected rare animals and birds: a crabeater seal from Antarctica, an albatross from the Southern Ocean, a condor from the Andes, parakeets from Samoa, flying squirrels from Australia, proboscis monkeys from Borneo, a Tasmanian devil, and flightless kiwis from the North Island of New Zealand. Never before had an expedition amassed such an exotic zoological collection.

In December 1839 the *Astrolabe* and the *Zélée* arrived in Hobart, Tasmania. As a result of nearly two years' cruising in the tropics many of their crew were now suffering from dysentery or malaria. The governor, Sir John Franklin, put the colony's hospital at the disposal of his visitors. Once again there was a brief period of rest and recuperation, then D'Urville set out on the final stage of his voyage, his search for the great bight of ice-free water which, according to sealers, reached deep into the Antarctic at about the 180° meridian. His departure was without doubt hastened by the knowledge that British and American expeditions were already heading for the same area. Sadly, he sailed without Goupil, who died only a few hours before the ships weighed anchor. How one wishes that this gifted artist could have been aboard the *Astrolabe* to record the remarkable discoveries to come. For unexpectedly, after heading south from Hobart for only a fortnight, the French sighted land.

On the afternoon of 19 January 1840, *Astrolabe* and *Zélée* crossed the Antarctic Circle. There were the usual crossing-the-line celebrations: according to D'Urville's Diary, 'a banquet, fancy-dress, and singing and dancing as the Antarctic Father Neptune welcomed us to his kingdom'. Later that evening several of the ships' company thought they could see in the south 'a distant appearance of mountains'. This was reckoned at first to be an hallucination; then the lookouts reported, drifting down on them, an unusual number of icebergs. Very prudently the ships hove-to.

Next morning the weather for once was magnificent; no wind, no cloud and the sea a rich Mediterranean blue. And the land was clearly visible, a vast unbroken coastline running from west-north-west to east-south-east as far as the eye could see. The shoreline appeared to consist of a sheer cliff of ice, about 200 feet high, and above and beyond this the snow on the receding slopes was piled up in huge symmetrical drifts, like the dunes of a desert. As his ships picked their way through a network of icebergs towards the shore, D'Urville realized in amazement that *Terra Australis Incognita* – the Great Southern Continent which for centuries had adorned maps of the Pacific – had materialized at last. At midday he was able to fix his position – 66° 30′S, 138° 21′E –

which placed him no more than a couple of miles from the coast of Antarctica. His compasses were swinging wildly; no two were reading alike, and this made him think that the South Magnetic Pole lay only a few miles inland. He was right, and his estimate of the Pole's position – 72° 00′S, 136° 45′E – was remarkably accurate.

For several days the two ships picked their way through the ice parallel to a coast of awesome beauty. Some of the ice consisted of fragments no larger than the petals of a flower, but there were also whole armadas of huge flat-topped bergs more than a mile in circumference. 'At times,' wrote D'Urville, 'it was as though our ships were threading their way through the narrow streets of a city between tall buildings.' The officers' orders echoed and re-echoed from the vertical walls of ice. The sea, rushing in and out

The *Astrolabe* in a storm off the Powell Islands. Antarctica, a drawing from D'Urville's *Voyage*.

of the ice-caves, created dangerous currents and whirlpools, and so great was the heat of the sun that cascades of water were constantly streaming down the sides of the bergs.' On 22 January, the *Astrolabe*'s longboat managed to land on a rocky island about a hundred yards offshore – this was as close to the mainland as the ice allowed them to get. The Tricolour was unfurled, rock samples were collected, a bottle of Bordeaux was ceremonially drunk, and in D'Urville's own words, 'following the ancient custom kept up by the English, we took possession of the island and the adjacent coast in the name of France'.

This was one of the great moments in the history of exploration. It may well be that some little-known sealer had landed a few years earlier on the coast of Antarctica – John Davis of New Haven has the likeliest claim – but this is impossible to prove. To D'Urville must go the honour of being the first person who, beyond doubt, sighted and landed on the most isolated of the world's continents. He describes the land he discovered as 'a formidable layer of ice, rather like an envelope, which forms the crust over a base of rock', a definition which, in essence, could hardly be improved on. He was following the coastline west when the weather brought his exploration to a premature end. The coast of Adélie Land – D'Urville, with refreshing gallantry, had

Adélie Land, Antarctica, a drawing from D'Urville's *Voyage*.

named his discovery after his wife – is probably the most desolate and windswept shore on Earth. Often the sun isn't seen for weeks at a time, and the wind *averages* 50 knots and frequently gusts to over 100. Ever since D'Urville's arrival the weather had been uncharacteristically benign; now suddenly it showed its true colours. On 24 January the ships were struck by a violent blizzard. They became separated, their canvas was torn to shreds, and in six hours they suffered more damage than in the previous six months. Next day they managed to come together again, but in the weeks that followed, as snowstorms and hurricane-force winds alternated with thick banks of fog, they were too preoccupied with survival to spare a thought for exploration. By the end of the month D'Urville had had enough. His vessels were leaking and near-foundering; his crew, yet again, were suffering from frostbite and scurvy; and he was thinking of heading for home, when about the last thing he could have expected very nearly took place: he almost collided with another ship.

Suddenly, out of the rolling mist and the driving snow, an unknown vessel was sighted bearing down on them. Both ships altered course – and both, subsequently, accused the other of deliberately avoiding contact. According to the French commander, the other ship, which was flying the American flag, veered away and disappeared into the spindrift. According to the American commander – Charles Wilkes of the US Exploring Expedition who was also in search of Antarctica – the French ship 'made sail so as to escape us'. Common sense, however, leads one to suppose that the reason why the two commanders failed to come together and exchange information was the appalling weather.

This was the last incident of note in D'Urville's three-year voyage. He returned, via Tasmania and New Zealand, to France and at once set about preparing his report. This was the type of work at which he was happiest and most skilled, and certainly the 23 volumes and 7 atlases of his *Voyage au pôle Sud et dans l'Océanie sur les corvettes l'Astrolabe et la Zélée* are graced not only by illustrations of outstanding merit but also by passages of great descriptive beauty, well worthy of the pen that first described the classical outlines of the Venus de Milo. Sadly, he didn't live to see his *magnum opus* published for he was killed in a train accident in the spring of 1842.

It would be hard to imagine two more contrasting expeditions than those of Bougainville and D'Urville, and the fact that they *were* so different was an indication of how the pattern of exploration in the Pacific was changing. Bougainville belonged to the old school; primarily interested in the discovery of new lands, he had been happy to accept the people of the Pacific at face value, and to endow them with characteristics not wholly substantiated by facts. D'Urville belonged to the new school; primarily interested in the discovery of facts, he viewed both the islands and the islanders with the eye of a scientist, and was content to collect information about them without passing judgement. It is difficult to say which of these two great expeditions was the more important. Bougainville's promoted the concept of the Noble Savage which may have been partly fallacious but which did at least promise the islanders a measure of protection from Europeanization. D'Urville's proved that the southern reaches of the Pacific were bordered by a major land mass; a *Terra Australis* very much reduced in size and very different from the mythical 'Land of Brazil Wood, Elephants and Gold', but nonetheless a land of continental proportions.

One reason why D'Urville's last voyage took place deep in the sub-Antarctic is that the French were late arrivers in the Pacific, and by the time they got there, the tropical and temperate reaches of the ocean had few secrets left to explore. Equally late to arrive were the Russians and the Americans. It was therefore around the polar extremities of the Pacific that Russian and American activities were concentrated.

D'Urville's discovery of 20 January 1840, from a painting by Le Breton.

THE FARTHEST ENDS OF THE EARTH

1. RUSSIAN EXPLORERS IN THE ANTARCTIC

'By now our gums had swollen up like dark brown sponges and had grown over our teeth so that we were quite unable to eat .. Want, cold, exhaustion, sickness, despair and death were our daily guests. Our dead, before we had time to bury them, were mutilated by foxes, who soon became so bold as to molest even the helpless living.' Georg Wilhelm Steller

The North Pacific has never had quite the same glamorous image as the South Pacific. In the south – at least in popular imagination – lay *Terra Australis Incognita*, 'the Land of Brazil Wood, Elephants and Gold'; and when this turned out to be myth there still remained the treasures of the Spice Islands, the delights of Tonga and Tahiti, and the mysteries of Easter Island. In the north lay darker and more enigmatic coastlines: not only Swift's Brobdingnag, with its 'flies the size of larks' and its 'volcanoes 30 miles high', but the almost equally mythical Compagnie Landt and Gamaland, the residue of early Dutch reports of land to the east of the Sea of Okhotsk, and the highly dubious straits of Anian and Juan de Fuca, the residue of early British and Spanish dreams of a seaway, linking the Pacific and the Atlantic, through North America. There extremities of the habitable world were shrouded in both mist and mystery.

One reason why exploration in the North Pacific lagged behind exploration in the South can be seen from the map. The South was an open seaway; as soon as it became known to Europeans, it was integrated into the great trade arteries of the world; across its waters the treasures of the East were carried to Europe. The North, in contrast, was a bottleneck, desolate coastlines converging into a desolate strait which led to nothing but yet more desolate pack-ice. There was little incentive here for exploration.

Other disincentives were the people and the climate. In the north-west Pacific the people of Korea and Japan firmly, and some might say wisely, closed their doors to 'the Western barbarians'. In Korea foreigners were never welcome. In Japan there was a brief honeymoon, during which traders and, to a greater degree, missionaries enjoyed some success. However, early in the seventeenth century the Tokugawa Shoguns established a highly efficient and highly exclusive regime which effectively isolated Japan from the rest of the world; foreigners were *persona non grata*. On the other side of the Pacific, the people of British Columbia and Alaska were not unfriendly, but they were few in number and had little to attract the attention of explorers. Their country, it is true, was rich in oil, gold, timber, salmon and furs, but only the last of these was instantly exploitable. In other words, ships venturing into the far north of the Pacific had to face a hostile people to port and an unrewarding people to starboard, while ahead lay little but sea-cows, walruses and pack-ice. They also had to face sailing

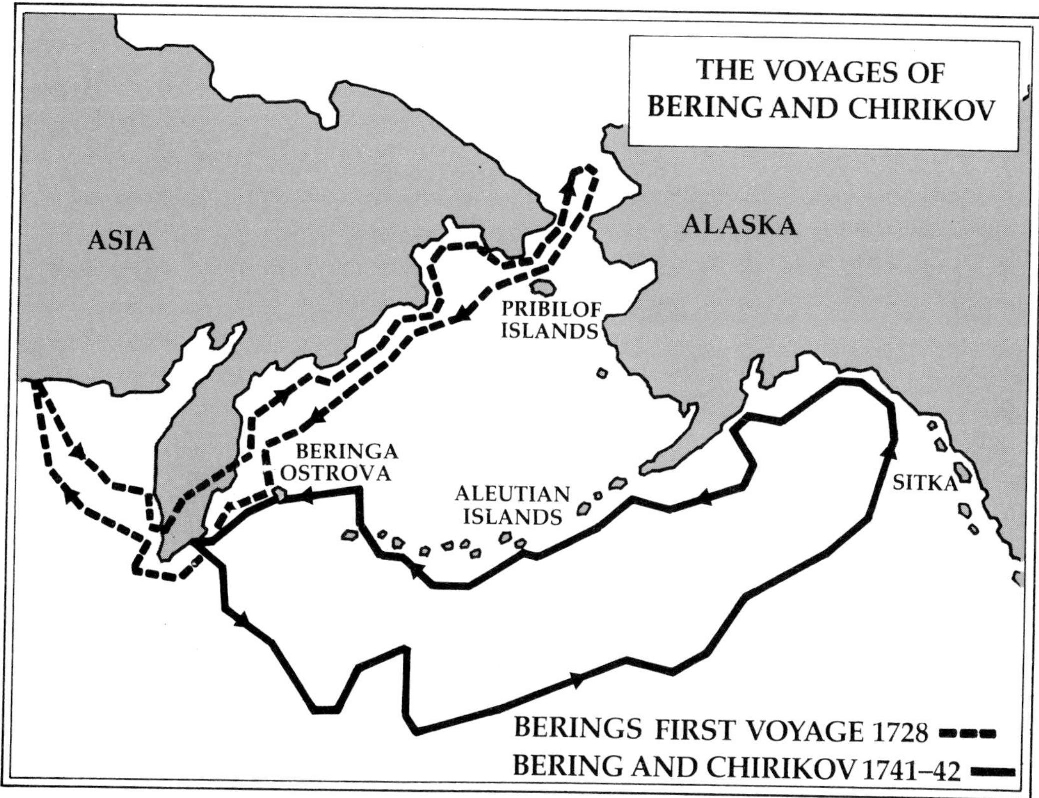

conditions which were exceptionally difficult and hazardous.

The climate in the extreme north of the Pacific has been nicely described in *The Geography of the Pacific* as 'a succession of unpleasant weather: cyclonic storms with winds of gale violence, sudden squalls, low cloud, dense fogs and drizzling rain or driven snow for days on end'. This is confirmed by the experience of the explorers. In one month – October 1741 – Bering in the *Saint Peter* recorded that on 23 days out of 31 there were winds of gale force or over, and on 27 days out of 31 there was rain. In another month – July 1778 – Cook in the *Resolution* recorded 17 days out of 30 as foggy and 21 out of 30 as wet. These conditions would have made for difficult sailing in the open sea; in coastal waters peppered with islands, shoals and reefs they made exploration a daunting business.

First into these dangerous waters were the Russians.

Not many figures in history have been accorded the simple epithet 'the great': Peter I of Russia is one of them, and deservedly; for out of barbaric feudalism he forged a modern world power. One of his most cherished projects was the creation of a Russian navy, and this in turn involved the establishing of ice-free ports. Most of his energy was centred on Saint Petersburg (present-day Leningrad). Here, in the desolate swampland where the River Neva enters the sea, he built, at the cost of more than 200,000 lives, what is arguably the most beautiful city in the world – 'Russia's window to the west'. He then turned his attention to the opposite extremity of his kingdom. What chance was there, he asked his advisers, of establishing an ice-free port in the Pacific? No one could tell him. For Russia's Pacific seaboard, divided from the country's main centres of government and culture by some 6,000 miles of desert, forest and steppe, was virtually *terra incognita*; it shared with Alaska the distinction of being the least-known coastline of the habitable world. In 1719 Peter sent two geodesists, Evreinov and Luzhin, to compile a report on this remote corner of his empire.

Historians have debated at some length what was expected of Evreinov and Luzhin. Were they to discover whether Asia and America were joined together; were they to look into reports that gold had been found in the Kurils; or were they to search for the mysterious Gamaland which, on ancient charts, spread amoeba-like over the sealanes east of Kamchatka? Peter would certainly have liked to know the answer to these questions; but his chief concern was more likely to have been to establish on the Pacific seaboard a port from which his embryo navy could operate. Unluckily, from the Russian point of view, the Chiang Dynasty had recently established themselves throughout present-day Manchuria and Korea, so the most southerly part of Peter's

Vitus Bering (1681-1741), the only known portrait of the Danish seaman who, in the service of Peter the Great of Russia, discovered the Bering Strait and the Aleutian Islands.

Pacific territory was the peninsula of Kamchatka. This was not very promising terrain: a great arm of barren mountains stretching out of the frozen wastes of the Arctic towards ice-free water. Stretching out towards ice-free water, but not altogether reaching it; for during much of the year the coast of Kamchatka is sheathed in a veneer of ever-shifting ice. The tiny port of Bolsheretsk clung precariously to the south-west tip of the peninsula, facing the Sea of Okhotsk, but so dangerous were the coastal waters off Kamchatka that local ships never ventured out of the Sea of Okhotsk into the main reaches of the Pacific. The geodesists therefore recommended the expansion of two tiny settlements on the south-east coast of Kamchatka – Petropavlovsk and Nizhne-Kamchatsk. It was from these remote outposts of the known world that Peter launched his first probe into the waters of the north. And the man he appointed to command his expedition was not a Russian but a Dane.

Vitus Bering was born in 1681 in Horsens on the east coast of the Danish mainland. He joined the Russian Baltic fleet at the age of 22, and over the next couple of decades built up the reputation of being a careful and competent seaman. He had little experience of waters outside the Baltic, and no experience at all of exploration – but this could be said about virtually all the officers in Peter's newly formed navy. He was a safe choice rather than an inspired one, and this was to be reflected in his achievements.

The story of his first expedition is soon told.

He left Saint Petersburg in February 1725, but was unable to begin actual exploration for three-and-a-half years, so great were the difficulties facing him. It was July 1728 before he finally set sail from Nizhne-Kamchatsk, for the logistics of mounting even a modest expedition from Kamchatka were daunting. Timber for building his ship had to be first felled then hauled over the snow by dog-teams. Equipment and stores had to be either carried some 6,000 miles across the steppes of Eurasia, or shipped some 25,000 miles across half the oceans of the world. In Kamchatka itself the native population (to quote Bering) 'did as it pleased and was by no means under Russian control'; while the port from which he had to operate consisted of 'no more than a couple of dozen rude dwellings'. Small wonder it took him three years simply to get his ship, the *St Gabriel*, built and under-way.

After so long a gestation, the voyage itself proved something of an anti-climax. It lasted less than two months and resulted in no spectacular discoveries.

Bering sailed from Nizhne-Kamchatsk on 14 July, and began immediately to survey the coast to the north-east. This was virgin territory and Bering showed great skill and patience in accurately mapping the Asian coastline right up to the Chukotskiy Peninsula. At the approaches to the strait which now bears his name he discovered Saint Lawrence Island. He then stood north, through thick mist, into the Arctic Ocean. By 16 August he had reached 67° 18′N. Here his expedition came to an uncertain halt. He had expected by this time to have made contact with the mainland of America, but for the last week the *St Gabriel* had been enveloped in mist 'so thick we could hardly see the length of the ship', and already there were signs that sea-ice was forming, as the brief Arctic summer drew to its close. Fearful of being trapped and forced to winter on an unknown shore which was likely to be devoid of both water and wood, Bering turned back.

On his homeward voyage, as on his outward, he passed through the narrow strait which divides Asia and America in thick fog. On both occasions he sighted the coast of Asia but not the coast of America, which, in normal weather, is clearly visible. He dropped anchor in Nizhne-Kamchatsk on 2 September 1728; but it was March 1730 before he was back in St Petersburg, his journey home via the forests of Siberia being almost a feat of exploration in its own right.

When Bering's report had been studied by the Tsar and his advisers, the general feeling was that although he had brought back a fine map of the coast of north-east Asia, he had achieved little else. In particular he had failed to find America. Another expedition was therefore planned, this time on a more ambitious scale. The whole coastline of Arctic Russia was to be surveyed, the interior of what might be loosely called Siberia was to be studied, the Kurils and the islands of Japan were to be charted, and, in particular, the north-west coast of America was to be located and placed on the map in its true relationship to Asia. Once this last objective had been achieved, the American coast would be followed as far south as California in the hope of opening up the area to Russian trade. Bering was in overall command, *and* had the major task of locating America. What a programme! Beside it the labours of Hercules pall to insignificance. For this was to prove the widest-ranging and longest-lasting expedition in the entire history of exploration. Fifteen years after its inception, many of its members were still in the field; twenty-five years after their return, many of its findings were still unpublished. No wonder the conscientious Bering was to wear himself out in his efforts to fulfil a task that was beyond the capabilities of any single man.

It is difficult to say exactly when this leviathan project got under way, but perhaps the date when Bering left St Petersburg – April 1733 – is as good a starting point as any.

Since Russia's Pacific ports could still boast virtually nothing in the way of ship-building or chandlers' yards, Bering was obliged to haul with him across Siberia all the nautical paraphernalia that was essential to a successful voyage – iron to strengthen his ships, sails, rigging, anchors, tar, navigational equipment, beacons, weapons, clothing, food, medical supplies . . . the list is endless – *and* he was expected to survey his route. No wonder it took three-and-a-half years and the efforts of some 3,000 men to get him even as far as Okhotsk, a port not far from the Manchurian border. And when he did at last reach Okhotsk he found 'that practically nothing had been done in preparation for our expedition'. Not only were his ships unbuilt, so were the yards in which to build them! It was another three-and-a-half years before he managed to construct and rig two 250-ton brigs, the *St Peter* and the *St Paul*. He was then held up by ice in the Sea of Okhotsk and by the difficulty of victualling his ships and training his crew. Eight years elapsed between the time he left St Petersburg and the time he arrived at – let alone set sail from – his final point of departure, Petropavlovsk. However, on 4 June 1741, after almost as many trials and tribulations as Job, he embarked at last on the most important of his many assignments – the search for America.

Before sailing, Bering had canvassed the views of his subordinates as to where America lay and what course they should set to reach it. The consensus of opinion was that they should head south-east; for they had found nothing on Bering's previous expedition to the north-east, and it was in the sealanes south-east of Kamchatka that maps showed the mysterious Gamaland, which, it was thought, must be a promontory jutting out from the American mainland. Gamaland had supposedly been sighted by Joao da Gama in 1590 when he was blown off course on passage from Macao to

Petropavlovsk, Russia's ice-free port in Kamchatka.

Harbour of New Archangel in Sitka, Alaska, centre for the *promyshlennika* (hunters-cum sealers) of the Russian American Company, from a painting by Y. Lisiansky, 1805.

Acapulco; and it shows how little was known about the North Pacific that for 150 years his report of 'high white mountains' (almost certainly clouds) was neither substantiated nor disproved. Bering's decision to head south-east was therefore perfectly logical. It was nonetheless unfortunate, for it meant that his expedition wasted time exploring an area in which there was nothing to discover. And in polar exploration, time, as Bering was to discover, is a matter of life or death.

Throughout the early part of June the *St Peter* and the *St Paul* headed into the featureless sealanes south of the Aleutians. Several times they *thought* they saw land; but the snow-white mountains on the horizon, when investigated, proved always to be cloud. To start with the weather was not too bad: 'light winds', 'drizzle' and 'chilly' are the three most common entries in the ships' logs; but towards the middle of the month these give way to 'storm', 'cold' and 'fog'. In worsening conditions the ships became separated. This, with inexperienced crews, was hardly surprising; but again it was unfortunate; for the ships wasted yet more time searching for one another before going their respective ways.

From now on the expedition consisted of two quite separate voyages: Bering's in the *St Peter*, and his second-in-command Chirikov's in the *St Paul*. Chirikov made the more important discoveries and survived; few people today have heard of him. Bering made less important discoveries and died; and such was the horror of his dying that his name today is remembered all over the world.

After the ships became separated, Chirikov altered course to the east-north-east. It was mid-July before they had their first hint that they were approaching land; then their lookouts spotted a duck and two floating tree-trunks. A couple of days later, on 15 July, they sighted 'some very high mountains, their summits covered in snow, their lower slopes, we thought, covered in trees. This', Chirikov wrote in his Diary, 'must be America.' He was right, and his landfall was almost certainly Prince of Wales Island, close to the 56th parallel, in southern Alaska.

For several days the *St Paul* followed the coast to the north searching for somewhere to land. On 18 July, as they were passing Baranof Island, they spotted a possible anchorage – what looked like the entrance to a sheltered bay – and their longboat was lowered and sent inshore to reconnoitre. What happened next will never be known. There were, during the next few days strong winds, heavy rain and fog. It was too dangerous for the *St Paul* to venture close inshore; so she beat up and down, at intervals firing her guns – the agreed signal for her longboat to return. But it didn't return; it was as though it had vanished off the face of the Earth; and eventually Chirikov, with some misgivings, sent a second boat inshore to investigate. It disappeared too. And there was not a lot Chirikov could do about it. He stood in as close as he dared to the shore – twice coming within a hairsbreadth of running aground – but could see no sign of his missing crew. He had almost given up hope of seeing them again when, very early one morning a week later, two boats were sighted leaving the shore. Joyfully the *St Paul* stood in to meet them. It was only as the vessels neared one another that Chirikov's lookouts realized the boats were being paddled not rowed. They were kayaks, and the men paddling them were Sitka Indians, who had almost certainly come to tell the Russians that some disaster had befallen their companions and to lead the *St Paul* to their help – why else should they continually have cried '*Agai*! *Agai*!, which is the Sitku for 'Come on' or 'Come here'? However, the Indians' timidity, the language barrier, and the fact that the *St Paul* couldn't have followed the kayaks inshore no matter how hard she had tried, precluded meaningful contact. The Sitka returned to the bay from which they had appeared. The *St Paul*, illuminated with lanterns, beat up and down for a further 24 hours; then reluctantly, Chirikov accepted the fact that his men were beyond any help that he could bring them. He thought they must have been attacked and killed by the Indians. It seems more likely, however, that they had fallen victim to the fierce-running tide-rips which make the inshore waters of Alaska a place of death. Years later the French explorer La Pérouse was to have two of his longboats wrecked and 21 of his men drowned in almost exactly the same area. One can't help thinking, however, that some of the Russians might have survived. If they did, one can only hope that the people of Alaska treated their involuntary guests as well as the people of Tierra del Fuego treated their Swiss watchmaker.

Chirikov now cut short his efforts to explore the coast of America and headed for home. The reason is stated very clearly in his Diary: 'because we had lost both of our ship's boats, we had no means of examining the shore, and no means of landing to procure water, of which we now had only 45 casks. . . Weather cloudy with rain. I told the crew to catch rain-water from the sails and store it for drinking. I also ordered water to be rationed.'

Their homeward voyage was an endless battle with fog, headwinds, scurvy and thirst.

Their course took them parallel to the southern fringe of the Aleutian Islands, which they sighted at intervals through the miasma of drizzle and fog – Kodiak Island on 2 August, Atka on 4 September, Adak on 9 September and Attu on 22 September. (These dates are those of the old-fashioned Julian calendar, which was still in use in Imperial Russia.) Off Adak they made contact with the Aleuts, who paddled their kayaks with great skill around the *St Paul* and exchanged bladders of water for knives, but could not be persuaded to come aboard. The meeting was cut short by a storm, which threatened to drive the *St Paul* ashore. 'It was only with much difficulty, with the loss of an anchor and with the help of God, that we were able to fight clear of the land.'

As the Russians struggled west, their ship's log gives us the bare facts of what conditions were like:

> *16 September. Captain Chirikov, Lieutenant Chikhachev and many members of the crew are seriously ill, due to a lack of water and the long and arduous voyage. More than half the crew are unable to work. This afternoon one of the strongest, the sailmaker Michael Usachev, died of scurvy. Only 9 small barrels of water left. . . 27 September. Osip Kachikov died of scurvy, and we lowered his body into the sea. Captain Chirikov, the Lieutenants Chikhachev and Plautin, the astronomer Delisle de la Croyère and many members of the crew are quite unable to move because of scurvy; others can get about only with the greatest difficulty. We have 6 small barrels of water left, and can no longer use water for cooking.*

When, on 10 October, they at last sighted Petropavlovsk they had only a single barrel of water remaining, more than half their ship's company were unable to stand, two died before the ship could be brought alongside, and six, including their commander, were so ill that they had to be carried ashore on stretchers.

Chirikov was a highly competent explorer who deserves to be better known. He discovered the north-west coast of America and placed it accurately on the map in its relationship to Asia. He also discovered the great chain of the Aleutian Islands. He had, it is true, to pay a high price for his discoveries, but his commander, Vitus Bering, was to pay even more dearly for his.

After the *St Peter* and the *St Paul* became separated Bering held course for a couple of days, then he too turned to the north-east. This didn't please his German naturalist, Georg Steller, who reckoned that he had more than once seen land to the south. Steller was a constant thorn-in-the-flesh of the Russians, for although he was a fine naturalist he was devastatingly unaware of his shortcomings as a seaman. He may have been right in thinking that the standard of nautical expertise aboard the *St Peter* was not very high, but on the many occasions when he and the Russians differed, it was usually Steller who was in the wrong – on this occasion, for instance, although he insisted he had seen 'snow-capped mountains' to the south, the nearest land in that direction was in fact Hawaii, and that was 1,500 miles away!

Bering had been on his new heading for some three weeks when he too sighted the American mainland. '17 July,' his Diary reads, 'at 12.30 a.m. we saw a chain of high snow-covered mountains, among them a great volcano.' His landfall was a couple of days later than Chirikov's, and several hundred miles to the north, at a part of the coast dominated by the 18,008-ft (5,489-metre) cone of Mount Elias. He was more successful than his second-in-command had been in his efforts to land, and next day his longboat put ashore on Kayak Island. Here his crew discovered 'an underground hut, rather like a cellar; but no people'. They left gifts for the inhabitants, who had almost certainly fled into the nearby woods; then they refilled their water-barrels, while Steller collected as many plants as possible on this their only landing. 'Ten years getting to America, and a miserable ten hours ashore!' the naturalist complained bitterly, this time with some justification. For Bering showed little interest in exploring the land he had discovered. The fact is that he was 62, and worn out with the vicissitudes of an impossible command. He had found America. That was his brief. And now his one wish was to get back as fast as possible to safety. 'Took onboard 35 barrels of fresh water,' his Diary reads. 'Then set course SW by compass for Kamchatka.'

This may have seemed at the time an over-cautious decision, but events were to prove, in no uncertain manner, that it was justified; for it would be difficult to imagine anything much more terrible than the events of the next few months.

At first the *St Peter* followed much the same track as the *St Paul*, only a shade farther to the south. Perhaps because she *was* that shade to the south, away from the shelter of the Aleutian Islands, she seemed to run into even worse weather. Soon the Russians were suffering from scurvy; by the end of September, 19 men were too weak to work, and they were still a thousand miles from Kamchatka. The westerly winds now set in with relentless fury – on some days they were blown literally backwards. They began to run short of water. The log of the *St Peter* records their suffering. The entry for any particular day may not appear all that traumatic; it was the combination of storm, rain and fog day after day, week after week, without respite, which transformed their voyage into a purgatory. Here is a precis of the *St Peter*'s log for October:

1 October. a.m.: Rain and squalls. Reefed trysail. Terrible storm with heavy seas. Lanyards and stays torn loose. p.m.: Storm continues. Gunport bulwark carried away. Waves constantly washing over the deck.
5 October. a.m.: Another storm, heavy swell, squalls and heavy rain. p.m.: Storm continues. Violent winds. Obliged to heave-to under trysail.
9 October. a.m.: Light wind with drizzle. Wind freshening to strong gale. Trysail stay parted. p.m.: Terrific storm with heavy swell. Hove-to under reefed trysail. Lee side of ship almost constantly under water.
13 October. a.m.: Cloud, drizzle, fog and occasional heavy rain. p.m.: Weather as before. Have 21 men on sick list.
17 October. a.m.: Clear with passing cloud. Repaired damage caused by storm. p.m.: Cloud, drizzle and fog.
21 October. a.m.: Thick cloud, hail and rain. Squalls, which obliged us to heave-to. Nikita Kharitonov died by the will of God. p.m.: Thick cloud, with hail and snow.
25 October. a.m.: More storms, with squalls of rain, hail and snow. Land sighted on starboard bow. p.m.: Strong winds, thick cloud and huge hailstones. The land we sighted this morning bears N by W¼W, about 8½ miles; we take it to be an island. (Almost certainly it was Kiska in the Rat Islands, a westerly extension of the Aleutians.) *Have now 30 on the sick list.*
29 October. a.m.: By the will of God, Stephen Buldirev, the cooper, died of scurvy. Sighted high land, N by W½W, 2 miles. Sounded, got 63 fathoms. Drizzle wet and foggy. p.m.: Sounded, got 35 fathoms. Because of fog we could not see anything, so hove-to. When the fog cleared, we sighted a small island. (Almost certainly Agattu in the Semichi Islands, the most westerly group in the Aleutians.)
31 October. a.m.: Light wind, drizzle and fog. p.m.: Weather as before, with frequent falls of snow. By the grace of God died the soldier Karp Pashennoi, and we lowered him into the sea.

On 4 November they sighted a small island and a couple of days later 'a high mountainous and continuous ridge covered with snow'. They were now at the end of their tether. They had, it is true, a fair amount of food left, but they had virtually no water; their rigging was rotten; their sails were in shreds; their ship was leaking and labouring, and each day men were dying of scurvy. It was agreed that their only hope was to land. As they stared at the shore which, they could see, would at least provide them with solid ground, water and wood, they thought that the worst of their agony must be over. In fact it was about to begin.

They tried to anchor in deep water; but gale-force winds and a heavy sea drove the *St Peter* over a sandbar and into a shallow lagoon. Those who were able to walk landed, and set about choosing a site where they could winter. They found a small valley, sheltered from the worst of the wind, with running water and a scattering of dwarf alder and birch. There seemed, at least for the moment, to be plenty of food – ptarmigan,

ptarmigan, sea-otters, fur-seals, foxes and (best eating of all) the soon-to-be-extinct sea-cows. They started to hack pits out of the frozen sand, 'like a grave for two people'. These they covered with driftwood, birchwood and all the blankets they could lay hands on. By 15 November they had everything ready for bringing the sick ashore. It was then that things started going wrong.

> *That day,* writes Steller, *the sick were brought up on deck. Some died as they were carried into the cold air, and this was the case of the master-gunner Ilya Dergachev; others died in the boats as they were being rowed ashore, and this was the case of the soldier Vasili Popkov; others died on the beach, and this was the case of the sailor Seliverst Tarakanov. The shoreline became a pitiful and indeed a terrible sight. Before our dead could be buried, they were mutilated by the foxes, who even became so bold as to molest the helpless living. Some of those who were sick were in tears because of the cold, others because they were hungry and thirsty but could neither eat nor swallow because of the agony of the scurvy. Soon the foxes gathered about us in great numbers; they ripped open our baggage, ate our provisions and dragged away our clothing. We killed them and we tortured them – skinning them, putting out their eyes, cutting off their ears and tails and part-roasting them – but this seemed to make them even more audacious and malevolent.* Bering's second-in-command, Sven Waxel, takes up the gruesome story. *Men were continually dying, and there was no one strong enough to drag away the corpses; nor were those who were still living able to move away from the dead. We all had to remain mixed up together in a circle with a fire in the centre. Bering was dying, and there was nothing we could do to help him; as he lay half-buried in sand in the hollow that had been dug for him, he begged to be left this way for warmth. He died on 8 December. . . Khitrov shared a hollow with me; between us lay our catering officer, Ivan Lagunov, dead.*

However, with the benefit of fresh food, fresh water and unlimited wood for their fires, those who survived the first few weeks managed slowly to come to terms with their desolate environment. They built 'five underground dwellings against the severity of the winter', sited close together, and each with its individual fire and fox-proof storehouse. They then set themselves three tasks: to kill enough animals and birds to provide them with food for the winter, to get together sufficient wood for them to have permanent fires, and to plan their daily routine so that all ranks and all nationalities had their fair share of hunting, wood hauling, cooking and resting. On Bering's death, his first-lieutenant Sven Waxel took over command. And a fine leader he was to prove, working largely by consensus, arriving at all the right decisions and managing to keep up the morale of his disparate ship's company. It was largely due to his good sense that the majority of his crew survived.

Survival was never easy, and many men many times that winter came close to death. On one occasion a hunting party was trapped in the open by a blizzard.

> *Six feet of snow fell overnight,* writes Steller, *and the men who had gone hunting came near to perishing. After passing the night in 'snow holes', they had by morning barely enough strength to dig themselves out. Three staggered back to us, unable to speak, and so stiff from the cold that, like rigid machines, they could scarcely move their limbs, while the assistant surgeon had gone totally snowblind. A fourth member of the party, a marine, was found wandering half-insensible along the beach; he had fallen into a river, and not only his clothing but his limbs were frozen virtually solid.*

By a near-miracle all survived. A few weeks later a group hunting sea-otters were forced by blizzards to shelter in a cave. Here they found themselves trapped by a succession of high tides, 'and were obliged to spend 7 days in cold uncomfortable surroundings with neither food nor firewood; they returned to us on the 9th day, by which time we felt sure they had been either drowned or crushed to death by an avalanche'.

People of the coast of North West America. *Top left* Eskimo mother and child; *top right* Nootka method of spearing; *above* on the shores of Nootka Sound.

They had one stroke of luck. Waking one morning after a particularly violent storm, they found the *St Peter* had been tossed up like so much driftwood on to the beach. This gave Waxel the opportunity he had been hoping for. All winter he had been regretting that the *St Peter* was too badly damaged ever to sail again; but her wreck now provided him with easily accessible stores and tools and, above all, with sufficient seasoned timber from which to build a completely new vessel. This proved a Herculean task, with everything having to be improvised – the 'tar' for caulking their seams, for example, was made by cooking the juice of laboriously gathered berries – but with their lives depending on their efforts the crew set to work with enthusiasm. 'No one,' wrote Steller in his Diary, 'wants to be idle, because all are exceedingly anxious to be delivered from this desolate island.' And by the middle of July, a 40-foot vessel stood on the improvised stocks ready for launching, a new *St Peter* risen Phoenix-like from the timbers of the old. She was launched, with much difficulty and apprehension, on 7 August and a week later was ready to put to sea.

'So,' writes Steller, 'we left our huts for the last time with much emotion, and crowded into the tiny vessel to which we had entrusted our fate.' And 'crowded' is an understatement; for the 42 survivors and their possessions were crammed so tightly together that it was physically impossible to lie down. Their home-built vessel, however, was their one hope of survival; and on the morning of 14 August, after prayers for a safe voyage, the anchors were weighed and they set course for Kamchatka.

They were lucky with the weather. The autumn storms had not yet started, and indeed there was so little wind that for much of the voyage they used oars rather than sails. This was just as well, for on their third night at sea the *St Peter* sprang a terrible leak, their pumps became clogged-up, and they had to hand-bail and throw overboard just about everything moveable. But the end of their ordeal was in sight, and on 27 August 1742, near-foundering, they half-sailed half-drifted into 'the long desired haven' of Petropavlovsk.

It would be hard to imagine a more gruesome chronicle of suffering, or a more indomitable epic of survival.

These voyages of the Russians epitomize the dark face of exploration. No golden girls, no sun-drenched beaches, no worldly treasures; only storm and ice, scurvy and death, and at the end of it all a desolate mist-encompassed shoreline inked in around the edge of the known world. Yet the voyages of Chirikov and Bering were not without significance, in both the short and long terms.

Their short-term significance was that they established Russian suzerainty over the extreme north of the Pacific. A cynic might say that this was a part of the world the Russians were welcome to, but that would be altogether too facile a judgement. The Russians were secretive about their voyages – Chirikov's and Bering's charts were not made available to the rest of the world until the following century, and even today much of the data collected by Bering's expedition has never been published outside the USSR. As a result of this secrecy it was mainly *Russian* fishermen, *Russian* sealers and *Russian* trappers who, over the next 100 years, were to reap so rich a harvest from the waters and forests of the north. Without this harvest – the whales, the salmon and the fur of seals, fox, beaver, sable, marten and bear – European Russia might well have lost interest in its Pacific territories. As it was, wealth gleaned from the North Pacific helped to bind the vast kingdom of the Tsars together – it is worth remembering that right up to the purchase of 1867 Alaska was a department of Imperial Russia, known simply as Russian America.

Once the Russians had established a sphere of influence in the North Pacific, it was inevitable that they should seek also to establish a naval presence. Petropavlovsk may not have been an ideal or entirely ice-free port, but during the next hundred years it served as the hub from which there radiated a large number of Russian voyages, the most important being those of Krusenstern (1803-6), Kotzbue (1815-18) and Lutke (1826-9). Indeed about the only major Russian explorer *not* to use Petropavlovsk was the greatest of them all, von Bellingshausen, whose exploits in the Southern Ocean rival those of Cook, but belong to the history of Antarctica more than the history of the Pacific.

These Russian voyages, crisscrossing the whole face of the ocean, helped to transform the dream of Peter the Great to reality and to establish Russia as one of the major sea powers of the world. So it might perhaps be said that the crew of the *St Peter* who died in such terrible circumstances on Bering Island didn't die in vain.

---

2. AMERICAN EXPLORERS IN THE ANTARCTIC

"Swerve me? The path to my fixed purpose is laid with iron rails whereon my soul is grooved to run."
Ahab in *Moby Dick*

The last of the great explorers to delineate the Pacific were the Americans.

Until the latter part of the nineteenth century the people of America took little interest in exploration by land outside the confines of their own vast territory, while exploration by sea was left almost entirely in the hands of individual sealers and whalers. In the 1820s, however, the administration did take a brief paternal interest in the affairs of the whalers – it was, after all, whale oil which kept the wheels of American industry turning and the street-lamps of American cities burning – and government officials were disturbed to hear of the losses whalers were suffering in the Pacific. Ships, it seemed, were being wrecked on uncharted reefs; crews were being attacked by hostile islanders – one ship's company, rumour had it, had actually been eaten! In 1821 the House of Representatives recommended, 'it is expedient that one of our public vessels be sent to the South Pacific to examine the coasts, islands, harbours, shoals and reefs, and ascertain their true description'.

From this seed, after years of painful labour, was born America's first national maritime expedition.

American expeditions today tend to be characterized by the excellence of their equipment and the camaraderie of their personnel. It is therefore something of a shock to find this first venture was castigated by its contemporaries as 'the most ill-prepared, the most controversial and probably the most unhappy which ever sailed.' Yet this is not an exaggeration. It took fifteen years to get the expedition off the ground; its gestation was marred by political intrigue, personal vendetta, corruption, larceny and fraud; and at the end of it all, its ships were unsuitable, its budget inadequate and its aims uncertain. There would seem to be two reasons for this. Since it was America's first government-backed venture there were no precedents to work from and the planners had to learn from their mistakes as they went along. Also too many people

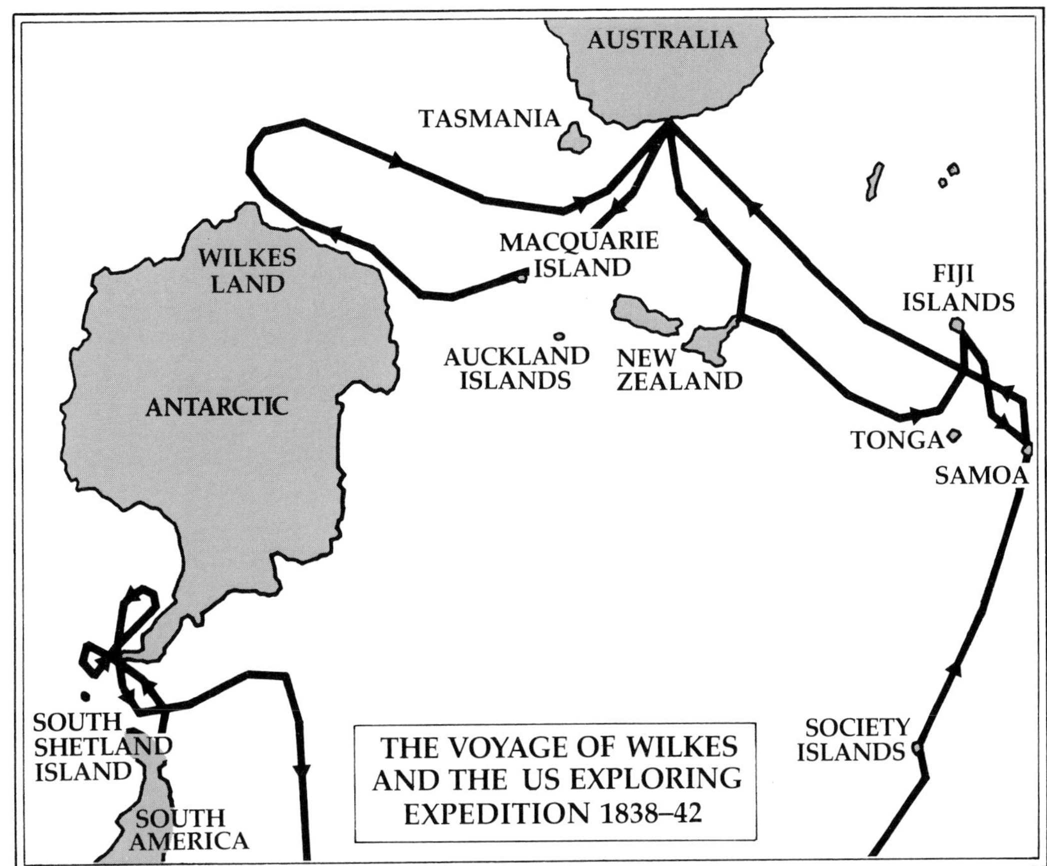

THE VOYAGE OF WILKES AND THE US EXPLORING EXPEDITION 1838–42

became involved in the expedition and expected too many different things from it. One lobby thought 'its primary object must be the promotion of the whaling industry'; another thought it should 'extend the bounds of science and promote the acquisition of knowledge'; some favoured exploring the Antarctic, others favoured exploring the coast of North America. As a result of these dissensions none of the high-ranking officers of the US Navy wanted anything to do with the expedition. However, in the spring of 1838 an officer, albeit a very junior one, came forward who was not only willing but eager to take command.

Lieutenant Charles Wilkes was head of the Depot of Charts and Instruments. His ancestry and his portrait provide us with clues to his character. He was a descendant (a grand-nephew) of John Wilkes, that champion of the peoples' rights and the American colonists who had been such a thorn in the flesh of King George III and the eighteenth-century Tories. His portrait shows a man with a firm mouth, a dominant nose, a stubborn jaw, and sad disillusioned eyes. He looks, as indeed he was, a born leader of lost causes.

Wilkes's appointment caused a furore, partly because of his junior rank, and partly because his precocious ability and ambition had already earned him enemies in naval and scientific circles. However, in the face of the new commander's determination and energy, his enemies were as chaff to the whirlwind. For fifteen years the US Exploring Expedition had been nothing but talk. Within fifteen weeks of Wilkes being put in command, it was at sea – albeit with leaking ships, inadequate equipment and discontented crews. Should we applaud Wilkes for his courage or condemn him for his impetuosity? Here – as with so many aspects of the expedition – there has always been controversy.

Wilkes's detractors argue that he was anxious to get to sea before he was relieved of his command, and that he sailed before his ships were ready. His apologists argue that he did all he could to get his ships and his equipment improved, but was repeatedly refused funds by the Navy Department. A balanced judgement would probably be that Wilkes submitted his requisitions with a singular lack of tact, and the Department got fed up with him and withdrew cooperation. Their whole unhappy relationship is encapsulated in miniature in the drama of the *Sea Gull*'s pumps. The *Sea Gull* was a wretched vessel, an ancient 100-ton New York pilot-boat which leaked like the proverbial sieve; her timbers were rotten and her pumps rusty. Wilkes requested new pumps. They were not sent. So, as a gesture of protest, Wilkes mailed one of the rusty pump-hoops to the Secretary of the Navy. For this 'act of consummate insolence' he was severely reprimanded. One doesn't want to inflate this minor incident to undue proportions, but it does raise an issue of some importance – who was to blame when, nine months later, the luckless *Sea Gull* foundered with the loss of her entire ship's company?

On 18 August 1838 Wilkes led his expedition out of Hampton Roads. He knew very well that his six vessels, the *Vincennes*, *Porpoise*, *Peacock*, *Sea Gull*, *Flying Fish* and *Relief* were ill-found and ill-provisioned, and that his 345 men were ill-tempered and ill-equipped. Yet he was determined to fulfil his orders – and in particular his orders as regards the Antarctic – not only to the letter but 'to such a degree that no person shall ever be able to say I ought to have done more'. In the disparity between his ambitions and his resources lay the seeds of tragedy.

Charles Wilkes (1818-77), commander of the US Exploring Expedition (1838-42) which discovered a large part of the coast of Antarctica, and his ship the *Vincennes* in Disappointment Bay, after a sketch by Wilkes.

It has been said that Wilkes devoted too much of his time to exploring the Antarctic, that he was obsessed with Antarctica in the same way that Melville's Captain Ahab was obsessed with Moby Dick. This is an interesting comparison: all the more so since it seems certain that Melville read Wilkes's *Narrative of the US Exploring Expedition*, and loosely based his character of Ahab on the character of Wilkes. This is how David Jaffé sees it in *The Stormy Petrel and the Whale*:

> *Melville read in the Narrative of a mysterious white ocean, with cathedral-like icebergs looming over the vessels; of flashing coruscations of supernatural brilliance; of the white terror of an Antarctic gale. Above all he read of a grim-faced sea-captain, persisting in his quest in the face of all these dangers, at extreme risk to ships and crew. . . Clearly here was a man who could have been a great national hero. But the hero was a tarnished one. Melville must have perceived that here was a great man with a tragic flaw – a will that was unbending to the point of monomania. A comparison of Wilkes with the evil-tinged heroes of Shakespeare is inevitable.*

This is good scholarship. It should, however, be pointed out that just because a literary character is loosely based on a real-life character, it doesn't follow that the latter has all the traits of the former. Melville was the most factual of novelists – parts of *Moby Dick* read like an instruction manual on whaling – but he still created *fictional* characters with *fictional* traits to suit the plot of his story. No one who has read *Moby Dick* would deny that Ahab was obsessed with getting the better of the great white whale; but it by no means follows from this that Wilkes was obsessed with getting the better of the great white continent. Indeed statistics seem to prove otherwise. For he spent comparatively little time in the Antarctic and less time writing about it. Out of the 48 months his expedition was at sea, only four were spent in the extreme south (two months on his first ice-edge cruise and two on his second). While out of the 2,500 pages of his official report only 100 deal with the Antarctic (12 pages on his first ice-edge cruise and 85 on his second). In other words no more than one-twelfth of his time and no more than one-twenty-fifth of his *Narrative* were devoted to Antarctic exploration. The idea that Wilkes neglected his more mundane duties in order to indulge in a personal battle with the great white continent would therefore seem wide of the mark.

By January 1839 Wilkes and his six ships were anchored in Orange Harbour, at the approaches to Cape Horn. From this well-sheltered base they set out on the first of their ice-edge cruises, Wilkes leaving the *Vincennes* and *Relief* in harbour and taking the *Porpoise* and *Sea Gull* with him towards the South Shetland Islands, while his second-in-command, William Hudson, took the *Peacock* and *Flying Fish* south-west into the area where some 65 years earlier Cook had reached the 71st parallel. These voyages, as Wilkes makes clear in his *Narrative*, were not intended to be major probes into the unknown, but to give his crews experience of ice-edge cruising and so prepare them for the more extensive exploration planned for the following summer.

Porpoise and *Sea Gull* spent three weeks among the ice-capped protuberances of the South Shetland Islands. These were little-known but by no means unknown waters, for throughout the previous 25 years they had been the killing ground for large numbers of British and New England sealers. These skilled and ruthless predators had come south in search of the fur seals (*Arctocephalus*) which breed in vast numbers on the sub-Antarctic islands; and within the span of a single generation they had not only all but exterminated the fur seals, they had sighted and landed on the Antarctic Peninsula. And if one wonders why such important discoveries were not at the time widely acclaimed, the answer lies in the nature of sealing. It was a secretive calling. For as J. C. Furnas puts it in his *Anatomy of Paradise*, 'Whalers could afford to swap information about their quarry. But sealing was wholesale massacre on a deserted shore; and a newly discovered rookery (breeding ground) was like a vein of precious metal, too easily exhausted to tell rivals about.'

So as Wilkes picked his way that autumn among the mist-wreathed islands, his Diary records no great new discoveries. It does, however, record in often evocative prose the wonders and hazards of ice-edge navigation:

> *4 March. By 8 a.m. we had penetrated among the numerous icebergs until it was impossible to go farther. I have rarely seen a finer sight. The sea was literally studded with these beautiful masses, some of pure white, others showing all the shades of the opal, yet others emerald-green, and here and there some of a deep black forming a striking contrast. It was a day of great excitement to all, for we had ice of all kinds to encounter, from the berg of huge quadrangular shape to the sunken deceptive mass that it was difficult to perceive before it was under the bow. Our situation was critical, but the weather favoured us till evening, when it became so thick with mist and fog as to render it necessary to lay-to till daylight. We then had a heavy snowstorm and a strong gale. The deck was soon covered with ice and snow . . . 5 March. The gale increased, and both vessels were now in imminent danger. At 3 a.m. we narrowly missed several icebergs. At 4 a.m. the ice was forming rapidly on deck, and so covered the rigging as to render it difficult to work the ships. The men suffered from the inadequacy of the clothing with which they had been supplied. Although purchased by the government at great expense, it was found to be unsuitable and in every way inferior to the samples exhibited.*

The entries of the next few days prove it wasn't only the crew's clothing which was unsuited to the Antarctic; the ships themselves were altogether inadequate. *Porpoise*'s timbers were rotten, and her gunports were open to the sea so that she was almost continually awash, and it was impossible for her crew to keep either dry or warm. Conditions aboard the *Sea Gull* were even worse; witness her captain's report for 6 March: 'Water freezing all over the deck: icicles enveloping everything: shipping huge seas every few minutes: jib hanging overboard: it is next to impossible for us to make sail: our foresheets are the size of a sloop-of-war's cables from being so covered with ice; there is scarce a sheave that will traverse.'

It was late March before *Porpoise* and *Sea Gull* limped back to Orange Harbour, the ships battered and near-foundering, the crews enfeebled by exhaustion, exposure and scurvy.

The *Peacock* and *Flying Fish*, meanwhile, were exploring some thousand miles to the west. Soon after leaving Orange Harbour they were separated by a series of violent gales, and for the better part of March worked their way south independently through the Bellingshausen Sea.

The *Peacock* was as ill-suited to polar voyaging as her sister sloop-of-the-line, the *Porpoise*. To quote her commander, William Hudson:

> *Her upper works were rotten, and due to her bad and defective refit no vessel could be more uncomfortable; although every precaution was taken to make her gunports tight, yet it was found quite imposssible to do so.* (His Diary records a constant battle with fog, ice, snow and blizzard.) *From 19-25 March we were in thick fog, without a sight of the sun or the sky, and completely surrounded by ice and icebergs. During a brief lift of the fog on 22 March, aided by the light from an iceblink, we discovered an extended range of bergs and field-ice in mass, presenting an absolute barrier. I was compelled to carry all possible canvass to work into a more open position . . . The ship became coated with ice, every spray thrown over her freezing solid, so that her bows and head were fairly packed with it.*

On 26 March Hudson very prudently gave up. He had penetrated as far south as the 68th parallel, and this, considering the bad weather and the state of his ship, was all that could have been expected of him.

The diminutive *Flying Fish* did even better. Indeed, this tiny unstrengthened vessel of under 100 tons came close to bettering Cook's *ne plus ultra* of 71° 10′S, for she somehow managed to force her way through the ice almost to within sight of the inaccessible Marie Byrd Land – a truly heroic achievement. Her commander, William Walker, was prepared to take more risks than Hudson, and his report is a hair-raising catalogue of disasters narrowly avoided:

> *Weather thick and foggy with heavy falls of snow . . . hail and snow in every watch for the last three days . . . intensely cold, and fog so thick we could not see twice the length of the ship. Huge ice-islands, which we frequently passed at dangerous proximity owing to their number and our limited view – with the sea breaking on them with the roar of thunder and to the height of full one hundred feet. I would not have believed a ship could pass through such dangers. . . We could see nothing; but the thunder of crashing ice to the northward made us apprehensive we were embayed . . . I came on deck to find the ice formed a complete circle round us, stretching in every direction as far as the eye could reach, and beyond, icebergs packed tight into field-ice. I did not know how I should proceed, but deemed it necessary at all hazards to extricate ourselves, so decided to try and force a way through by ramming.* (There follows a highly technical account of this manoeuvre – a dangerous business in a small unstrengthened sailing vessel.) *At last the ice cracked, we pushed through and got into a tolerably clear sea. Here, fatigued with labour and anxiety, we hove-to; and I believe all returned thanks to Heaven for our deliverance.*

Twice they had hopes of bettering Cook's 'farthest south', but were brought up short at the last moment by consolidated pack-ice at about the 70th parallel.

On both these occasions Walker suspected – rightly – that he was close to land. He reported that the water was 'much discoloured', that some of the ice 'had the appearance of being but lately detached from land', and that in several of the icebergs there were dark streaks 'which seemed to amount to an earthy stain'. Prior to this – apart from the sealers' reports of mountains seen dimly beyond the South Shetland Islands – there had been no hint of land in the Antarctic; and it was another year before D'Urville, Wilkes and Ross were to make what are usually regarded as their near-simultaneous first discoveries of the continent. It would be quite wrong to suggest that Walker, that autumn, predated these discoveries, but he deserves credit for being one of the first people to come up with evidence that an Antarctic land mass existed. If the weather had been better he might well have sighted the continent, for on 21 March and again on 23 March he was less than a couple of hundred miles from the coast of Lesser Antarctica.

Probably not one person in a million today has heard of Walker or the *Flying Fish*, but happily their names are remembered in a range of mountains and a cape, cemented into the near-inaccessible iceshelf of what is probably the bleakest shoreline on Earth.

By the middle of May Wilkes's squadron had reassembled in the Chilean port of Valparaiso – all except the luckless *Sea Gull*, which was last seen off Cape Horn fighting for her life in 'a very severe gale'. It was obviously a losing battle, for she was never seen again. One can't help wondering if new pumps might have saved her.

By the middle of June a somewhat depleted US Exploring Expedition was heading into the Pacific – they were now without the *Relief* as well as the *Sea Gull*, the former having been sent home as 'unfit for service'. Wilkes was to spend the greater part of the next two years in the Pacific, visiting places as far apart as Tierra del Fuego, New Zealand, Australia, Singapore, Samoa, Tonga, Tahiti, the Tuamotus, Wake, the Philippines, Hawaii and the coast of British Columbia. At the time this was regarded as the most important part of his expedition. And it is true that during Wilkes's two years in the Pacific his ships did valuable work showing the American flag, his scientists did valuable work collecting botanical and zoological data, and he himself wrote a valuable book, *Narrative of the US Exploring Expedition*, which gives an illuminating picture of Polynesia midway between its primordial innocence and the final collapse of its culture – the local chiefs were now demanding 'landing fees', and the girls were no longer offering themselves but selling themselves. Wilkes's descriptions of Polynesia in transition are among the more interesting parts of the *Narrative*. Entry after entry shows with tragic clarity the effect that Westernization was having on the once-generous islanders.

> *In one village,* Wilkes writes, *which had little communication with foreigners, the people were open and honest. They appeared virtuous and happy, and the youngsters were full of animation. However, in a nearby village that was much frequented by foreigners, the houses were dirty and full of vermin, and the people idle, crafty and covetous. Our men in their rambles were met by a number of these people who kept repeating 'walk about one hilling'; by which our men soon understood they were required to pay one shilling for the privilege of walking along the beach and collecting shells.*

What a contrast to the welcome accorded to Cook and Bougainville!

Wilkes and his squadron arrived in Sydney in November 1839; and again his *Narrative* gives an illuminating picture of a community in transition, only changing this time for the better.

Some 50 years had passed since Captain Arthur Phillip and his first convict fleet came ashore in 'what is surely the finest harbour in the world'. The settlement that they founded didn't take root easily. Year after year the crops failed, the sheep and cattle died and the people came close to starvation. However, in the last decade of the eighteenth century, prosperity came to Australia from an unexpected source. It was found that the coastal waters to the south-east of the continent were one of the finest whaling grounds in the world. By 1800 Sydney could boast more whalers than convicts, and its future was assured. By the time Wilkes got there it was a boom town.

> *There is now a great influx of people of all kinds,* he wrote. *Everything has a new look about it, and the people manifest great busle and activity. . . This is a glorious colony of which the whole Anglo-Saxon race may well be proud,* though ever the Puritan he goes on to castigate the people of Sydney for *licentiousness, debauchery and drunkenness . . . everywhere there are low taverns and grog shops. Even persons of the fair sex are to be seen staggering about the public streets, and the consumption of rum amounts to eight gallons annually for every individual in the colony.*

He spent a month in Sydney, preparing his ships for their coming battle with the Antarctic, though no amount of preparation could compensate for their basic defects. They were too small, half-rotten and their equipment was inadequate.

> *All who visited us seemed disappointed at not seeing the same complete outfits as they had found in the vessels of the English expedition. They inquired whether we had* (watertight) *compartments to keep us from sinking? How we intended to keep ourselves warm? What kind of antiscorbutics we were to use? Where were our great ice-saws? To all these questions I was obliged to answer, to their*

great surprise, that we had none, and to agree that we were unwise to attempt Antarctic service in ordinary cruising vessels. Most of our visitors considered us doomed to be frozen to death. However, we had been ordered to go, and go we should... Though the necessity I felt of subjecting so many lives in such unworthy ships caused me great anxiety.

One can't help feeling sympathy for Wilkes. Although this sympathy is somewhat lessened by the fact that he so often gives the impression of positively revelling in the trials, tribulations and injustices by which he seems ever beset. On this occasion, however, his forebodings were well-founded and obviously shared by his crew. For during the month they were in Sydney a full 25 per cent of them deserted! It was therefore with a reduced complement that on Boxing Day, 1839 his four ships stood south out of the Heads.

Wilkes's reputation as an explorer stands or falls on how we interpret the events of the next couple of months. Was he a brave man who overcame the poor state of his ships, who was the first person to sight the main bulk of the Antarctic continent, and who added some 2,000 miles of unknown coastline to the maps of the world? Or was he a braggart who, in the words of his subsequent court martial, 'needlessly hazarded his ships . . . and made a false entry as to the date on which he sighted Antarctic Land'?

As his squadron headed south, Wilkes took advantage of a spell of fine weather to complete the caulking of portholes and hatches, to test his makeshift stoves and to issue protective clothing. And it was as well he did; for early in the New Year he ran into a succession of electric storms. His *Narrative* contains several descriptions of such storms:

We had this evening a remarkably severe storm of thunder and lightning; the ship appeared filled with electric fluids; the points of the conductors, the mastheads and yardarms were all illuminated with Corpo Santos (Saint Elmo's Fire) *and several officers declared that they felt electric shocks.*

This, it has been pointed out, is very similar to a passage in Melville's *Moby Dick.*

'Look aloft!' cried Starbuck. 'The corpusants! The corpusants!'

All the yard-arms were tipped with a pallid fire, and touched at each tri-pointed lightning-rod-end with three tapering white flames; each of the three masts was silently burning in that sulphurous air, like three gigantic wax tapers before an altar.

Wilkes's detractors have used such similarities in the two books to help substantiate the parallel between Ahab in obsessive pursuit of the great white whale, and Wilkes in obsessive pursuit of the great white continent. And this obsession, they suggest, was now made manifest, when during the week commencing 11 January Wilkes made a false and premature claim to have discovered the continent of Antarctica.

That Wilkes *did* claim to have discovered Antarctica is beyond dispute. 'My *Narrative* [he writes] must leave no doubt in any unprejudiced mind of the correctness of the assertion that we have discovered a vast new continent.' Here is his account of how the discovery took place:

11 (January). *The fair wind from the northwest (accompanied with a light mist, rendering objects on the horizon indistinct), still enabled us to pursue our course southerly. Icebergs became so numerous as to compel us occasionally to change course. Towards 6 p.m. we began to perceive smaller pieces of ice, floating as it were in patches. As the icebergs increased in number, the sea became smoother and there was no apparent motion. Between 8 and 9 p.m. a low point of ice was perceived ahead, and in a short time we passed within it. There was now a large bay before us. By 10½ p.m. we had reached its extreme limits, and found our progress stopped by a compact barrier, enclosing large square icebergs. The barrier consisted of masses closely packed, and of every variety of shape and size. We hove-to until full daylight. The night was beautiful, and everything seemed sunk in sleep, except for the sound of the low rustling of the ice. We were now in 64° 11′S, 164° 30′E; and one and all felt disappointed that the way was blocked for further progress. What surprised me most was a change in the colour of the water to an olive green, and some faint appearances resembling distant land; but as it was twilight, I put no faith in these indications, although some of the officers were confident they were not occasioned by icebergs. We lay to until four o'clock.*

12. As it grew light a fog set in so thick that we lost sight of the Porpoise. . . I determined to work along the barrier to the westward. We were all day beating in a thick fog, with the barrier of ice close to us and occasionally right under our bow; at other times we were almost in contact with icebergs. During the whole of the day we could not see at any time further than a quarter-of-a-mile, and seldom more than the ship's length. Fog and thick mist was forming into ice in our rigging. From the novelty of our situation and the excitement produced by it, we did not think of the danger.

For the next ten days Wilkes's ships worked their way independently along the edge of the barrier in thick fog. Each of them reported discoloured water, sea-elephants and large numbers of birds – all of which often indicate the proximity of land. On the evening of the 15th the weather cleared, and the ships met up and continued together to the westward. Now comes the controversial entry in Wilkes's *Narrative*:

On the 16th the three vessels were in longitude 157° 46′E, and all within a short distance of each other. The water was much discoloured, and many albatrosses, Cape pigeons and petrels were seen about the ships. . . On this day appearances believed at the time to be land were visible from all three vessels, and the comparison of the three observations, when taken in connection with the more positive proofs of its existence afterwards obtained, has left no doubt that the appearance was not deceptive. From this day, therefore, we date the discovery which is claimed for the squadron.

This, to controversy, was as timber to a bush fire. Wilkes's advocates point out that his 'appearances believed at the time to be land' may sound vague, but that they were based on independent reports by three of his officers from two of his ships. They point out also that claims of first sightings around Antarctica were often couched in vague and hesitant terms; this was partly because the appalling weather made visibility uncertain, and partly because the ice-capped mainland is almost identical in appearance to the consolidated pack-ice that surrounds it. These are valid points. And Wilkes's advocates say that another point in his favour is his character. They don't deny that he was obstinate, highly-strung, quick to take offence and disdainful of authority. But they insist he was also a man of integrity and Christian principles: not the sort of man who would deliberately falsify official records.

His detractors, however, point out that there are strange omissions and discrepancies in his report, in particular that he omits to give his position at the time of his alleged sighting. All he tells us is that during that morning he was in longitude 157° 46′ East. In addition to this, we know that a couple of days earlier he had been close to the 64th parallel, and that a couple of days later he was close to the 66th parallel. Yet within the viewing-range of these positions there was no land which, in the prevailing weather conditions, he could possibly have sighted! To sight land in longitude 157° East he would have needed to be well beyond the 67th parallel, and he never claimed to have penetrated that far to the south. His detractors don't dispute the fact that a week or so later he undoubtedly did sight Antarctica, and then followed its coastline westward for hundreds if not thousands of miles. But they claim that he fabricated the earlier sighting so as to deny the Frenchman D'Urville the honour of being first to discover the

Two engravings from the *Narrative of the US Exploring Expedition* by Charles Wilkes. *Top* Fiji Village with dancers; *above* view of the Antarctic Continent.

new continent. (The *Astrolabe* and *Zélée*, it will be remembered, had definitely sighted Adélie Land on 20 January.) And if today it seems unlikely that so petty a motive should have given rise to so monumental a deception, it must be remembered that throughout the nineteenth century Jingoism was an adjunct of exploration – and Wilkes was a child of his times. It is difficult to arrive at the truth; but the verdict of history has been that Wilkes's claim must in this instance be regarded as non-proven. He makes great play in his *Narrative* of the fact that his men at the masthead (Midshipmen Eld and Reynolds) sighted 'two black peaks, in a conical shape, which I have named after those officers who discovered them'. Yet in today's atlases there are no peaks marked Eld or Reynolds; and the boundary of Wilkes Land (i.e. the land that Wilkes discovered) is to be found not in longitude 157° but in longitude 137°, hundreds of miles to the west.

So were his claims to have sighted land that January no more than moonshine? I think not. I think that he probably *did* sight mountains, only not at the time and place over which there has been such controversy. I suggest he saw land not on 16 January, but on 11 January and not in longitude 157°, but in longitude 164°. Remember the entry in his *Narrative* for the evening of 11 January: 'We were now in 64° 11′S, 164° 30′E. . . What surprised me most was a change in the colour of the water . . . and some faint appearances resembling distant land; but as it was twilight, I put no faith in these indications, although some of the officers were confident they were not occasioned by icebergs.'

According to his calculations – and we have no reason to doubt their accuracy – Wilkes's position that evening was less than 100 miles from the Balleny Islands. These five islands lie about 150 miles to the north of the Antarctic mainland; they are volcanic, thickly covered with ice, and rise to a height of over 4,000 feet. In good visibility – and Wilkes described the weather that evening as beautiful – it is quite possible in the clear Antarctic atmosphere to see mountains from a distance of 100 miles. By next morning we are told that 'a fog [had] set in', and we can picture Wilkes's ships groping their way westward along the barrier, and leaving behind the bleak little archipelago on which they had unwittingly stumbled.

This discovery still leaves us with the problem of what to make of Wilkes's subsequent 'false' sightings of the following week. In the witch-hunt and court-martial that followed his return, many people seemed eager to believe that his sighting reports were simply a pack of lies, for Wilkes had a penchant for making enemies. However, looking at things dispassionately after a cooling-off period of some 150 years, it seems unbelievable that, even if he had wanted to, Wilkes could have coerced several of his officers and several of his crew, under oath, into making false statements. It seems to me far more likely that some of his ships' company genuinely thought that they had sighted land, but (like many others, both before them and after them) they mistook the consolidated pack for the mainland. It could perhaps be argued that Wilkes, anxious to substantiate his claim to an early sighting, gave undue credence to these reports. This would not be out of keeping with his positive and impetuous character. However, the controversy seems barely worth the heat it has engendered, for soon afterwards the US Exploring Expedition not only undoubtedly sighted the mainland but landed on an 'ice island' a little way offshore.

As his expedition now built up to its climax, Wilkes evokes the wonders they saw, the dangers they faced, and the hardships they suffered.

The beauty of the new-found continent illuminates the somewhat pedestrian prose of his *Narrative*:

That night we were gratified with a splendid exhibition of the aurora australis. It exceeded any thing of the kind I have heretofore witnessed. Its activity was inconceivable, darting from the zenith to the horizon in all directions in the most brilliant coruscations; rays proceeding as if from a point in the zenith flashed in pencillings of light like sparks of electric fluid, reappearing again only to vanish; forming themselves into one body like a fan, shut up; again emerging to flit across the sky showing all the prismatic colours at once or in quick succession. So remarkable were the phenomena that our sailors were constantly exclaiming in admiration of its brilliancy. . . The character of the ice now changed. Tabular-icebergs prevailed, and there was little field-ice. Some of the bergs were of magnificent dimensions, one third of a mile in length, and from 150 to 200 feet in height, with sides perfectly smooth, as though they had been chiselled. Others, again, exhibited lofty arches of many-coloured tints, leading into deep caverns, open to the swell of the sea, which rushing in produced loud thunderings. The flight of birds passing in and out of the caverns, recalled the recollection of ruined abbeys, castles and caves; while here and there a bold projecting bluff, crowned with pinnacles and turrets, resembled some Gothic keep. Every noise on board, even our voices, reverberated from the massive white walls. These tabular bergs are like masses of beautiful alabaster. If an immense city of ruined alabaster palaces can be imagined, of every variety of shape and tint, and composed of huge piles of buildings grouped together, with long lanes or streets winding irregularly through them, some faint idea may be formed of the grandeur and beauty of the spectacle.

The dangers that beset them are also chronicled in meticulous detail:

The ship had rapid way on her and was much tossed about, when in an instant all became perfectly quiet; the transition was so sudden that men were awakened by it from sleep, and we all knew that we had run within a line of ice – an occurance from which the feeling of great danger is inseparable. The watch was called, to be in readiness to execute such orders as might be necessary for the safety of the ship. The feeling is awful and the uncertainty most trying thus to enter within the ice, blindfolded by fog; (but) on we went until we heard a low and distant rustling, and suddenly a dozen voices proclaimed the barrier, just ahead. The ship, which a moment before had seemed as if unpeopled from the stillness of all on board, was instantly alive with the bustle of performing the evolutions to bring her into wind. But after awhile the ice was again (met with) ahead, and the full danger of our situation was realized. The ship was embayed.

What was liable to happen to vessels that became embayed is described by William Hudson. . . His sloop the *Peacock* had worked her way through broken field-ice almost up to the barrier. Here, on the morning of 24 January, in worsening weather, she came into contact with an ice-floe

so forcibly that it seemed from the shock as if we were entirely stove-in; the wheel ropes were carried away, and the rudder twisted and split. We immediately commenced working the ship with sails and ice-anchors into more open sea. In this we were successful for a time, until an increase of wind and a change in its direction brought down upon us masses of ice. These completely beset the ship, finished the destruction of our rudder, and forced us up against an ice island some 8 miles in extent, with an elevation equal to that of our masthead. We furled all sails, and clung on by our ice-anchors. But the pressing masses of ice drove us stern-first against the island, carrying away our boom and stern-davits, and breaking all the bulwark-stanchions on that side of the ship. Soon Peacock was labouring in the swell, with ice grinding and thumping against us on all sides. Every moment something was carried away – chains, bolts, bobstays, bowsprit, shrouds; even the anchors were lifted up, and coming down with a surge carried away eyebolts and lashings. Towards midnight sea and snow increased, there was every indication of a gale, and the ice was rapidly accumulating outside of us, and forming a compact mass. There was therefore no choice left, but to try and force a way out, even though we thumped the ship to pieces in the attempt.

For 48 hours *Peacock* fought for her life. 'The destruction of the vessel', wrote Wilkes, 'seemed almost inevitable, with the loss of everyone on board'. However, thanks to the courage and almost superhuman efforts of her crew, and the skill of her commander, she at last fought her way free. She managed to repair and rehang her rudder, and limp, battered but still afloat, into the comparative safety of the open sea. For the moment she was out of danger. She was, however, far too badly damaged to remain in Antarctic waters. Wilkes ordered her to head for Australia, which she reached 'after a boisterous and difficult passage' on 21 February.

Wilkes and his three remaining ships, meanwhile, continued to claw their way westward along the edge of the pack-ice.

It would be difficult to overstate the hardships they suffered. I doubt if any ships' companies, before or since, were ever asked to endure such terrible conditions in such ill-found ships. They were battered by gale-force winds, shrouded in mist-cum-fog, and beset with ice in every conceivable form, size and shape; their rations contained no antiscorbutics; their quarters were never dry; they were never warm. On the last day of January the *Vincennes*'s doctors handed Wilkes a document which might be described as a cross between a petition and an ultimatum:

> *Sir,*
> *It becomes our duty, as medical officers of this ship, to report to you in writing the condition of the crew at the present time.*
> *The number upon the* (sick) *list this morning is fifteen; most of these cases are consequent on the extreme hardships and exposure they have undergone during the last gales, when the ship has been surrounded with ice.*
> *Under these circumstances we feel obliged to report that, in our opinion, a few days more of such exposure as they have already undergone, would reduce the number of the crew by sickness to such an extent as to hazard the safety of the ship and the lives of all on board.*
> *Very respectfully, your obedient servants,*
> (signed) *J.L. Fox,*
> *J.S. Whittle*
> *Assistant-Surgeons.*

Elephant Island in the South Shetlands,
from a painting by Ernest Goupil.

Curiously-shaped icebergs seen close to the South Orkney Islands, from a painting by Ernest Goupil.

Wilkes asked his other officers for their comments. Reading between the lines, it is clear that he hoped they would recommend him to ignore the doctors' report. But they didn't. They endorsed it – 'in my opinion the watch officers and crew [are] unfit for the arduous duties required of them . . . the report of the medical officers is a sufficient reason for putting back . . . the health of the crew demands an immediate return to a mild climate.' Most commanders would have bowed to the consensus of opinion. But it was ever in Wilkes's nature to fly against the wind. We can picture him alone in his cabin, wrestling with his conscience, obedient at the last to that 'stern daughter of the voice of God', duty. His convoluted prose reflects the indecision that racked him:

> *Notwithstanding these opinions, I was not satisfied that there was sufficient cause to change my original* (plans) *and after full consideration of the matter, I came to the conclusion, at whatever hazard to ship and crew, that it was my duty to proceed, and not give up the cruise until the ship should be totally disabled, or it should be evident to all that it was impossible to persist any longer. In bringing myself to this decision, I believe that I viewed the case on all sides with fairness, and allowed my duty to my country, my care for those whom it had committed to my charge, and my responsibility to the world, each to have its due weight.*

One is torn between admiration for Wilkes's tenacity, and pity for his long-suffering ships' companies. For as the brief Antarctic summer drew to its close, the crew of the *Vincennes*, *Porpoise* and *Flying Fish* were not only almost constantly cold, wet and exhausted, they broke their backs as they fell on the ice-rimed deck, they were swept overboard by gargantuan seas, they were frozen solid into the sails as they struggled to furl them.

And still Wilkes, like some daemonic Flying Dutchman, held course to the west, edging ever closer to the snowbound shore which was now intermittently visible almost every day along the southern horizon.

Soon his three vessels were reduced to two. For the crew of the *Flying Fish* handed their commander, Lt Cdr Pinkney, a petition:

We, the undersigned, wish to let you know that we are in a most deplorable condition; the bed clothes are all wet; we have no place to lie down in; we have not had a dry stitch of clothes for seven days; four of our number are very sick; and we, the remaining eight, can hold out no longer. We hope you will relieve us from what must terminate in our death.

Pinkney, like Wilkes, consulted his officers. And their opinion was unanimous. They pointed out that the *Flying Fish* was close to foundering, with her pumps having to work flat-out to keep the water at bay, and that her crew were so weak they were unable to work the sails. 'We express our most thorough conviction,' they wrote, 'that the condition of both vessel and crew loudly demand an immediate return to milder latitudes.' Pinkney had a less exalted concept of duty than Wilkes. He set course for New Zealand.

The *Vincennes* and *Porpoise* were now catching a glimpse almost every day of the mainland of Antarctica. The entry in Wilkes's Diary for 12 February is typical. 'Land was distinctly seen, from 18 to 20 miles distant: a lofty mountain range covered with snow and bound by perpendicular icy cliffs.' He was eager to land, but found the way ashore blocked by ice that was always too close-packed to be penetrated. He had therefore to content himself with landing on an island: a huge conglomeration of rock-cum-ice, many miles in circumference, which had broken away from the mainland.

14 February. Position at noon 106°18′E, 65°59′S. On running in (towards the land) *we passed several icebergs greatly discoloured with earth, and finding we could not approach the shore any nearer, I determined to land on the largest. On coming up with it, I hove the ship to, lowered the boats and effected a landing. We found embedded into the ice boulders, stones, gravel, sand, mud and clay. The larger specimens were of red-sandstone and basalt, the largest being about six feet in diameter. Many samples were obtained, and it was amusing to see the eagerness of all hands to possess a piece of the Antarctic Continent; these pieces were in great demand during the remainder of the cruise. In the centre of the ice-island was found a pond of most delicious water; we obtained from it about 500 gallons. We remained on the island several hours, the men amusing themselves to their hearts' content . . . while* (our scientists) *found many species of zoophytes and small crustacea. This day, notwithstanding our disappointment in being still repelled from treading on the new continent, was spent with much gratification, and gave us many new specimens from it.*

This was the climax of the expedition. The two ships continued to follow the coastline westward for another week. But the temperature was falling, the sea-ice was thickening, and Wilkes knew that their chance of setting foot on the mainland was lessening with each passing day. On 21 February he set course for Sydney. 'Seldom', he tells us, 'have I seen so many happy faces!'

The US Exploring Expedition was to spend another year in the Pacific. It did useful work, particularly in making a detailed survey of the coast between Vancouver and San Francisco. Such work, however, cannot really be classed as exploration, for the islands and coastlines visited were by now well-known and well-delineated. It is by his exploits in the Antarctic that Wilkes must be judged as an explorer.

On his return to America, instead of the hero's welcome which he might have expected, Wilkes found himself in trouble. It was pointed out that he had lost three ships, that 23 of his men had died and no fewer than 127 deserted. He was hauled in front of a court martial, and accused of 'hazarding his ships, the oppression and illegal flogging of his men, cruelty to the natives, and scandalous conduct in making a false entry as to the date on which he sighted Antarctic Land'. Considering the number and influence of the enemies he had managed to make, this was not altogether surprising. What *does* seem surprising is that he was found guilty, was sentenced to be publicly reprimanded, and was denied funds to publish his report.

Wilkes reacted with his usual vigour. Within two years, largely at his own expense, he had published his apologia, the six volumes of his *Narrative of the US Exploring Expedition* (a further 19 scientific volumes were to follow). This, at the time, was fulsomely praised by the few and savagely attacked by the many – 'Throw it into the Potomac; that is the best thing!' a well-known senator suggested. It was difficult then and it is still difficult today to arrive at a balanced judgement of Wilkes. Indeed this can only be done if we forget his character and concentrate on his achievements.

On his first ice-edge cruise he confirmed the existence of the South Shetland Islands, and one of his vessels found evidence of the proximity of land some thousand miles to the south-west of Cape Horn. On his second ice-edge cruise his achievements were more meaningful. Setting aside the controversy as to exactly where and when he first sighted Antarctica, the fact is that for six weeks he was in intermittent contact with a continent that was previously unknown, and that he followed the coast of this continent westward for more than 1,500 miles. He therefore added to the map of the world a new coastline of equal length to the Pacific coast of the United States from Mexico to Alaska. Under any circumstances this was a commendable achievement. In the appalling sailing conditions of the Antarctic it was a great achievement; in small and ill-found ships it was an achievement that can only be described as heroic. Indeed if asked to sum up Wilkes's exploits in the Antarctic in a single word, 'heroic' is the one I would choose.

The importance of his discoveries was recognized at the time by almost every country except his own. In Europe he was showered with honours, including that most sought-after of explorers' accolades, the gold medal of the Royal Geographical Society. Yet in America, when he died, many newspapers failed to mention in his obituary that he had ever been to the Antarctic. Only recently has scholarship begun to suggest he may have been more sinned against than sinning. However, perhaps the final word should be left with someone who went with him on his expedition yet managed to stay aloof from the jealousies of naval and political intrigue, the multi-talented scientist James Dwight Dana. 'Wilkes', this eminent scientist wrote, 'was a man without conciliation, inclined to be arbitrary in minor matters as well as those that were important, and often at variance with some of his officers . . . and yet withal an excellent commander, probably no better could have been found in the Navy at that time.'

Wilkes's expedition discovered the last, remotest and least-habitable region of the Pacific, and so completed the exploration of the ocean which had begun 3,000 years earlier when the first Polynesians pushed eastward through the islands off south-east Asia.

The final stages of this exploration had been dominated by people from outside the Pacific, and it was inevitable that this influx of foreigners should alter the lives of the indigenous people. What was *not* inevitable – unless one takes a very pessimistic view of history – is that the indigenous people should have been decimated and their culture obliterated. This was brought about not so much by the explorers as by those who came in their wake – the exploiters.

THE EXPLOITERS

'The Aleuts were made to work as slaves, without redress. They lived and died in squalid barracouns (shelters), *half-underground, cold and filthy . . . and it seemed the policy of the Russians to keep them so, and to treat them not near so well as the dogs they brought there for company.'*
H.W. ELLIOTT: *Alaska and the Seal Islands.*

It was the ill-fortune of the Pacific islanders that the exploiters who descended on them in the wake of the explorers were particularly predatory and undisciplined. Predatory because they all wanted to take something away – the fur of the seals, the baleen of the whales, the wood of the rain-forests or the oil of the coconuts – and give nothing in return; undisciplined because most of them worked for themselves, and were unshackled by the restraints of government or company. There was no one to curb their excesses.

The most destructive and, to modern eyes, the least attractive of these predators were the sealers. In the South Pacific their exploits were largely confined to the uninhabited islands of the sub-Antarctic, although their brigs were not unknown in the harbours of New Zealand and Tasmania. They had a devastating effect on the southern wildlife, but only a marginal effect on the southern people.

Their quarry were the fur seals (*Arctocephalus*), elephant seals (*Mirounga leonina*) and Weddell seals (*Leptonychotes weddelli*) which came ashore each summer, literally in their millions, to mate and give birth on the sub-Antarctic islands. These seals were well able to look after themselves in water; but on land they were utterly defenceless, and were massacred by the hundred-thousand. The sealers' technique was simple and effective. A parent-ship, usually a brig of 250-300 tons, would find a beach on which the seals were breeding, and anchor offshore. She would then use her shallop to land about half her crew. For the men put ashore, what followed was not so much a hunt as a massacre. The British sealer, Robert Fildes, describes many of the breeding beaches as 'fur-lined, so close-packed it is impossible to haul up a boat without killing your way ashore . . . And when one has landed, it is impossible to push through the creatures unless one has a weapon with which to clear a path.'

The sealers didn't lack weapons – 14-inch stabbing knives and long, specially weighted clubs – and with these they made short work of their victims. The seals made little effort to escape; for millennia of immunity to any type of predator had atrophied their suspicions. A bull in his harem might occasionally rear up and bellow defiance; but the mild-eyed cows simply watched the slaughter with incurious passivity, lying and even mating among the carnage until it was their turn to be clubbed, stabbed and flayed to death. An expert could kill and skin 50 seals an hour, at the end of which, if he was working on rock, he would be literally up to his knees in blubber and blood. It would be hard to imagine a more callous business. And the callousness of man to seal was paralleled in the callousness of man to man. Fights between rival sealing-ships were frequent; shore-parties were frequently marooned. Captain Althearn of Nantucket is quite explicit about this marooning: 'If I got to a rookery early,' he writes 'and found a great show of seals, I would get as many aboard as I could. I would then leave on the rocks all the men I thought might blab, go to the most convenient port and sell my skins. This way I should expect to have another season without company.'

One remembers the Swiss watchmaker and his companion rescued by D'Urville, and wonders how many potential blabbers died of exposure and starvation, waiting in vain for a skipper who valued his profits more highly than the lives of his crew.

Men such as Captain Althearn were not, it might be felt, the ideal ambassadors of Western culture. Yet according to their lights they were good men: sober, hard-working Puritans from Scotland and New England, men whose creed encouraged them to combine commercial acumen with strict morality. Their drink was water, their literature was the Bible, their ships were among the most beautiful and seaworthy ever built, and as practical seamen they have had few equals and no superiors. According to the tenets of their day they were doing no wrong. Yet within the span of little more than a generation (between roughly 1790 and 1830) they butchered something like four-and-three-quarter-million seals. It wasn't long before the species was close to extermination. 'Our men gleaned every beach,' the sealer Williams wrote despondently in the 1830s, 'and searched every rock, but not a remnant of the species was found. Thus in wretched and wanton destruction has gone for ever from the Southern Ocean a whole race of animals useful to man.' Williams in fact was over-pessimistic; although some species were indeed hunted to extinction, others survived and are today increasing in number. No one, however, could deny that in the South Pacific the sealers brought carnage to the wildlife and no benefit to the people.

In the North Pacific their depredations had a tragic effect on wildlife and people alike. The people of the north – the Inuit of Alaska, the Aleuts of the Aleutians and the Ishutski of the USSR – had hunted seals, whales, walrus and sea-otters from time immemorial. Their lives depended on them. Yet even if these so-called primitive people had had the ability to exterminate any one species in any one area they would never have done so. They were too dependent on the Earth and its flora and fauna to be anything other than good conservationists. However, with the advent of the white man attitudes changed, and first the Russians, then the Americans, reaped a rich but wanton harvest from the waters of the north.

One result of Bering's ordeal on Beringa Ostrova had been that his naturalist Georg Steller published a panegyric on the island's wildlife, and a warning against the folly of over-hunting. The panegyric was heeded, the warning was not. Soon Russian adventurers, literally by the thousand, were descending on the coasts of Alaska and the Aleutian Islands in search of a fortune in fur. Fur-fever was heightened when, in the late 1760s, a furrier in Canton perfected a method of separating the coarse outer-fur of a seal from its smooth and valuable under-fur. The result was sealskin – uniquely warm, perennially fashionable – and a consequent rise in the price of a seal-pelt from 50 cents to 5 dollars. By 1780 more than 60 separate Russian companies had vessels 'trading' in the sealanes between Kamchatka and Alaska. To quote Henry Elliot's classic work, *Alaska and the Seal Islands* (written almost exactly 100 years ago):

> *The success of the early fur hunters was so great that soon every Siberian merchant who had a few thousand roubles was putting out a craft or two to engage in* (this) *remunerative business. They all carried on their operations in the same manner. The owner of the sloop or schooner engaged a crew*

Top Seal Hunting in the northern seas, from a sketch by J. W. Hayward, 1871. *Left* Seals being driven to the killing grounds, in the Bering Straits.

on shares. The cargo of furs brought back was divided into two equal divisions: half to the owner, the other half divided between the captain and his crew as could be agreed between themselves. After this division, every participant gave one-tenth of his portion to the Government at St Petersburg, which, stimulated by this generous swelling of its treasury, never failed to keep an affectionate eye on its Pacific subjects, and encouraged them to every exertion.

From this arrangement there always emerged one certain winner: the Russian government. And it is an indication of how important the northern fur trade was to St Petersburg, that in 1821 Tsar Alexander issued an *ukase* (arbitrary decree) which virtually sealed off the extreme north of the Pacific to foreign shipping. Under this decree foreign vessels were prohibited from approaching within 100 miles of the shore in a huge arc which ran from Vancouver Island in the east, past the entrance to the Bering Strait, and to the Kurils in the west. Any foreign ship seized within this area was taken to Petropavlovsk, where its cargo was confiscated and its crew repatriated – at their own expense! Whatever profit accrued from the seizure was shared between government and captor – usually a warship of the Imperial Navy. So here was another incentive for St Petersburg to keep a paternal eye on the exploits of its *promyshlenniki* (hunters-cum-fur-traders.)

Most books about this little-known part of the world stress the squalor of the life and the brutality of the *promyshlenniki*, and there is certainly evidence of both. There was, however, another side to the coin. In 1799 the various trading groups were merged, by order of the Tsar, into the single all-powerful Russian-American Company – a conglomerate which may have been relatively short-lived, but whose splendours in its heyday surpassed even those of its rival colossus, The Company of Adventurers of England trading into Hudson's Bay. During the first decade of the nineteenth century the Company's governor, Alexander Baranov, established his headquarters on the Alaskan island of Sitka. And what a magnificent if overtly feudal emporium he created! Within ten years more than 1,000 Russians had settled in a town they called 'The New Archangel': a town with shipbuilding yards, brick-works, iron and brass foundries, machine shops, and both Roman Catholic and Greek Orthodox churches, all overlooked by 'the castle of Baranov', a fortress which, with its turrets and palisades, might have been lifted straight out of the Middle Ages. Overlooked too by some of the most spectacular coastal scenery on Earth. In its heyday Sitka was the home of an élite who, in a harsh environment, lived lives of bizarre luxury.

Their houses, writes a contemporary, *were often 150 feet in length and 80 feet in depth, three stories high with huge attics. They were constructed of spruce logs, trimmed down to 12 by 12 ft timbers, beautifully dovetailed. The windows were in tasteful casements, with double sashes. The floors were of parquet, tongued and grooved by hand, and highly polished. The inner walls were showily papered and hung with tapestries. Heavy Russian furniture stood upon rugs of rich fur . . . All travellers bear witness to the hospitality of the Russians and the comfort of their living conditions.*

The living conditions of the Aleuts were another matter; for many of the *promyshlenniki* treated them as less-than-human serfs, forcing the hunters and trappers to provide them with a demanding quota of sea-otter and seal pelts; hunters and trappers who failed to come up with their quota found their women raped and their homes burned. Few robber economies have caused such destruction to both wildlife and people as that of the fur trade. What happened in the Pribilof Islands is typical.

The Pribilof Islands are one of the remotest archipelagos in the Pacific, situated between the Aleutian Islands and the Bering Strait. For much of the year they are shrouded in mist and extremely difficult to find. Perhaps that is why the northern fur seals had for millennia used them as a breeding ground; it has been estimated that each summer between three-and-a-half and five million seals used to haul ashore on to the rocky beaches of this one small archipelago to mate and give birth. The islands were discovered in 1787 by Gerassim Pribilof, whose brig 'in thick mist was regaled by the sweet music of the seal-rookeries'. For a few years exploitation was haphazard and small-scale. Then Baranov and his Company took control of the fur trade, and the breeding beaches became big business. Aleuts were brought in and forced to work in the previously uninhabited islands. 'Here,' Elliott tells us, 'they were made to work as slaves, without redress. They lived and died in squalid barracouns [shelters] half-underground, cold and filthy . . . and it seemed the policy of the Russians to keep them so, and to treat them not near so well as the dogs they brought there for company.'

One of the tasks of these Aleuts was to kill the 'holluschickie', or bachelor-seals, which as soon as they had hauled ashore hovered hopefully around the periphery of the breeding beaches. The holluschickie congregated instinctively into huge droves, and it proved an easy matter to drive them like sheep to the killing-grounds.

> *I was impressed*, writes Elliott, *by the singular amiability of these animals when driven. They never show fight, and no sign of resistance is ever made. As the drive progresses they all move along in the same manner: a kind of walking, sliding, shambolling gallop, with the seals pausing every few minutes to catch their breath and make, as it were, a plaintive survey and mute protest. Finally they arrive and are left to cool off in the slaughtering ground, close to the village. At about six or seven o'clock the whole able-bodied male population turn out to engage in the work of killing them. These men are armed with stout bludgeons, made specially at New London* (Connecticut), *about 5½ feet in length; also with stabbing knife, skinning knife and whetstone. The men drive about 150 seals at a time into what they call a pod, which they surround in a circle, huddling the seals close together until they are directly within reach of and under the clubs. The leader gives the word 'Strike!' and instantly the heavy clubs come down, until every animal is stretched out, stunned and motionless.* (Elliott adds in a footnote that the seals' heads are often *stricken so hard that the crystalline lenses of their eyes fly out from their sockets like hail-stones, frequently striking me in the face as I stood watching the killing.) The clubs are dropped, the men seize the prostrate seals and lay them out on the ground; then every sealer takes his knife and drives it into the animal's heart; its blood gushes forth, and its quivering presently ceases. After bleeding is finished, the bodies are spread out over the ground just free from touching one another, and the men then turn to and strike down another pod, until a thousand or two are laid out. Then they skin them.*

There follows a detailed description of the skinning, salting, storing and finally the shipping of the pelts. The carcasses were simply left from one year to the next to rot in the killing-grounds, 'polluting the air to a sad degree and causing great punishment to our nostrils'. Elliott estimates that in the one killing-ground in one village on one island upward of 80,000 seals were butchered in a single season. No wonder the species was soon in danger of extinction.

Hair-seals, walrus, sea-lions, whales, sea-otters and – until their extermination – sea-cows were hunted with equal efficiency and ruthlessness. Is it surprising that the Inuit and the Aleuts were bewildered then and are even more bewildered today? For thousands of years they had hunted the mammals of the north, who had provided them with food, warmth, clothes, shelter, weapons and just about every necessity of life. No one could pretend that their hunting methods were not cruel, but they were highly selective, on a small scale and *never* wasteful; not in a thousand years would they have endangered a single species. Then came the white men who taught them – and indeed forced them – to participate in a butchery that was unbelievably wasteful and on a scale hitherto undreamed of. The creatures of the north were decimated; some were made extinct. Then came the supporters of Greenpeace, who today try to stop the Inuit, once a year, from making not a wanton killing but a selective culling; this, the supporters of Greenpeace say, is 'murder'. No wonder so-called primitive people often feel that the white man's opinions are no more constant than the wind.

It would be foolish to pretend that the European and American sealers who reaped so rich a harvest from the Pacific caused one of the major tragedies in world history. But it would be even more foolish to pretend that both the people of the Pacific and the creatures of the Pacific would not have been a great deal better off without them.

The same could be said of those other blood-soaked predators, the whalers.

Whaling is an emotive subject. It is hard to be dispassionate about a creature, noble and sentient as a horse, writhing in agony at the end of a rope or cable until it is stabbed to death. Most people today regard whalers with abhorrence. There can be no denying, however, that they played an important role in opening up the Pacific. At the beginning of the nineteenth century they were active in the south of the ocean, where they helped to establish a British presence in Australia and New Zealand, and to explore the approaches to Antarctica. In the middle of the century they were active in mid-Pacific, where they played a leading role in familiarizing the islanders with the less desirable aspects of Western life – cupidity, drunkenness, venereal disease and prostitution. And towards the end of the century they were active in the north, where they helped to establish an American presence on the Pacific seaboard, and to open up the approaches to the Bering Strait and the Arctic Ocean.

The first whalers from the outside world to enter the Pacific arrived via Cape Horn towards the end of the eighteenth century. Their vessels were often the latest products of the New England shipyards, beautifully built and eminently seaworthy; but their technique of whaling was unbelievably old. Whales have been hunted for longer than history has been recorded. We know this because their bones, together with Stone Age harpoon heads, have been found in middens dating back to 4500 BC. Modern whaling, however, is usually considered to have begun with the Basques. By about AD 800 the people of northern Spain were putting to sea in shallow-draft rowing-boats known as *chaloupes* (the derivation of shallop) to hunt the Biscayan Right whales, which, in their heyday, used to migrate in huge numbers past the coasts of south-west Europe. A *chaloupe* would row as stealthily as possiisble and as close as possible to its quarry. Then, from a range of 15 to 20 feet, a harpooner would fling a lance-with-a-rope-attached into the glistening cliff of the whale's body, his object being not to kill the great creature (for that would be almost impossible with a single thrust) but to secure it, so it could be played like a gargantuan fish. Once transfixed by harpoon-and-rope, the luckless whale had little chance to escape; no matter how many times it dived, and no matter how far or how fast it swam, whenever it surfaced men with harpoons and lances were waiting. F. D. Ommanney in *Lost Leviathan* describes the last moments of a Biscayan right:

> *Now the boat had to back away quickly, for the whale, mortally wounded, would begin its terrible and pathetic death agony, threshing the water with its tail in fear and pain, snapping its jaws and wallowing in a smother of foam, crimsoned with blood. If the boat did not pull away fast enough it was liable to be struck by the tail or snapped by the jaws. Sometimes a whale had to be approached and attacked a second or even a third time before it was killed.*

This was almost exactly the technique used a thousand years later by the first whalers to enter the Pacific, the only difference being that instead of launching *chaloupes* from the shore they launched shallops from the deck of a parent-vessel which had located its quarry in mid-ocean. Their first victims were the playful and monogamous greys which migrated each summer along the west coast of America. Then, crossing the ocean to Australia, they found a harvest richer than any they had dreamed of. They found the Southern Right whales.

It was the convict-transports who were first to notice the *Eubalaena australis*, black, slow-moving, peaceful creatures, which came in great herds each season to the coast of south-east Australia. Soon it became standard practice to equip convict-transports with whaling gear, so that having landed their human cargo they could load up with something more lucrative for the passage home. And how lucrative the Southern Rights were! They were big – about 60 feet in length and 60 tons in weight – and each carcass yielded almost two tons of oil and a ton of baleen (whalebone). Both, in the nineteenth century, were in great demand – the former as fuel for street-lamps and for candles, the

An engraving showing the hazards of whaling.

latter as whalebone for corsets, stays and hooped skirts. A ton of baleen would fetch £2,500 in London, enough to pay the entire cost of a voyage to Australia and back. No wonder the brigs of British and American whalers were soon descending by the hundred on the coastal waters of the newly settled continent.

There are two ways of seeing what happened next. From the point of view of the British and Americans there was a boom in trade, a surge in profits, and the establishment of a permanent white presence in Australia and New Zealand – for 'the whale-ship', as Herman Melville shrewdly observed, '[was] the true mother of that mighty [Australian] colony'. However, from the point of view of the indigenous people, the outcome was not so happy. In Australia, the growth of European settlements along the south-east seaboard sounded the death knell of the Aborigines' traditional way of life; for they, like the Polynesians, lacked the physical and mental resources to withstand the impact of Westernization. In Tasmania the establishing of hundreds of bay-whaling stations around the coast sounded, literally, the requiem of the Aborigine race. For unpalatable as it may be to Western readers, the fact is that the Tasmanian Aborigines were poisoned with arsenic and hunted with packs of dogs until the race was obliterated; not one survived. In New Zealand the whalers met with more resistance. When they burned one of the islanders' villages and raped their women, the Maori retaliated by seizing a whaling vessel (the *Boyd*) and not only killing the entire crew but eating them! There followed several decades of sporadic violence, with the whalers setting up fortified and heavily defended camps. Probably no one will ever know how much blood was shed round the Bay of Plenty and the Bay of Islands, not only by direct confrontation, but by whalers selling the Maori firearms, and deliberately fanning the flames of their inter-tribal wars.

Whaling in the South Pacific was a two-edged instrument, bringing prosperity to the Europeans and the Americans, but conferring virtually no benefit on the indigenous people.

A lithograph of
San Francisco in 1847

In the Central Pacific the story was the same. Whaling here was almost entirely sperm whaling. Sperm are the most numerous and ubiquitous of the whale family, being found in every ocean, as far north as the Arctic and as far south as the Antarctic. They have been described as 'the most unique form of animal life on Earth', a full third of their bodies being taken up by an enormous asymmetrical head which contains not only a well-developed brain, but a buoyancy chamber filled with up to a ton of waxlike spermaceti, which acts as a stabilizer during deep-water dives. Sometimes, enmeshed in their 450-odd feet of intestines, you will find lumps of mucus secreted by the whale over the irritating beaks of octopus which it has eaten but can't digest. This is ambergris, the only natural fixative in the world for perfume; in the days before synthetic fixatives, a lump of ambergris was worth quite literally its weight in gold. There were therefore plenty of incentives for catching and killing a sperm. But there were also dangers. For most of the time the great creatures were gregarious and playful, but if attacked they would sometimes show fight, and there are many well-documented cases of a so-called 'ugly' sperm staving in and sinking vessels of up to 400 tons. In addition to this, they were strong and resilient – any whaler will confirm that sperm are by far the most difficult species to kill. Yet incredible as it sounds, nineteenth-century whalers in the Pacific continued to use the old Basque technique of hunting them: stabbing the great creatures with a hand-harpoon, being towed after them (sometimes for days) in their flimsy shallops, and finally stabbing them to death in a frenzy of churned-up water and blood, their boats often being swamped, capsized or splintered to matchwood in the process. This has been dubbed the 'golden age' of whaling: an age of long voyages, desperate encounters, harsh conditions and fabulous rewards; the age of *Moby Dick*.

The New Englanders were the most active sperm-whalers, and statistics prove the scale of their activities. In its heyday, *c.* 1840, the New England fleet consisted of some 750 vessels, of which more than 500 were likely in any one year to be sperm-whaling in mid-Pacific. Assuming each had a crew of 40 – which is conservative – then from New England alone some 20,000 whalers would be at work each year among the Pacific islands. And a more cosmopolitan or more unruly lot it would be hard to imagine! One vessel, we are told, had a Russian captain, a Dutch purser, an Arab first-mate and a Nigerian boatswain, while among its crew were ten other nationalities. As for the sort of men they were, who should know better than Herman Melville, who himself served for several years aboard a New England whaler? In his Preface to *Omoo*, Melville writes:

> *Nowhere are the proverbial characteristics of sailors shown under wilder aspects than in the South Seas. For the most part the vessels navigating these remote waters are engaged in the Sperm Whale Fishery: a business peculiarly fitted to attract the most restless seamen of all nations, and to foster in them a spirit of the utmost licence. For their voyages are unusually long and perilous, and the only harbours accessible are among the barbarous islands of Polynesia or along the lawless coast of South America. Here scenes the most novel frequently occur among the crews.* ('Scenes the most novel' was a nineteenth-century euphemism for orgies. And Melville goes on to describe one.) *In the evening after we had come to anchor, the deck was illuminated with lanterns, and a picturesque band of sylphs, tricked out with flowers, and dressed in robes of variegated tappa, got up a ball in great style. These females are passionately fond of dancing, and in the wild grace of their style excel everything I have ever seen. The dances of the Marquesan girls are beautiful in the extreme, but there is an abandoned voluptuousness in their character which I dare not attempt to describe. Our ship was now wholly given up to every species of riot and debauchery. Not the feeblest barrier was interposed between the passions of the crew and their unlimited gratification. The grossest licentiousness and the most shameful inebriety prevailed, with occasional and short-lived interruptions, through the whole period of our stay. Alas for the poor savages when exposed to the influence of these polluting examples! Unsophisticated and confiding, they are easily led into every vice, and humanity weeps over the ruin inflicted upon them by their European 'civilizers'. Thrice happy are they who, inhabiting some yet undiscovered isle in the midst of the ocean, have never been brought into contaminating contact with the white man.*

Now Melville knew what he was talking about. He was not a prim and proper missionary who thought the Polynesians were evil because they went about half-naked, nor was he a romantic like Commerson who thought they were Noble Savages because that is what he would have liked them to be. He was a practical adventurous man-of-the-world, who had served below-decks in a whaler, deserted, and spent several months living with the Polynesians, as one of them, on one of the remoter islands (in the

Marquesas). So what he writes of them carries weight. He admits they were cannibals. He admits they had frequent wars; and he admits they were 'somewhat inclined to be lazy'. But the word that he uses most often to describe them, the word that appears again and again in his writing, is that they were 'happy'. This happiness he ascribes to two factors – their attitude to women, and the all-embracing nature of their love.

Of their attitude to women he writes:

If the degree of consideration in which women are held is – as the philosophers affirm – a criterion of the degree of refinement among a people, then I may truly pronounce them (the Marquesans) *to be as polished a community as ever the sun shone upon. Nowhere are ladies more assiduously courted; nowhere are they better appreciated; and nowhere are they more sensible of their power. Far different is their condition from that among many rude nations where they are made to perform all the work . . . here they pass their days in one long round of happiness.*

While of their love he tells us, *During my whole stay on the island I never witnessed a single quarrel, nor even a dispute. The natives appeared to form one household, whose members were bound together by ties of strong affection. The love of kindred I did not so much perceive, for it seemed blended into the general love, and when all were treated as brother and sister it was hard to tell who were actually related by blood. . . All worked together, actuated by an instinct of friendliness that was beautiful to behold.*

This traditional and seemingly happy way of life the whalers helped to destroy, both directly and indirectly. They helped to destroy it directly by debasing the Polynesian women, by using them as sex-objects, whom they bought for liquor or cash and did as they liked with. By the 1830s as many as 150 whaling vessels were visiting Tahiti each year. Life aboard was squalid, hard and dangerous, and when the men came ashore they wanted girls. Frederick Bennett, a surgeon from one of the whalers, writes:

The indiscriminate sale of spirits and the laxity of the laws which permitted sensuality to be carried to a boundless extent, caused scenes of riot and debauchery to be exhibited at Papeete that would have disgraced the most profligate purlieus of London. By partaking in these, the natives degraded their physical no less than their moral state, and in the slovenly and diseased inhabitants of the port, it is vain to attempt to recognise the prepossessing figure of the Tahitian as pictured by Cook.

It might be thought that this was painting too black a picture, that seamen-on-leave have been a problem ever since voyaging began, and that what went on in Papeete was no different from what had been going on for thousands of years in thousands of ports-of-call all over the world – and there is a grain of truth in that. Yet in the Pacific the consequences of sexual intercourse between whalers and islanders were particularly injurious. This is partly because of the length and frequency of the whalers' visits, partly because of the small size and relatively small population of the islands, and partly because the Polynesians' penchant for casual sex made it likely that any diseases given them by the whalers would be passed on. This indeed is what happened. And it would be no exaggeration to say that when a whaling ship dropped anchor within a lagoon, the shock-waves sometimes rippled outward to rock the lives of just about every family on an island.

The whalers also had a disastrous effect indirectly on the Polynesians; for they often brought with them a tatterdemalion rabble of escaped convicts, deserters and adventurers, who had hitched a ride to the islands in their overcrowded fo'c'sles.

Throughout much of the nineteenth century the archipelagos of the Pacific were considered too remote and unimportant for the great powers to take much interest in

The Reverend and Mrs Creed
landing at Taranaki, New Zealand.

them. They were ungarrisoned and unvisited by officials, and whaling ships were their principal contact with the outside world. When these whaling ships stood out to sea, after the usual 'scenes the most novel', they frequently left behind not only anything up to a third of their crew who had deserted, but also a jetsam of undesirable characters who, for one reason or another, were anxious to escape from the conventional world.

So a new type of man appeared in the islands, the beachcomber, the reject of the West. Not all of them were evil. Some wanted only to liaise with the Polynesian women, and some wanted only to soak up the sun and the rum and opt out. But there were also among them a fair number of destructive characters, men who reckoned that with a couple of stolen muskets they could set themselves up as petty latter-day warlords. As early as 1806 Banks was writing of Tahiti that the island

> *is said to be in the hands of about one hundred white men, chiefly English convicts, who lend their assistance as warriors to the chief, whoever he may be, who offers them wages payable in women, hogs etc; and we are told that these banditti have, by the introduction of diseases, by devastation, murther, and all kinds of European barbarism, reduced the population of this most interesting island to less than one-tenth of what it was when the Endeavour visited it in 1769.*

Banks was exaggerating; but the essence of what he writes is true. And his *cri-de-coeur* comes down to us through the years, its message crystal clear. Paradise was being defiled: defiled by 'European babarism'.

In the North Pacific the whalers were comparative late-arrivers, handicapped by the vast distance between the killing-grounds and their bases on the Atlantic seaboard. F. D. Ommanney writes:

> *The story of whaling is made up of a number of chapters each repeating the same pattern. Each begins with discovery and enterprise, passes through a phase of fierce competition and ruthless*

exploitation, and ends in diminishing resources, exhaustion and failure. In his pursuit of the whale man has been both blind and ignorant.

What is true of whaling in general is true of whaling in the North Pacific in particular.

The first whales to be hunted by Europeans in this part of the ocean were the sperm. For about thirty years (1815-45) the sperm-industry flourished, employing hundreds of ships and tens of thousands of men, and 'turning the Pacific from a vast *aqua incognita* into a whalers' pond'. However, the sperm were hunted with such ruthlessness that they became scarce; a ship's average annual catch dropped from over 30 to under 3, and the whalers were forced to seek pastures new. It was probably a Siwash Indian who led them to the kelp beds off California, the feeding and breeding ground of the grey whales. The grey (*Eschrichtius glaucus*) are the most ancient of the whale family, and used to be found all over the world – a skeleton dating back to 50,000 BC was recently unearthed in the Zuider Zee. They are not very prepossessing to look at, being slightly hump-backed and often covered in barnacles, crustaceans and lice, which is why the ancient whalers nicknamed them Devil Fish. The name, however, is singularly inappropriate; for the grey are friendly, gregarious and family-orientated creatures, who mate for life and are devoted to their young. This latter trait the whalers were quick to notice and take advantage of. Armed with explosive harpoons, they made their first target the baby whales as they played in the inshore lagoons, knowing that once they were killed, their distraught parents wouldn't leave their bodies and would themselves become easy victims. For perhaps twenty years large numbers of grey were slaughtered each breeding season. Inevitably their numbers declined. By the 1870s no more than a handful were coming south each season to the kelp beds of California and by the 1890s they were believed to be extinct. (In fact a handful were subsequently found – and declared a protected species – off the coast of Japan.)

Once again the whalers were obliged to seek new killing grounds. By now they had hunted the greater part of the ocean to exhaustion and were forced to search for their quarry in the remote and dangerous waters of the extreme north. Here they found the bowheads, first in small numbers in the Sea of Okhotsk, then in far greater numbers in the Arctic Ocean. There followed one of the most wasteful episodes in the whole history of man's extirpation of fauna. A bowhead yielded roughly a ton of oil and a ton of baleen. The oil fetched less than 30 cents a gallon, the baleen fetched over $4 a pound. Why, the whaling companies argued, should they bother with the laborious business of cutting up and rendering down the bowheads' blubber? Why didn't they simply hack out the baleen and leave the carcass for the gulls? Soon the approaches to the Bering Strait were littered with the putrifying bodies of literally thousands of whales. The bowheads retreated deep into the ice-leads of the Arctic, but even here the men from New England sought them out. The rewards in this frozen cul-de-sac of the world were enormous, but so were the dangers. In 1871 almost the whole of the New England Arctic fleet got itself trapped, off the north coast of Alaska, between the thickening ice and the shore. Out of 40 vessels only 7 survived. It was disasters like this which, together with the discovery in 1859 of petroleum, brought about the decline of the North Pacific whaling industry. It lingered on into the early 1900s, but more as an anachronism than a vital force.

Yet in its heyday what a force it was! A force which may have been blind and wanton in its spoliation, but which nonetheless played a major role in the Westernization of the North Pacific. It helped to draw Hawaii into the orbit of America. It helped to establish San Francisco as one of the major ports of the world. It helped to substitute American influence for Russian influence in Alaska. And it is pleasant to record that here on the rim of the known world, the whalers and the people of the extreme north met, if not in harmony, at least with a degree of tolerance and camaraderie. There were of course misunderstandings and skirmishes, but the two races had a common adversary – the cold, a common objective – survival, and a common prey – the whales; and the tough and resilient Eskimos were better able to look after themselves than the gentle and easy-going Polynesians. In the North Pacific the activities of the whalers affected the fauna more than the people.

One last piece of evidence underlines the major role these whalers played in opening up the Pacific: the large number of islands they discovered. In his *Discovery of the Pacific Islands*, Andrew Sharp lists more than fifty atolls and small islands which were first sighted by whaling vessels, most of them American. Few of these New England captains – Ingraham, Cary, Barrett, Allen, Clark, Starbuck, Gardner, Mooers – are remembered today, but the ocean is littered with their discoveries. And as well as these known and proven first-sightings, how often must explorers have been led to their discovery by the verbal report of a whaler? Swains Island in a case in point. . . When Captain Hudson (of the US Exploring Expedition) was in Samoa in 1841, the master of a whaling vessel told him of a hitherto unknown island which he had sighted while in pursuit of a sperm whale. Hudson went in search of it; and about 200 miles to the north-north-west of Samoa, in 11° 5′S – 170° 55′W, he found a coral formation which was several miles in circumference but nowhere more than 25 feet above sea level. This discovery is usually attributed to Hudson, although he generously named it Swains Island, after the master of the whaler whose report led him to it. A story which must have been repeated many times during the exploration of the Pacific.

It could therefore be said of the whalers – as of the buccaneers – that although their deeds were dark they helped to shed light on a part of the world that was little known.

A very different sort of light was shed on the Pacific islands by a very different people: the missionaries.

Of all those who came to the Pacific in the immediate wake of the explorers, I would rate the whalers and the missionaries the most important. Other groups of people may have had a transitory influence in this or that archipelago – sealers in the Aleutians, slave-traders in the New Hebrides, sandalwood cutters in the Marquesas, pearlers in the Tuamotus – and towards the end of the century government officials and troops began to play an increasingly important role. But the missionaries, like the whalers, were persistent and ubiquitous; and they were no birds of passage, they had come to stay. It would have been pleasant to record that their influence was as benign as that of the whalers was malevolent. The truth, however, is not so simple.

The impact of Christianity on the Pacific islanders was every bit as traumatic mentally as was the impact of whaling physically. For the doctrine propounded by the missionaries was so totally at variance with the islanders' traditional beliefs as to be almost incomprehensible to them, and this difference was accentuated by the fact that the islanders and the missionaries were so totally different in character. The islanders didn't like working unless they had to; the missionaries believed in the efficacy of labour, in 'drudgery divine'. The islanders were content with the status quo; the missionaries were ever striving to bring about a better world. Above all, the islanders were a physical people who regarded sex as an innocent pleasure; the missionaries were cerebral and equated casual sex with sin.

With so great a gulf dividing them, the wonder is not that the missionaries some-

Top Timor: a scene near Kupang from Freycinet's *Voyage de l'Astrolabe. Above* A painting by Garneray of Dumont D'Urville's ship surrounded by ice.

Hibiscus rosa sinensis, painted in 1769 by Sydney Parkinson, artist on Cook's *Endeavour* voyage.

Parrot with a blue back and two pygmy parrots, from D'Urville's *Voyage*.

Top Painting by Charles Wilkes of his flagship *Vincennes* in the Antarctic. *Above* The harbour of St Paul in the island of Cadiak (now Kodiak Island, in the gulf of Alaska), the site of the first Russian colony in America, by Y. Lisiansky.

Passage de Tahiti painted in 1892 by Paul Gauguin, who spent the latter part of his life in Tahiti and the Marquesas.

Tourism has brought about a welcome if emasculated revival of Polynesian and Melanesian traditions. Warrior at Sing-Sing in Papua New Guinea.

Top Va Huka dancers in the Marquesas; *above* pageant of the long canoes at Oahu in Hawaii.

Of all the evils that white people brought to the Pacific, perhaps the greatest is still being practised there today. A thermonuclear fireball bursts over an unnamed atoll in the Tuamotus.

Baptism of the Prime Minister of the King, on board the *Uranie,* Sandwich Islands, by L. P. Crespin after J. Arago, published in Freycinet's *Voyage.*

times failed, but they they achieved the success they did. For remarkable as it sounds, within a generation of their arrival more than 100 mission-stations had taken root in the Pacific islands, and several archipelagos, at least on the surface, had been reformed and evangelized. As Alan Moorehead succinctly puts it, 'Venus was supplanted by Mary Magdalene' – although it must be pointed out that the islanders' conversion was often a matter of convenience rather than conviction, and it was not achieved without loss. What happened on Tahiti was typical.

In March 1797 the schooner *Duff* put ashore on the sands of Matavai Bay a boat-load of incongruous immigrants. There were 39 of them; four ordained clergymen, and a couple of dozen lay-preachers, five of whom had their wives with them and two their children. They were members of the London Missionary Society – 'a Set of Tinkers', according to their class-conscious contemporaries, 'men of little education, selected from the dregs of the common people' – and they had come to Tahiti with the intention of bringing God's word to the islanders and reshaping their lives in the image of lower-middle-class Protestant England. Now it is easy to ridicule these self-appointed messengers of grace. Most people today would regard them as narrow-minded, sometimes absurd and nearly always repressive. They were forever telling the Polynesians not to do this and not to do that: not to play on their flutes, not to sway their hips as they danced, not to tattoo their bodies, not to make love. It was as though they reckoned God's greatest commandment was 'thou shalt *not* love thy neighbour'. Yet thanks to circumstances that were partly tragic, partly comic opera, they achieved a sort of triumph. And indeed it is worth pointing out that in the long-term they provided the Polynesians with a lifeline, not only a spiritual but an educational plank to help them through the transition from an old culture to a new.

Not one of the 39 who landed that autumn in Matavai Bay had ever left England before – most had never even left their parish – and they had little idea of what to expect in Tahiti. Some thought it quite on the cards that they were going to be killed and eaten, and if this was God's will they were prepared to accept it; martyrdom was not, in their eyes, too high a price to pay for spreading His word. One virtue they were not short of was courage. In the event, of course, far from killing them and eating them, the Polynesians made them welcome, and indeed quite overwhelmed them with hospitality. They offered them a house, a large area of land, food and a selection of young girls – all but the last of which were accepted with grateful bewilderment. 'Their generosity is boundless,' wrote one of the missionaries, 'and appears excessive. Not only are cart-loads of provisions sent in for our whole community, but individuals have received the most surprising abundance of gifts, without return being expected or even thought of . . . they are friendly and generous to a fault.'

This reaction tells us quite a lot about the missionaries. The Polynesians had welcomed them in the most friendly and generous manner imaginable, yet the missionaries nonetheless found fault with them, describing their very virtues as faulty and excessive – as though love was something it was dangerous to have too much of. And if one asks *why* the missionaries were so determined to fault the Polynesians, the answer seems to be that they regarded them as children of the devil, steeped in original sin. As Niel Gunson points out in his excellent book, *Messengers of Grace*:

> *The Evangelical missionary had little doubt that Satan, adversary of God and man, reigned as absolute sovereign over the South Sea Islands. . . Critics have often marvelled at the perverse way in which the missionaries adopted a stern attitude towards the islanders, and at the ruthless way in which they set about overturning their existing society.*

An easily exploitable resource of the
Pacific: cutting copra in Fiji,

They acted this way, Gunson suggests, because they believed not only that all primitive people were depraved, but that the South Sea Islanders in particular were *totally* depraved. And we need only look at what the missionaries wrote about the islanders to see that Gunson is right. Of the Fijians:

> *They are in one word the very dregs of mankind, dead and buried under the primeval curse* (the sin of Adam) *and nothing of them alive but the Brutal part, yea, far worse than the Brute-Savage, quite unfit to live but more unfit to die.* And of the Marquesans: *In point of morals they must be classed with the lowest of our species. Nothing we have beheld in the shape of human depravity in other parts of the world will compare for a moment with their shameful and shameless iniquities. The blackest ink that ever stained paper is none too dark to describe them.*

Whatever, one wonders, had the Polynesians been up to, to be on the receiving end of such a broadside?

There seem to have been four facets of Polynesian life which particularly outraged the missionaries: cannibalism, human sacrifice, infanticide and something they called 'onanism', although it is pretty certain that what they were complaining of was homosexuality. One could have understood and indeed shared the missionaries' outrage if the first three of these practices had been widespread, but they were not; they were rare. Cannibalism was practised in New Zealand, the Marquesas and in a small number of islands in Melanesia. Nowhere was it widespread, and it seems to have taken place only in time of war. It was certainly a stigma on the Polynesians' way of life, but not one that affected many people. The same was true, only to an even greater degree, of human sacrifice; this was *taboo* on most islands, and in islands where it wasn't *taboo* it was resorted to only in exceptional circumstances – impending war or prolonged famine. Infanticide was a problem in just the one archipelago (the Society Islands) and among just the one class (the aristocracy-cum-*arioi*). The idea of infanticide is particularly repugnant to Christian and Western eyes, and one can understand the evangelists' revulsion when they found it being practised on their doorstep. . . The wife of Pomare – one of the major kings on the island – became pregnant by her lover who was a servant. It was unthinkable to the Tahitians that the child should be allowed to live, and in spite of the impassioned pleading of the missionaries, who even offered to look after the baby themselves, Pomare's wife duly killed it – an act which confirmed the missionaries in their belief that the Polynesians were completely and utterly depraved. Further evidence of this depravity, it seemed to the missionaries, could be observed daily in the islanders' sexual promiscuity in general and their tolerance of homosexuality in particular. Homosexuality was, to the men from the *Duff*, something so wicked that they couldn't bring themselves even to write of it openly. They could only hint that some men on the island are not so purely masculine as they ought to be, and some women not so purely feminine . . . and this 'leads to many unnatural crimes, which we dare not name, being committed daily without the slightest sense of shame or guilt.' There is also an occasional reference in the missionaries' Diaries to the *mahus*, 'a set of men of the most execrable cast, affecting the manners, dress, gestures and voice of females, and too horrid to be described,' so 'horrid' that when one of the *mahus* expressed the desire to become a Christian, the missionaries refused to baptize him.

All this would seem to indicate that since cannibalism, human sacrifice and infanticide were rare, what the missionaries disapproved of most strongly about the Polynesians was their attitude to sex; and as evidence of this they were forever trying to persuade them to dress more modestly, to dance less abandonedly and above all not to have casual sexual intercourse.

Their feelings about the latter come across very strongly in an incident related by the Reverend John Orsmond. Orsmond tells us that he spent weeks of 'prodigious toil' making a pulpit for the mission church in Papeete. It had been installed only a few days when the missionary 'caught a man and woman, actually within the pulpit, in an act of adultery'. It is clear from what Orsmond tells us that they were having sexual intercourse, although why this was described as adultery is less clear. Be that as it may, the missionary was so convinced that his pulpit had been defiled, that he smashed it to pieces and burned it.This incident, it seems to me, tells us a lot about Orsmond, as does his claim, when writing to his superiors in London, that 'our brethren, by their example, have already done much to restrain the natural levity of the natives'.

How, one wonders, did such melancholy shepherds attract a flock?

The answer is that for many years they didn't. The Tahitians soon came to accept the missionaries as part of their everyday lives, and it would seem that they thought of them as rather pathetic figures who needed looking after – when they put to sea they forgot their paddles and had to be rescued, when they went swimming they were too prudish to take their clothes off and nearly drowned. It quickly became obvious that these strange white men in their strange black clothes wanted the Tahitians to accept their God; but the Tahitians had gods of their own and saw no reason for apostasy – especially as the white man's God was always threatening to burn them in everlasting flames. Some Tahitians, out of politeness, attended the missionaries' church services and rather enjoyed the hymns. Some, again out of politeness, took to covering up their bodies when they visited the mission; and a very small number listened to readings from *Pilgrim's Progress* which, since they had no concept of sin, was totally incomprehensible to them – although one islander is reported to have set out earnestly in search of Apollyon with the intention of killing him.

At the end of ten years little had been achieved; Tahiti was in the throes of a series of wars, and many of the evangelists had either moved or were about to move to other islands. 'By 1810,' writes the historian of the London Missionary Society, 'to all human appearance the Tahitian mission was at an end.' The church had been dismantled; the lead in its printing-press had been melted down for bullets, its Bibles had been torn up for cartridge paper.

Yet before another ten years had passed, Tahiti had been evangelized. It was not, however, the eloquence and the example of the missionaries which established God's word on the island. It was the powder and shot of muskets.

It all started with Pomare's conversion. Pomare II was a self-indulgent debauchee and drunkard who was suspected by the missionaries (and with good reason) of 'unnatural crimes'. He may have been an unattractive character, but he was remarkably astute, and he realized that by becoming a Christian he would gain the backing of the white establishment – the missionaries and the more repsonsible sea-captains, traders and whalers. The white establishment all had muskets. And muskets won wars. In 1813 Pomare was living in exile on Huahine, having been defeated by his fellow chiefs in a series of local skirmishes. Within eighteen months of his conversion he had returned to Tahiti at the head of a macabre musket-toting Crusade, defeated his enemies, and made himself king of the island. A less intelligent man might, at this stage, have ditched his Christian supporters. Pomare realized that to stay in power he was likely to need them. So he made them his advisers.

What an opportunity this afforded the missionaries! To be fair to them, they had always done their best to keep out of the island's wars, and the authority they sought had been spiritual rather than secular. But now the latter was offered them, they realized that here was a unique opportunity to create a gospel-based society, a latter-day Protestant and more practical version of Quiros's New Jerusalem. David Howarth explains very well how they set about doing this:

> *Everything they disapproved as sinful was made illegal. They did not have to preach against sin and threaten punishment in a life to come: they only had to tell Pomare to make a new law forbidding each sin and they could punish it then and there. They themselves lived in perpetual melancholic remorse for the sin of the world, and they expected everyone else to do the same. They equated beauty with sin, and suspected that any sign of happiness, such as laughter – 'unseemly levity' they called it – was a symptom of sin. If they heard anyone laughing, they asked what he had to laugh at, and whatever it was, it was likely to be wrong.*

Joylessness-imposed-by-law spread like a cancer through the fabric of Polynesian life, eroding traditional values, stifling spontaneity, and denying the islanders those physical pleasures which for thousands of years they had taken as their birthright. It is almost unbelievable how many things the missionaries made *taboo*. Under their Puritanical regime there could be no singing – except of hymns. No dancing. No wrestling. No acting of plays. No beating of drums. No playing on the flute. No drinking of spirits. No tattooing. No weaving garlands of flowers. No flowers to be worn in the hair – and the 'long sinful hair' itself to be cut short. By night morality police combed the woods for illicit lovers. On what the missionaries reckoned was the Sabbath (although ironically they were a day out in their calculations) everything ground to a halt except for church services, where vigilantes with bamboo-sticks ensured a good attendance.

All this produced a society which was more well-behaved than happy, a fair assessment of it being made by the Russian explorer von Kotzebue, who visited Tahiti in 1816.

> *The religion of the missionaries,* Kotzebue writes, *has indeed reduced incontinence and theft; however, it has introduced in their place bigotry, covetousness and hypocrisy. . . Also it is a shame that every pleasure should be punished as a sin, especially among a people whom Nature endowed with such a capacity for enjoyment.*

One would have hoped that with the passing of time, the harshness of the missionaries' regime might have been relaxed. But it wasn't; and a generation later Melville was delivering a more impassioned (but perhaps also more unbalanced) denunciation of the missionaries.

> *Distracted with their sufferings, the people brought forth their sick before the missionaries while they were preaching, and cried out 'Lies! Lies! You tell us of salvation, and behold we are dying. We want no other salvation than to live in this world. Where are there any saved by your speech? We are all dying with your cursed diseases. When will you give over? . . . When will you leave us alone?'*

Melville of course was baying to the moon. The Pacific Ocean had been discovered. The Pacific islands had been explored; and now, as surely as sun-up gives way to morning, the Pacific islanders were going to be exploited. There could be no turning back the clock, no retreat into the past, no matter how happy that past might have been.

The missionaries were by no means the last purveyors of Western culture to help bring about the collapse of Polynesian culture. After the men of the cloth came the men of the sword, and after them the administrators, the businessmen, and in our own generation the scientists and the tourists. However, these more recent interlopers could hardly be called explorers. The age of exploration ends with the whalers and the missionaries; and although the contribution of the latter was not great, neither was it negligible. Two ships alone – the *Duff* in 1797 and the *Endeavour* in 1823 – discovered more than a dozen islands: James Wilson in the former was the first person to sight Timoe Mangareva and Pukarua in the Tuamotus, Vanua-Mbavalu Ongea and Fulanga in the Fiji group, and Satawal Lamotrek Elato Ifalif and Woleai in the Western Carolines; while John Williams in the latter discovered Mitiaro and Mauke in the Cook Islands. By the time the whalers and the missionaries stopped voyaging, there was hardly an island, atoll or reef in the Pacific that had not been discovered. The exploration of the ocean, which had begun 3,500 years earlier as the first *pahis* stood east from Indonesia, was complete.

Our story began with the Polynesians, and it is only right it should end with them, for the Pacific is their ocean.

The European and American seamen who opened up this greatest of oceans to the rest of the world include some of the most famous explorers in history. Who could better Magellan for endurance, Cook for seamanship, Bougainville for rapport with the indigenous people, or Wilkes for courage? The exploits of many of these explorers were nothing short of heroic. Yet wherever they went they found that the Polynesians had been there before them. When a European first sighted Easter Island, the remotest island on Earth, he found the Polynesians living there. When Europeans landed in the Line Islands on some of the most barren and insignificant outcrops of coral in the world, they found evidence that the Polynesians at one time had settled there.

The first and greatest explorers of the Pacific were the Polynesians. And not only did they explore the ocean, they established throughout it a network of island-kingdoms in which people led, in the true sense of the word, civilized lives; that is to say they were 'enlightened in the art of living'; they were happy. It is true that Polynesian civilization was lacking in ambition and material expertise and was far from perfect – though David Howarth reckons 'it came nearer to perfection than any other that has been recorded' – but, perfect or imperfect, few thinking people today would deny that its obliteration was a tragedy. Yet obliterated it was. There can be no doubt about that. The beauty of the Polynesian islands was never of course obliterated; many of them today are still unspoilt and lovely as dreams. Nor were the Polynesians themselves obliterated; they were decimated, but they survived, and the men today are still handsome and virile and the women still beautiful and charming, and both are still cheerful and good-natured to one another and to strangers. But their traditional way of life has been swept away, swept away beyond recall; and the world is poorer without it.

This is a side to the exploration of the Pacific that tends to be conveniently forgotten. Most people regard the conquest of the Ocean as a great Western achievement. They think of sailing ships anchored off palm-lined beaches, of long voyages with men racked by hunger, thirst and scurvy, of the hazards of storm, ice and sheer distance, of the pursuit of great whales and golden girls; and they are proud to think that this great Ocean has, by such efforts, been transformed from a sleepy backwater into a dynamic tide-race – now one of the fastest-growth areas in the world. This is one point of view. However, the nineteenth-century people of the Pacific doubtless saw things differently; and so, I suspect, will historians of the twenty-first century. For already, when conservationists and ethnologists write of the Pacific, one word is beginning to appear with increasing frequency in their reports; that word is rape.

Two men who witnessed the death throes of Polynesian culture were Melville and Gauguin; and since the islanders lacked the ability to write their own requiem, perhaps these two Westerners, who lived among them and knew what they were talking about, might be allowed to write it for them.

Melville tells us of a conversation between one of the *arioi* and a visiting missionary. This was in the 1840s; and the *arioi* said to the missionary, 'Your ancestors came here in the time of men, but you have come at a bad time, when only a remnant of my people are still alive.' And he went on to quote a Polynesian saying – 'I have frequently heard it myself,' Melville adds, 'chanted in a sad low tone by aged Polynesians':

> *'A haree ta fow,*
> *A toro ta farraro,*
> *A now ta tararta.'*
> The palm tree grows,
> The coral spreads,
> But man shall vanish.

Gauguin didn't write a great deal about the Polynesians, but he painted them; and his portraits, like those of all great artists, are a social comment. He came to Tahiti in the hope, he tells us, of painting the islanders in their natural state. 'These nymphs, I want to perpetuate them, with their golden skin and their animal odour.' But everywhere he went – this was a generation later than Melville – he was appalled by the degradation of the Tahitians and the desecration brought about by the white man.

> *There used to be many strange and beautiful things here,* he wrote, *but no trace of them now remains. The natives have nothing to do, and think of one thing only, drinking. There is much prostitution. Day by day the race vanishes . . . they are dying of despair.*

Nevermore by Paul Gauguin. 'In Gauguin's Tahitian paintings no man or woman ever smiles. Supine, defeated, despairing, beautiful . . . they long for a paradise once familiar but now forever lost.'

And in their despair he painted them, Alan Moorehead puts it very well:

In Gauguin's Tahitian paintings no man or woman ever smiles; supine, defeated, despairing and beautiful, his people gaze in a reverie into the lost past. They see nothing but the broken stones of their marae, their fallen idols, the great legendary war-canoes with their tattooed warriors in their elaborate robes, and the forgotten dances and rituals of the arioi.

What is probably Gauguin's most famous portrait, that of a nude girl, has an enigmatic one-word title. The girl's body is beautiful, but there is nothing beautiful about her expression. She lies inert and naked on her bed, utterly inanimate, hoping for nothing, caring for nothing. In the background a dark conspiratorial couple are whispering things that can't be spoken of openly; about her bed are scattered the starlike petals of the *tiare Tahiti*, while looking down on her from the walls are all the mystical creatures and symbols of a tropical paradise once familiar but now forever lost. On the back of his canvas Gauguin wrote in English one word – 'Nevermore'.

APPENDIX I

PRINCIPAL VOYAGES IN THE EXPLORATION OF THE PACIFIC

POLYNESIAN

c. 1400-1100 BC	Purposeful migration from Indonesia to Fiji, Samoa and Tonga.
c. 1100 BC-200 AD	Drift-voyaging to Society Islands, Marquesas, Tuamotus, Cook and Tubuai archipelagos.
c. AD 200-AD 1000	Purposeful migration to Hawaii, Easter Island and New Zealand.

SPANISH

16th century	MAGELLAN (1521) first crossing of the Pacific. Discoveries in Tuamotus and Marianas.
	SAAVEDRA (1528) first crossing of Pacific from North America. Discoveries in Marshall and Caroline Islands.
	ARELLANO (1565) first to cross Pacific from west to east.
	MENDANA (1568) discovers Guadalcanal and Wake; discoveries in Ellice Islands and Solomons; (1595) discoveries in Marquesas, Santa Cruz and E. Carolines.

BRITISH

16th century	DRAKE (1578) first commander to complete successful circumnavigation of the world.

SPANISH

17th century	QUIROS (1606) discovers Henderson, Ducie and Rakahanga Islands. Discoveries in Tuamotus, Banks, New Hebrides and Gilbert Islands.

DUTCH

17th century	LE MAIRE (1616) discovers seaway to the Pacific south of Cape Horn. Discoveries in Tuamotus, Tonga group, Horne Islands, Bismarck Archipelago. Proves insularity of New Guinea.
	TASMAN (1642) discovers Tasmania and New Zealand. Discoveries in Tonga group, Ringgold Islands and Ontong Java. Proves Australia does not extend far eastward into the Pacific.
18th century	ROGGEVEEN (1722) discovers Easter Island. Discoveries in Tuamotus, Society Islands and Samoa.

RUSSIAN 18th century	BERING (1728) discovers Bering Strait and entry to Arctic Ocean. And (1741) with CHIRIKOV discovers coast of Alaska and Aleutian Islands.
BRITISH 18th century	WALLIS (1767) discoveries in Tuamotus, Society Islands – first landing in Tahiti – and Marshall Islands. CARTERET (1767) discovers Pitcairn Island. Discoveries in Tuamotus and Solomon Islands.
FRENCH 18th century	BOUGAINVILLE (1768) discoveries in Tuamotus, Society Islands, New Hebrides and Solomon Islands. His report on the Polynesian way of life in Tahiti promotes the concept of the Noble Savage. Possible first sighting of east coast of Australia.
BRITISH 18th century	COOK (1769) discoveries in Tuamotus, Society Islands and Austral Islands. First circumnavigation of New Zealand; delineates east coast of Australia.
SPANISH 18th century	BOENECHEA (1772) discoveries in Tuamotus and Austral Islands.
BRITISH 18th century	COOK (1773) discoveries in Cook Islands, New Hebrides, Marquesas and New Caledonia. His close circumnavigation of Antarctica proves that no Great Southern Continent exists north of the pack-ice, between Australia and South America. (1778) discoveries in Cook, Tonga and Austral Islands. Discovery of Christmas Island and the Hawaiian Islands. First charting of the North American coast between Vancouver and the Arctic Ocean.
FRENCH 18th century	LA PÉROUSE (1787) discoveries in Samoa group. Discovers Necker Island and French Frigate Shoals, north of Hawaii.
BRITISH 18th century	BLIGH (1789) discovers Bounty Islands; discoveries in Fiji and Banks Islands. (*Bounty* mutineers discover Rarotonga in 1793.) Further discoveries in Fiji Islands. VANCOUVER (1791) discovers The Snares and Chatham Islands. Detailed survey of coast of British Columbia and Alaska.

AMERICAN 18th century	INGRAHAM (1791) discoveries in the Marquesa Islands.
RUSSIAN 19th century	KOTZEBUE (1815) discoveries in Tuamotus and Marshall Islands; discovery of Bikini Atoll.
	BELLINGSHAUSEN (1820) second circumnavigation of Antarctica. Discoveries in Tuamotus and Fiji Islands. Discovery of Vostok Island.
BRITISH 19th century	FITZROY (1831) discoveries in Tuamotus. The research work of his naturalist Charles Darwin results in publication of *The Origin Of Species*.
FRENCH 19th century	DUMONT D'URVILLE (1840) commands first expedition to sight the mainland of Antarctica. Discovery of Adélie Land (20.1.1840).
AMERICAN 19th century	WILKES (1840) controversial claim to be first to sight Antarctic mainland. Sights Balleny Islands. Discovers Wilkes Land and follows the coast for 1,500 miles, thus delineating the southern limits of the Pacific.

APPENDIX II

THE PRINCIPAL ISLANDS OF THE PACIFIC OCEAN

ADMIRALTY ISLANDS (1° 50′S – 146°E): an archipelago in Melanesia, north of New Guinea. First European sighting by Saavedra in 1528 and named by him 'The 21 islands'; renamed by Carteret in 1767 'in honour of the Lords of the Admiralty'. Most of the islands are low-lying atols with a poor soil that will grow little except coconuts. When first discovered by Europeans they supported a healthy Micronesian/ Melanesian population, but by 1900 were virtually uninhabited.
ALEUTIAN ISLANDS (53°N – 163° to 173°W): a chain of volcanic islands (the submerged peaks of the Aleutian Range) scattered for some thousand miles across the North Pacific between Alaska and Kamchatka. First European sighting by Bering and Chirikov in 1741, and named after the native inhabitants, the Aleuts. Susbequently charted by Cook and visted by La Pérouse, Kotzebue and Lutke. Although barren and suffering from 'a succession of unpleasant weather', the coastal waters are rich in fish and mammals. The islands were transferred from Russia to the USA at the time of the Alaska purchase (1867).
AUCKLAND ISLANDS (51°S – 166° 30′E): a small group of uninhabited islands south of New Zealand. Discovered by the British whaler *Bristow* and named in honour of the Earl of Auckland, First Lord of the Admiralty and Viceroy of India.
AUSTRALIA (12° to 38°S – 114° to 153°E): continent and largest island on Earth, situated between the Indian and Pacific Oceans, first populated about 25,000 years ago by a Negrito people crossing by land-bridges from Indonesia. The north and west coasts were 'discovered' by the Dutch and named New Holland; the east coast was 'discovered' by the British and named New South Wales. The first European sighting of the north coast was in April 1606 by Janszoon in the Gulf of Carpentaria; a further sighting may have occurred a few months later as Torres passed Cape York. The west coast was sighted many times in the decade 1610-20 by Dutch vessels on passage from Capetown to Batavia. The east coast may have been first sighted by Bougainville in June 1768, when he was turned back by the Great Barrier Reef opposite Cape Flattery; however, the usually accepted first sighting is by Cook who, between April and August 1770, surveyed and landed on the coasts of New South Wales and Queensland. The name Australia is derived from the Latin *australis* = southern. *Terra Australis Incognita* (the Unknown Southern Land) was the name given by ancient cartographers to the great land mass which, it was believed, must exist in the southern hemisphere to balance the land mass of Eurasia in the north. After Flinders had circumnavigated Australia in 1802/3 he wrote: 'Now that New Holland and New South Wales are known to form one land, there must be a general name [given] to the whole, and I have re-adopted the original name *Terra Australis*. Had I permitted myself any change it would have been to convert Australis to Australia.'
BANKS ISLANDS (13° 50′S – 167° 30′E): an archipelago in Melanesia between the New Hebrides and Santa Cruz Islands. First sighted by Quiros in 1606; renamed by Bligh in 1788 in honour of the naturalist Sir Joseph Banks.
BERINGA OSTROVA (55°N – 166° 40′E): a barren island, rich in aquatic mammals, 124 miles (200 km) east of Kamchatka. First sighted by Bering, who ran his ship, the *St Peter*, ashore on the east coast, thus enabling some of his ships' company to survive the sub-Arctic winter.

CAROLINE ISLANDS (8°N – 147°E): an archipelago in Micronesia consisting of some 450 atolls strung out between the Philippines and the Marshall Islands. First sighted by the Portuguese Diego la Rocha in 1527. Rediscovered in 1686 by the Spaniard Lazeano and renamed first 'Islands of the Gardens', then the Caroline Islands after Charles II of Spain.
COOK ISLANDS (20°S – 158°W): an archipelago in Polynesia, south-west of the Society Islands. One island (Rakahanga) was sighted by Quiros in 1606; but the group is named after Cook who visited it in 1773 and 1775. The islands were governed by New Zealand from 1901 until 1965 when they gained independence.
EASTER ISLAND (27° 10′S – 109° 30′W): the remotest island on Earth, lying in a vast expanse of featureless ocean 2,350 miles (3,790 km) from South America and 995 miles (1,600 km) from Pitcairn Island. Known to the Polynesians as Te-Pito-O-Te-Henua (the Navel of the World) and believed to have been first settled by Polynesians *c.* AD 400 – Heyerdahl's theory of its population from Peru is now generally thought improbable. First sighted on Easter Sunday, 1722 by Jacob Roggeveen, and subsequently visited by Cook, La Pérouse and Kotzebue. Famous for its large (9-yard) statues carved out of volcanic rock. The island has been governed by Chile since 1888; and the present population of 2,000 is largely of Chilean extraction, the original islanders having all been decimated by disease or abducted by Peruvian slave-traders.
FIJI ISLANDS (190°S – 17° 60′E): an archipelago in Polynesia, consisting of some 800 islands and atolls: the first stepping-stone of the Polynesian voyagers who, some 3,000 years ago, migrated into the mid-Pacific. Named after its largest island Viti Levu (derivation unknown). First European sighting by Tasman in 1643; subsequently visited by Cook (1774) and more thoroughly explored by Bligh (1789), Bellingshausen (1820), Dumont D'Urville (1838) and Wilkes (1840). Annexed by Great Britain 1874; gained independence 1970.

Harbour of Pago-Pago, Tutuila,
from a sketch by C. Wilkes.

GALAPAGOS ISLANDS (0° 10′N – 90° 30′W): a group of 19 volcanic islands straddling the equator, 602 miles (970 km) west of Ecuador. First sighted in 1535 by de Berlanga, bishop of Panama, and named after the giant tortoises (Spanish *galapago* = tortoise) which inhabit several of the islands. The group was often visited by seventeenth-century buccaneers who used them as a base from which to raid Spanish treasure galleons and ports on the mainland. A more welcome visitor, in 1835, was Charles Darwin, who found evidence among the unique fauna to support his theory of 'The Origin of Species'. Since 1832 the Galapagos have been a province of Ecuador.

HAWAIIAN ISLANDS (centred on 20°N – 157° 50′W): an archipelago in north Polynesia consisting of 8 inhabited islands and 124 uninhabited atolls. Originally peopled by the Polynesians, *c.* AD 500, who named the main island Hawaii = 'home of the gods', believing that their goddess of fire, Pele, lived in the volcanoes Mauna Kea and Mauna Loa. At one time it was thought that the first Europeans to sight the islands were Spaniards blown off course between Manila and Acapulco; however, this cannot be proved; and it is now generally thought that the islands were 'discovered' by Cook – Kauai, Oahu, Niihau, Lehau and Kaula in 1778 and Maui and Hawaii in 1779. He named them the Sandwich Islands after the First Lord of the Admiralty, the Earl of Sandwich, the islands reverting to their Hawaiian name when they were annexed by America in 1898. The group was subsequently visited by Gray, Vancouver, Krusenstern and Wilkes; also by many sea-otter and seal hunters and whalers. The decline in the islands' population is better documented than in most archipelagos: 300,000 in 1780, 135,000 in 1820, 85,000 in 1850 and 40,000 in 1890, when 'the heavy mortality was accompanied by orgies of drunkenness, prostitution and gambling'. Since Hawaii's annexation by the United States its prosperity and population have increased. It is now one of the most sought-after places in the world to visit or live in. It is, however, American rather than Polynesian. In 1959 it became the 50th State of the Union; and today over 80 per cent of its population is Caucasian, Japanese or Filipino; 19 per cent is mixed, and less than 1 per cent is Polynesian.

JUAN FERNANDEZ (33°S – 90°W): three small islands, 417 miles (670 km) west of Chile. First sighted by Fernandez, a soldier in Pizarro's army, in 1563. Settled by Spanish fishermen in 1591. A favourite watering place for expeditions, buccaneers, sealers and whalers. Early in the eighteenth century a buccaneer rescued from the islands a Scottish seaman named Alexander Selkirk and a Mosquito (Panamanian) Indian who had been marooned there, and who served Defoe as models for Robinson Crusoe and Man Friday. Since 1819 the islands have been governed by Chile.

KIRIBATI (0° 30′S – 174°E): formerly Gilbert Islands: an archipelago in Micronesia, consisting of some 33 islands, south-east of the Marshall group. First sighted by Quiros in 1606; subsequently visited by Byron (1765), Captains Gilbert and Marshall (1788), and Wilkes (1841). The islands were governed by Britain from 1892 to 1979 when they became an independent republic.

MACQUARIE ISLAND (54° 20′S – 159° 45′E): an isolated volcanic island south of New Zealand. First sighted by Hasselborough (1810), who reported a wreck 'high up on the coast'. Named after Lord Macquarie, Governor-General of New South Wales. Subsequently visited by Bellingshausen, and many sealers and whalers.

MARIANAS (12° to 20°N – 145° 30′E): an archipelago in Micronesia, consisting of a chain of 17 islands running north/south some 335 miles (540 km) to the east of the Philippines. Only 6 islands are inhabited; all are subject to earthquakes. First sighted by Magellan (1521) who called them sometimes 'The Islands of Thieves' and sometimes 'The Islands of the Lateen Sails' (lateen being the rig of the Chamorros' canoes). The islands were formally taken into Spanish possession by Legaspi (1565) who named them in honour of Maria of Austria, wife of Philip IV. They were subsequently annexed first by Germany, then by Japan, then by the United States, and are now a self-governing commonwealth.

MARQUESA ISLANDS (8° 50′S – 139° 40′W): an archipelago of 10 medium-sized islands in Polynesia, 746 miles (1200 km) east of Tahiti. Occupied by the Polynesians *c.* AD 300, probably via Tonga. First European sighting in 1595 by Mendana, who named the group after the Viceroy of Peru, the Marques de Mendoza. Subsequently visited by Cook, Ingraham, Marchand, and many sandalwood traders and whalers. Annexed first by Great Britain, then by USA, and finally in 1842 by France, who still retains jurisdiction. Population figures show the customary tragic decline: 80,000 in 1775, 50,000 in 1810, 20,000 in 1842, 6,000 in 1870 and 2,000 in 1920. Today, because of their spectacular and unspoilt beauty, the islands are a favourite port-of-call for yachtsmen on passage between America and Tahiti.

MARSHALL ISLANDS (9°N – 168°E): a scattered archipelago in Micronesia, consisting of 34 islands and over 850 reefs and atolls, well to the east of the Philippines. First sighted by Loaysa in 1526 and Saavedra in 1528. Subsequently visited by Wallis (1767), Marshall (1788), after whom the islands are named, and Kotzebue. Much used by whalers; and a favourite haunt of beachcombers. Annexed first by Germany, then by Japan and finally by USA, who used Bikini Atoll for atomic tests.

MELANESIA: collective name for the archipelagos north-east of Australia – Papua New Guinea, Admiralty Islands, New Ireland, New Britain, Solomon Islands, Santa Cruz Islands, New Hebrides, New Caledonia, Banks Islands and Fiji. Named from the Greek *melas* = black and *nesos* = island, because of the exceptionally dark skins of the inhabitants.

MICRONESIA: collective name for the multitude of islands extending east from the Philippines – Marianas, Caroline Islands, Marshall Islands, Gilbert Islands, Tuvalu. Named from the Greek *micros* = small and *nesos* = island. An area strewn with islets, atolls and reefs; there are more islands in the Philippines and Micronesia than in all the rest of the world put together.

MOLUCCAS (2°S – 128°E): an archipelago situated between Sulawesi and Western New Guinea (Irian Jaya), formerly known as The Spice Islands. These islands (Buru, Ambon, Seram, Talaibu, Obi, Bacan, Ternate and Halmahera) were the desideratum of European voyagers throughout the sixteenth and seventeenth centuries, and the heartland of the Dutch trading empire, producing camphor, quinine, dyes, cloves, nutmeg, ginger and above all pepper. First sighted by de Varthema in 1502 and visited by Serrão in 1511. It was Magellan's attempt to reach these islands by sailing westward rather than eastward which first made the Pacific Ocean known to the Western world.

NEW BRITAIN (5°S – 150°E): an island and a group of islands in Melanesia, off the north coast of Papua New Guinea, consisting of the Admiralty Islands, New Ireland and the Saint Matthias Group, formerly known as the Bismarck Archipelago. The large southernmost island of New Britain was discovered by Dampier in 1690; New Ireland was discovered by Carteret in 1767. Several islands were annexed by Germany in 1885 – hence the name Bismarck Archipelago. The archipelago is now part of Papua New Guinea.

NEW CALEDONIA (21° 30′S – 165° 30′E): a large island (the largest in the Pacific after New Zealand) and a cluster of small islands in Melanesia about 621 miles (1,000 km) east of Queensland, Australia. Before the arrival of Europeans, the population numbered about 70,000, and lived by subsistence farming; there were frequent tribal wars and some cannibalism. The island may have been sighted by Bougainville in 1768; but the first European to land on it was Cook (1774) who named it New Caledonia because the pine-clad hills resembled those of Scotland. Subsequent landings were made by La Pérouse and D'Entrecasteaux; and in 1850, after the entire crew of the French survey ship *Alcmene* had been captured and eaten, the island was annexed by France. For many years it was used as a penal settlement.

NEW HEBRIDES (16° 50′S – 168° 50′E): an archipelago in Melanesia (now Vanuatu) lying about 248 miles (400 km) north of New Caledonia and 1,118 miles (1,800 km) east of Australia; the main islands are Espiritu Santo, Maewo, Pentecost, Ambrim, Malekula and Efate. The first European to sight the islands was Quiros in 1606 who named the largest island Austrialia del Espiritu Santo (not Australia = austral = south, but Austrialia after the Queen of Austria). The group was subsequently visited by Bougainville (1768) and Cook (1774) who was the first to survey and chart it accurately. In the nineteenth century sandalwood-and-slave traders greatly reduced the population, islanders being shipped by the thousand to work and die in the sugar plantations of Queensland.

NEW ZEALAND (34° to 47° 50′S – 166° 50′ to 177°E): the largest and most southerly islands in Polynesia, 994 miles (1,600 km) south-east of Australia, probably settled by voyagers from Tonga *c.* AD 900. First European sighting by Tasman (1642) who named the islands Staten Landt, thinking them part of the southern continent so named by Le Maire in 1616; Tasman was dissuaded from landing by the warlike attitude of the Maori. In 1769 both islands were accurately surveyed by Cook, who used them as a base on each of his three Pacific voyages. Subsequent explorers to visit the islands include Surville (1769), Vancouver (1791), D'Urville (1827), FitzRoy and Darwin (1835) and Wilkes (1840). In the nineteenth century the islands were a frequent port-of-call for whalers and sealers. The first missionaries settled there in 1814; and by the treaty of Waitangi (1840) the Maori chiefs ceded sovereignty to Great Britain. In 1907 New Zealand became a dominion of the Commonwealth.

PAPUA NEW GUINEA (01°S to 11°S – 131°E to 151° 50′E): After Australia and Greenland, the largest island in the world, covering 312,862 sq. miles (810,000 sq. km); situated north of Australia, with Indonesia to the west and Melanesia to the east. First populated about 35,000 years ago by a dark-skinned Negrito (Papuan) people, who now live mainly in the interior, and subsequently by a Melanesian people, who now live mainly in the coastal plains and islands. The western half of the island, Irian Jaya (now part of Indonesia) was probably known to Europeans even before its first documented 'discovery' (1526) by the Portuguese Jorge de Meneses, who called it *Ilhas dos Papuas* (Islands of the frizzy-haired people, from the Malay *papuwah* = frizzy-haired). The eastern half of the island was 'discovered' by the Spaniard Ortiz Retes, who called it New Guinea because the people reminded him of the inhabitants of the Guinea coast of Africa. The most frequent early visitors were the Dutch – Janz, Le Maire, Carstenz and Tasman – but the island was also visited by Dampier, Cook and D'Urville. In the nineteenth century Germany proclaimed a protectorate over Irian Jaya, and the British proclaimed a protectorate over Papua New Guinea. Since 1973 the former has been part of the Republic of Indonesia, and the latter an autonomous state.

PHILIPPINE ISLANDS (6°S to 18° 50′N – 119° 50′E to 127°E): an archipelago of nearly 8,000 islands, situated north of Indonesia and bordered by the China Sea to the west and the Pacific Ocean to the east. The original inhabitants were probably Negritos who moved into the islands as long ago as 30000 BC. A few remnants of these Stone Age people can still be found in the remote rain forests, but the present-day population is almost entirely Malaysian. The first European sighting was by Magellan who landed on Samar on 16 March 1521, the Feast of Saint Lazarus – hence his name for the archipelago, *Ilhos dos Lazarus*. In 1524 the Spaniard Villalobos took official possession of the islands, renaming them after Philip II. Manila, founded in 1571, became one of the major emporia of the world, taking in gold and silver from South America and sending out in exchange silks, jade, porcelain, precious wood and spices. The Philippines were ceded by Spain to America in 1898, and are now an independent republic.

PITCAIRN ISLAND (25° 04′S – 136° 06′W): one of the remotest islands of Polynesia, situated roughly midway between the Tuamotus and Easter Island. First European sighting in 1767 by Carteret, who 'gave it the name of the young midshipman who first saw it'. It was colonized in 1790 by some of the mutineers from HMS *Bounty*.

POLYNESIA: collective name for the vast complex of islands and atolls within the triangle Hawaii, Easter Island, New Zealand. From the Greek *polus* = numerous and *nesos* = islands. All the indigenous people within this vast triangle (an area larger than the whole of the USSR) are of the same race, which makes them by far the most widely spread ethnic group on Earth. Principal archipelagos are: TONGA, or Friendly Islands, now Tongatapu Group; SAMOA; PHOENIX ISLANDS, now Kiribati; COOK ISLANDS; AUSTRAL ISLANDS, now Polynésie Française; HAWAIIAN ISLANDS, formerly Sandwich Islands, now a state of the USA; SOCIETY ISLANDS, including TAHITI and MOOREA, now Polynésie Française; TUAMOTU ARCHIPELAGO, formerly Low, Pearl or Dangerous Islands, now Polynésie Française; MARQUESAS, now Polynésie Française; EASTER ISLAND, now a dependency of Chile.

PRIBILOF ISLANDS (57°N – 170°W): an isolated volcanic archipelago of two small islands, Saint George and Saint Paul, and two rocky outcrops, Walrus Island and Otter Island, situated between the Aleutian Islands and the Bering Strait. Discovered in 1787 by Gerassim Pribilof, and subsequently the scene of the slaughter of anything up to half a million fur seals each breeding season.

SAMOA: Western Samoa = Palauli and Upolu; and American Samoa = Pago Pago and Tau (13° 50′N – 172°W): an archipelago in Polynesia consisting of 14 volcanic islands and many atolls, one of the first groups of islands to be occupied by the Polynesians, *c.* 1050 BC, as they migrated into the Pacific. First European sighting by Roggeveen (1722); subsequently visited by Bougainville (1768); a favourite haven of deserters and escaped convicts. The derivation of the name is uncertain, but it could be from the Polynesian *sa-moa* = the home of Moa, these being gigantic birds of the ostrich family, now extinct.

SITKA (57°N – 135° 15′W): an island off the coast of Alaska, headquarters of the Russian-American Company who established there a settlement known as The New Archangel.

SOCIETY ISLANDS (17°S – 150°W): Windward Islands = Tahiti, Moorea, Mehetia, Tetiaroa and Maiao. Leeward Islands = Huahine, Raiatea, Bora Bora, Maupiti and Tahaa. Now part of Polynésie Française: a fertile and eminently habitable archipelago famous for the beauty of its people and scenery, sometimes regarded as the heart of Polynesia. First European sighting by Wallis (1767); subsequently visited by Bougainville (1768) Cook (1769, 1773, 1774, 1777) and de Boenéchea, Bligh and Vancouver. Bougainville and Cook both wrote enthusiastic accounts of the islands and their people, which helped to promote the myth of the Noble Savage. Bougainville named the group *La Nouvelle Cythère*, after the island where the goddess Venus was thought to have risen from the sea. The more prosaic Cook called the archipelago the Society Islands in

Nanuya Lailai Island,
one of the Yasawa Group, Fiji.

honour of his patrons, the Royal Society. In the nineteenth century there was friction between British and French settlers, and the two countries came close to war. However, in 1847 the Tahitian Queen Pomare accepted French annexation, and Tahiti became the centre of French rule in Oceania.

SOLOMON ISLANDS (8°S – 159°E): an archipelago in Melanesia to the east of Papua New Guinea, consisting of a double chain of islands: to the north Choiseul, Santa Isabel and Malaita; and to the south Kolombangara, Rendova, Guadalcanal and San Cristobal; both chains surrounded by numerous atolls. First European sighting by Mendana (1568), who thought – incorrectly – that the inhabitants were wearing gold jewellery, and therefore assumed that he had found the Biblical Ophir of King Solomon. The Solomons have had a more than usually violent history; several ships disappeared there, nearly a dozen missionaries were killed, and slave-traders were responsible for much misery and depopulation. After being first a German then a British protectorate, the islands became a self-governing state in 1976.

SOUTH SHETLAND ISLANDS (62° 50′S – 60°W): a group of about 15 volcanic ice-capped islands situated between the tip of South America and the tip of the Antarctic Peninsula. First visited by sealers from New England; surveyed by D'Urville and Wilkes.

TASMANIA (42°S – 147°E): a large island about 112 miles (180 km) south of the south-east tip of Australia. Populated before the arrival of Europeans by descendants of the original Negrito people who came to Australia *c.* 25000 BC. First European sighting by the Dutchman Abel Tasman (1642) who landed briefly, but saw no people, and named his discovery Van Diemen's Land after the governor of the Dutch East India Company, a name it retained until 1853. Subsequently surveyed by Cook, D'Entrecasteaux, Baudin and Bass. Many of the first settlers on the island were convicts, soldiers or whalers, who so decimated the indigenous people that their numbers declined from an estimated 5,000 in 1800 to 203 in 1831; the race became extinct when the last Tasmanian died in 1876.

TIERRA DEL FUEGO (54°S – 69°W): a large island off the south tip of South America, divided from the mainland by the STRAITS OF MAGELLAN – a succession of spectacular fjords discovered by Magellan in 1520 and being for many years the only known entrée into the Pacific from the east. Named 'Land of Fire' by Magellan because its shores by night were illuminated by the camp fires of the Fuegian Indians. Off the south and west coasts are a plethora of smaller islands, among them Hoste, Navarino, Staten (separated from the mainland by a 12 mile (20 km) strait discovered in 1616 by Le Maire and offering an alternative sea-route to the Pacific) and Horn (whose south-facing cliffs, named after Le Maire's ship *Hoorn*, form the southernmost tip of the Americas).

TONGA (19°S – 176°W): an archipelago in Polynesia consisting of three main groups and many small islands and atolls, about 1,055 miles (1700 km) north of New Zealand. One of the first archipelagos to be settled by Polynesians migrating east into the Pacific – the earliest radiocarbon dating of human remains is 1140 BC. First European sighting by Le Maire (1616) who had skirmishes with the islanders of Tafahi and Niuatoputapu. Subsequent visitors were Tasman (1643), Wallis (1767), Cook – who named the archipelago The Friendly Islands because of the warm welcome given to his crew – (1773, 1774 and 1777), La Pérouse (1787) and Bligh (1789). The first missionaries arrived in 1797, and eventually converted many islanders to Christianity. For some time loosely affiliated to Great Britain, Tonga became an independent kingdom in 1959.

TUAMOTU ARCHIPELAGO (14° to 24°S – 135° to 149°W): the most widely scattered archipelago of Polynesia, lying east of the Society Islands and south of the Marquesas, and covering an area of some 300,000 sq. miles (777,000 sq. km). Except for the high volcanic islands of Mangareva, the archipelago consists of a multitude of low coral atolls (some only 10 feet [3 metres] above sea-level) together with numerous reefs – hence the name 'Dangerous Islands' given to the group by Bougainville. Between these islands and the coast of South America lies some 3,105 miles (5,000 km) of virtually empty ocean. The islands were probably first settled from the Marquesas *c.* AD 400, although there is some evidence to support the theory that there was also settlement from South America – the *Kon Tiki* expedition proved it was possible for rafts to drift from Peru to the Tuamotus. The first European sighting was by Magellan (1521) who landed on Pukapuka. Other islands were subsequently discovered by Loaysa (1525), Quiros (1606), Le Maire (1616), Roggeveen (1722), Byron (1765), Bougainville (1768), Boenéchea (1772) Cook (1774), Kotzebue (1816) and Bellingshausen (1819). In the nineteenth century the islands were much frequented by pearlers. They became part of Polynésie Française in 1849, and in recent years have been the site of nuclear tests.

BIBLIOGRAPHY

The literature of the Pacific is almost as vast as the ocean itself. I have listed only books that I have used.

Basic sources are *The Pacific Islands Year Book* (Pacific Publications, New York), the Admiralty *Pilot* series published by the hydrographer of the Navy (*South American Pilot, Pacific Islands Pilot*, etc), and the diaries and log-books of the explorers, many of which are held by the Royal Geographical Society.

The best single-volume history, although written 50 years ago, is still *The Exploration of the Pacific* by J. C. Beaglehole (A & C Black, 1966, 3rd edition). The best multi-volume history is *The Pacific Since Magellan* by O. H. K. Spate (Croom Helm, 1979), a scholarly and readable work on the grand scale, though not yet completed. Other good popular books are *Tahiti* by David Howarth (Collins Harvill, 1983) and *The Fatal Impact* by Alan Moorehead (Hamish Hamilton, 1966).

In the bibliography which follows, the place of publication is London unless otherwise stated.

Chapter One

Beiser, A. and the editors of *Life*, *The Earth* (Time-Life International, 1964).

Darwin, C., *Coral Reefs* (Pacific Science Board, Washington, DC, 1897).

Deacon, M., *Scientists and the Sea* (Scientific Committee on Antarctic Research, Cambridge, 1971), and *Oceanography* (Holt, Rinehart and Winston, 1978).

Drake, C. L., Imbrie, J., Knauss, J. A., Turekian, K. K., *Oceanography* (D. Van Nostrand, 1978).

Engel, L. and the editors of *Life*, *The Sea* (Time-Life International, 1963).

Freeman, O. W., *Geography of the Pacific* (Chapman and Hall, 1951).

Groen, P., *The Waters of the Sea* (D. Van Nostrand, 1967).

King, C. A. M., *Introduction to Marine Geology and Geomorphology* (Edward Arnold, 1975).

Maxwell, A. E., *The Sea* (John Wiley, New York, 1971).

Menard, H. W., *The Marine Geology of the Pacific* (W. H. Freeman, 1964).

Sears, M., *Oceanography* (American Association for the Advancement of Science, Washington, DC, 1961).

Shepard, F. P., *Submarine Geology* (Oxford University Press, 1973).

Van Dorn, W. G., *Oceanography and Seamanship* (Adlard Coles, 1975).

Wegener, A., *The Origin of Continents and Oceans* (Dover Publications, 1967).

Whipple, A. B. C. and the editors of *Time-Life Books, Restless Oceans* (Time-Life Books, Virginia, 1984).

Chapters Two and Three

Akerblom, K., *Astronomy and Navigation in Polynesia and Micronesia* (Stockholm, 1968)

Bellwood, P., *The Polynesians* (Thames and Hudson, 1984).

Dodd, E., *Polynesian Seafaring* (Conway Maritime Press, 1972).

Emory, K.P., Essays in honour of, Highland, G.A., *Polynesian Cultural History* (Bernice P. Bishop Museum, Special Publications, Honolulu, 1969).

Fornander, A., *An Account of the Polynesian Race, Its Origins and Migrations* (Trübner, New York, 1878-85).

Freeman, J. D. and Geddess, W. R., *Anthropology in the South Seas* (Thomas Avery, New Plymouth, New Zealand, 1960).
Heyerdahl, T., *The Kon-Tiki Expedition* (Allen & Unwin, 1950); *American Indians in the Pacific* (Allen & Unwin, 1952); *Aku-Aku* (Allen & Unwin, 1958); *Sea Routes to Polynesia* (Allen & Unwin, 1968); *The Art of Easter Island* (Allen & Unwin, 1976); *Early Man and the Ocean* (Allen & Unwin, 1978).
Hornell, J., *Canoes of Oceania* (Bernice P. Bishop Museum, Special Publications, Honolulu, 1936).
Langdon, R., *The Lost Caravel* (Pacific Publications, Sydney, 1975).
Lewis, D., *We, The Navigators* (Australian National University Press, Canberra, 1972); *The Voyaging Stars* (Collins, 1978).
McArthur, N., *Island Populations of the Pacific* (Australian National University Press, Canberra, 1968).
Sharp, A., *Ancient Voyagers in the Pacific* (Polynesian Society, Wellington, New Zealand, 1957); *The Discovery of the Pacific Islands* (Clarendon Press, 1960); *The Discovery of Australia* (Oxford University Press, 1963); *Ancient Voyages in Polynesia* (Angus and Robertson, 1964).
Taylor, E. G. R., *The Haven-Finding Art* (Hollis and Carter, 1956).
Vayda, D.P., *Peoples and Cultures of the Pacific* (American Society for the Advancement of Science, Bailey Bros and Swinfen, 1968).
White, J., *The Ancient History of the Maori* (Sampson Low, 1889).
Whitney, H. P., *An Analysis of the Design of the Major Sea-Going Craft of Oceania* (Thesis for master's degree at University of Pennsylvania, 1955).

Chapter Four

Amherst, Lord, *The Discovery of the Solomon Islands* (Hakluyt Society, 1901).
Baiao, A., *Historia de Expansao no Mundo* (Editorial Atica, Lisbon, 1937).
Cameron, I., *Magellan* (Weidenfeld & Nicolson, 1973).
Jack-Hinton, C., *The Search for the Islands of Solomon* (Oxford University Press, 1969).
Markham, C., *The Voyages of Fernandez de Quiros* (2 vols) (Hakluyt Society, 1904); *Early Spanish Voyages to the Straits of Magellan* (Hakluyt Society, 1911).
Parr, C. M., *So Noble a Captain* (Robert Hale, 1955).
Pigafetta, A., *Magellan's Voyage* (Translated Skelton, R.A., Yale University Press, 1969).
Renault, G., *The Caravels of Christ* (Allen & Unwin, 1959).
Visconde de Lagoa, the, *Fernao de Magalhais* (Vida e Viagem, Lisbon, 1938).
Zweig, S., *Conqueror of the Seas* (Cassell, New York, 1938).

Chapter Five

Boxer, C. R., *The Dutch Seaborne Empire* (Hutchinson, 1973).
De Klerck, E. S., *History of the Dutch East Indies* (Rotterdam, 1938).
Foster, Sir W., *England's Quest of Eastern Trade* (A. & C. Black, 1933).
Heeres, J. E., *The Life and Labours of Tasman* (Frederick Muller, Amsterdam, 1898).
Hough, R., *The Blind Horn's Hate* (Hutchinson, 1971).
Reisenberg, F., *Cape Horn* (Robert Hale, 1941).
Sharp, A., *The Journal of Jacob Roggeveen* (Oxford University Press, 1970); *The Voyages of Abel Janszoon Tasman* (Oxford University Press, 1968).

Simkin, C. G. F., *The Traditional Trade of Asia* (Oxford University Press, 1968).
Villiers, J. A. J., *The East and West Indian Mirror* (Hakluyt Society, 1906).
Wood, G. A., *The Discovery of Australia* (Macmillan, 1969 revised edition).

Chapter Six

Banks, Sir J., (ed Beaglehole, J. C.), *The Endeavour Journal of Joseph Banks* (Angus and Robertson, Sydney, 1962).
Beaglehole, J. C., (ed with Skelton, J. C.), *The Journals of Captain Cook on his Voyages of Discovery* (3 vols) (Hakluyt Society, 1955-68) (A scholarly, definitive and very readable work, with copious introductions, lesser-known diaries and notes).
Carrington, A. H., *Life of Captain Cook* (Sidgwick & Jackson, 1939).
Joppien, R., *The Art of Captain Cook's Voyages* (2 vols) (Oxford University Press, Melbourne, in association with the Australian Academy of the Humanities, 1985).
Muir, J. R., *Captain Cook* (Blackie & Son, 1939).
Parkinson, S., *A Journal of a Voyage to the South Seas* etc. (Printed privately for Stanfield Parkinson, ed, 1784).
Samwell, D., *Some Account of a Voyage to the South Seas* (1779) (in *The Journals of Captain Cook*, ed Beaglehole).
Villiers, A., *Captain Cook* (Hodder & Stoughton, 1967).

Chapter Seven

Brosses, C., *Histoire des Navigations aux Terres Australes* (Paris 1756/Da Capo Press, New York, 1967).
Brosses, J., *Great Voyages of Discovery* (Facts on File, New York, 1985).
Bougainville, L. A. de, *Voyage autour du monde par la frégate du roi la Boudeuse et la flûte l'Etoile* (Saillant & Nyon, Paris, 1771).
Cap, P. A., *Philibert Commerson, naturalistic voyageur* (Paris, 1861).
Diderot, D., *Supplément au voyage de Bougainville* etc (Paris, 1935).
Dumont d'Urville, J. S. C., *Voyage de la corvette l'Astrolabe exécuté pendant les années 1826-29* (19 vols) (J. Tastu, ed, Paris, 1835); *Voyage au pôle Sud et dans l'Oceanie sur les corvettes l'Astrolabe et la Zélée, 1837-40* (30 vols) (J. Tastu, ed, Paris, 1842).
Dunmore, J., *French Explorers in the Pacific* (2 vols) (Oxford University Press, 1965).
Forster, J. R., *A Voyage Round the World 1772* (translation) (F. Cass, 1967).

Chapter Eight

Part One

Coxe, W., *Account of the Russian Discoveries Between Asia and America, 1780* (Kelly, USA).
Fisher, R. H., *Bering's Voyages: Whither and Why?* (Seattle, 1977).
Forster, J. R., *History of the Voyages and Discoveries Made in the North* (translation) (G. G. J. & J. Robinson, 1786).
Golder, F.A., *Bering's Voyages* (2 vols) (American Geographical Society Research Series No 1 and No 2, New York, 1922).
Lauridsen, P., *Vitus Bering: Discoverer of the Bering Strait* (translation) (Chicago, 1889).
Steller, G. W., *Reise von Kamtschatka nach Amerika mit dem Commandeur – Capitan Bering* (John Pleifcher, Leipzig, 1774).
Waxel, S., *Report on the Voyage of the St. Peter* (Archives Department, Washington, DC).

Part Two

Haskell, D. C., *The United States Exploring Expedition, 1838-42, and its Publications* (New York Public Library, 1942).

Howard, L., *Herman Melville* (University of California Press, Berkeley, 1951).

Jaffé, D., *The Stormy Petrel and the Whale* (Port City Press, Baltimore, 1980).

Stanton, W., *The Great United States Exploring Expedition* (University of California Press, Berkeley, 1975).

Wilkes, C., *Narrative of the U.S. Exploring Expedition 1838-42* (Lea and Blanchard, Philadelphia, 1845); *Defence of Charles Wilkes to the Charges on Which he has been Tried* (Pamphlet for court-martial) (Washington, 1842).

Chapter Nine

Anderson, C. R., *Melville in the South Seas* (Columbia University Press, 1939).

Bockstoce, J. R., *Whales, Ice and Men* (University of Washington Press, Seattle, in association with New Bedford Whaling Museum, 1986).

Cameron, I., *Antarctica, The Last Continent* (Cassell, 1973).

Christie, E. W. H., *The Antarctic Problem* (Allen & Unwin, 1951).

Elliott, H. W., *An Arctic Province, Alaska and the Seal Islands* (Sampson Low, Marston, Searle & Rivington, 1886).

Gauguin, P., *Intimate Journals* (translation) (Crown, New York, 1936).

Gunson, N., *Messengers of Grace* (Oxford University Press, 1978).

Melville, H., *Typee* (John Murray, 1846); *Omoo* (John Murray, 1847); *Moby Dick* (New York, 1851).

Ommanney, F. D., *Lost Leviathan* (Hutchinson, 1971).

Priestley, R. (ed), *Antarctic Research* (Butterworths, 1964).

Sanderson, I. T., *Follow the Whale* (Cassell, 1958).

Stackpole, E. A., *The Sea Hunters* (Lippincott, 1953); *Whales and Destiny* (Lippincott, 1972).

Stonehouse, B., *Animals of the Antarctic* (Peter Lowe, 1972).

Williams, J., *Missionary Perils* (in *Missionary Annual*, 1835).

Wilson, J., *A Missionary Voyage to the Southern Pacific Ocean Performed 1796-1798 in the Ship Duff*, etc (Published 'for the benefit of the missionary society' by T. Chapman, 1799).

ACKNOWLEDGEMENTS

The Royal Geographical Society is an Aladdin's cave to those in search of books, diaries, maps and illustrations which have anything to do with exploration. I am very grateful to the Society for letting me use their library, map room and archives. In particular I should like to say a personal 'thank you' to the Librarian, David Wileman, and his assistants; their patience, kindness and help have made my research work a pleasure.

In the text, quotations from the Society's publications are made by permission of the Royal Geographical Society. I also acknowledge with thanks permission to quote from the following sources: *Ancient Voyagers in the Pacific* by Andrew Sharp, published by Penguin Books Ltd; *Captain Cook* by John Muir, published by Blackie & Son Ltd; *Captain Cook* by Alan Villiers, published by Hodder and Stoughton; *Darwin and the Beagle* by Alan Moorehead, published by Hamish Hamilton; *Discovery of the Pacific Islands* by Andrew Sharp, published by Oxford University Press (1960); *The Fatal Impact* by Alan Moorehead, published by Hamish Hamilton; *Geography of the Pacific* by O. W. Freeman (editor), published by Chapman and Hall; *Magellan* by Stefan Zweig, published by Cassell & Co.; *Messengers of Grace* by Niel Gunson, published by Oxford University Press (1978); *Polynesian Seafaring* by Edward Dodd, published by Conway Maritime Press; *The Stormy Petrel and the Whale* by David Jaffé, published by Port City Press, Inc.; and *Tahiti* by David Howarth, published by Collins Harvill Publishers. The quotations from *Darwin and the Beagle* and *The Fatal Impact* are made by permission of the Estate of Alan Moorehead. The quotation from *Lost Leviathan* by F. D. Ommanney is reproduced by permission of Curtis Brown Ltd.

PHOTOGRAPH ACKNOWLEDGEMENTS

The author and publisher would like to thank the following individuals and institutions which have kindly provided the illustrations. They are from the collections of the Royal Geographical Society, with the exception of the following: *7* Royal Commonwealth Society; *11T* Melanesian Mission; *B* BBC Hulton Picture Library; *12* British Library; *19* Compix; *23T* J. Allan Cash; *B* New Zealand Information Service; *26TR* Axel Poignant Archive; *BL* Axel Poignant Archive; *28L* Axel Poignant Archive; *30B* Melanesian Mission; *35T* BBC Hulton Picture Library; *B* National Library of Australia; *37* Axel Poignant Archive; *40* Axel Poignant Archive; *42B* Australian Museum, Sydney; *45* Melanesian Mission; *49L* Museum of Mankind; *R* Werner Forman Archive; *54TL* Axel Poignant Archive; *TR* Werner Forman Archive; *B* Axel Poignant Archive; *59* BBC Hulton Picture Library; *63* Bulloz; *65* Dieter & Mary Plage/Survival Anglia; *66* Bryan & Cherry Alexander; *67T* Walter Deas/Seaphot; *67B* Bryan & Cherry Alexander; *68* Geraldine Prentice; *69TL* Museum für Völkerkunde, Basel; *TR*, *B* Axel Poignant Archive; *70/71* Bridgeman Art Library; *72* National Maritime Museum; *74T* BBC Hulton Picture Library; *74B* National Maritime Museum; *87T* Collection Viollet; *101T* Koninklijk Instituut voor de Tropen; *101B* Mansell Collection; *103L* BBC Hulton Picture Library; *103R* Axel Poignant Archive; *106T* New Zealand Government; *106B* BBC Hulton Picture Library; *111* Mansell Collection; *114L* Mansell Collection; *114R* Australian Information Service; *117T* Axel Poignant Archive; *117B* Mansell Collection; *121* Mansell Collection; *127T* National Maritime Museum; *127B* British Library; *132L* Mansell Collection; *133R* Bridgeman Art Library; *137B* National Maritime Museum; *138/139* Bridgeman Art Library; *140T* National Art Gallery, New Zealand; *140B* Musée de la Marine; *141T* Axel Poignant Archive; *141B* National Maritime Museum; *142/143* National Maritime Museum; *144T* Mitchell Library; *144B* National Maritime Museum; *147L* Bulloz; *147R* Musée de la Marine; *149* BBC Hulton Picture Library; *152* Musée de la Marine; *156* BBC Hulton Picture Library; *170* Novosti; *172* BBC Hulton Picture Library; *178* Cambridge Museum of Archaeology & Anthropology; *182L* US Naval Academy Museum; *189T* Bettmann Archive; *198T* BBC Hulton Picture Library; *198B* Mansell Collection; *202* National Maritime Museum, San Francisco; *203* Mansell Collection; *206* National Library of Australia; *209T* Giraudon; *209B* Bulloz; *210* British Museum (Natural History); *212T* Peabody Museum; *213* Bridgeman Art Library; *214* Ian Griffiths/Robert Harding Picture Library; *215T* Victor Englebert/Susan Griggs; *215B* J. Allan Cash; *216* J. Allan Cash; *217* National Library of Australia; *219* Royal Commonwealth Society; *224* Courtauld Institute of Art; *235* J. Allan Cash.

Maps and diagrams by Ian Sandom.

INDEX

Numbers in *italics* refer to pages on which illustrations occur

M

N

O

P

U

V

W

Z